RACISM AND ETHNIC INI
IN A TIME OF CRI!

Findings from the
Evidence for Equality National Survey

Edited by
Nissa Finney, James Nazroo, Laia Bécares,
Dharmi Kapadia and Natalie Shlomo

P

First published in Great Britain in 2023 by

Policy Press, an imprint of
Bristol University Press
University of Bristol
1–9 Old Park Hill
Bristol
BS2 8BB
UK
t: +44 (0)117 374 6645
e: bup-info@bristol.ac.uk

Details of international sales and distribution partners are available at
policy.bristoluniversitypress.co.uk

British Library Cataloguing in Publication Data
A catalogue record for this book is available from the British Library

ISBN 978-1-4473-6884-7 paperback
ISBN 978-1-4473-6885-4 ePub
ISBN 978-1-4473-6886-1 ePdf

Cover design: Andrea Pazos
Front cover image: Andrea Pazos
Bristol University Press and Policy Press use environmentally responsible
print partners.
Printed in Great Britain by CMP, Poole

Contents

List of figures, tables and boxes

Figures

Tables

Boxes

Notes on contributors

Andrea Aparicio-Castro is a PhD candidate in Social Statistics at the University of Manchester (UoM) and a Fellow of the Higher Education Academy. She is also a scholar of the ESRC North West Social Science Doctoral Training Partnership and a Cathie Marsh Institute research member. She graduated as an MSc in Social Research Methods and Statistics from the UoM, and as a Specialist in Statistics and Sociologist from the National University of Colombia. Her career has focused on applying quantitative methodologies in social sciences, specialising in data integration, imputation of data, multilevel and hierarchical modelling, and forecast from a Bayesian perspective.

Laia Bécares is Professor of Social Science and Health in the Department of Global Health and Social Medicine, King's College London. Her research interests are in studying the pathways by which the discrimination and marginalisation of people and places lead to social and health inequalities across the life course, with a specific focus on racism and heteronormativity as systems of oppression. She is a member of the ESRC Centre on the Dynamics of Ethnicity (CoDE).

Neema Begum is Assistant Professor in British Politics at the University of Nottingham. Her research uses mixed-methods approaches to analysing British ethnic minority political attitudes, voting behaviour and political representation. She was formerly a research associate at CoDE, where she analysed ethnic minority representation in UK local government. She has also conducted research on ethnic minority voting behaviour and immigration attitudes in the 2016 EU referendum, decolonising the university curriculum and ethnic minority women's political activism.

Magda Borkowska is Senior Research Officer at the Institute for Social and Economic Research, University of Essex. She has conducted research on inequalities experienced by ethnic and immigrant minorities, social cohesion, civil society, neighbourhood effects and political attitudes. In her research she primarily uses quantitative, longitudinal approaches to study life course outcomes. She previously worked in the Policy Unit of Understanding Society (UK Household Longitudinal Study), where she frequently collaborated with government departments researching gender inequalities in labour market outcomes, immigrant integration and residential segregation.

Ken Clark is Senior Honorary Research Fellow at the Department of Economics and a member of the Centre on the Dynamics of Ethnicity at the University of Manchester. He is also an IZA Research Fellow. His published work is broadly in the area of labour economics, where he specialises in the analysis of employment and wage differentials between different ethnic and immigrant groups. As well as being published in academic journals, his work has contributed to considerations of the best policies to improve labour market equality for government and other policy makers.

Daniel Ellingworth is Researcher at CoDE at the University of Manchester, working on the design and analysis of EVENS. His previous work has focused on crime and criminal justice, addressing patterns of repeat victimisation and area crime rates, and the evaluation of a range of offender interventions.

Nissa Finney is Professor of Human Geography at the University of St Andrews. She has published and taught widely on ethnic inequalities, residential mobility and housing, neighbourhood change and segregation. She is a Fellow of the Royal Geographical Society, former Chair of the Royal Geographical Society (with the Institute of British Geographers) Population Geography Research Group, member of the ESRC Centre for Population Change (CPC) and a founding member of CoDE. On ethnic inequalities, her work has brought new understandings in population scholarship, evidencing differential opportunities and experiences of ethnic groups in residential choices, underlying processes of racism and discrimination, and policy narratives that marginalise groups and places.

Joseph Harrison is Research Associate at CoDE. Alongside this, he is studying for a PhD at the University of St Andrews. His research uses quantitative methods and longitudinal data to focus on Pakistani immigrants and their descendants in the UK and Norway, particularly relating to their family dynamics and health. Previously he has worked as a research assistant at Stockholm University Demography Unit (SUDA) from where he also graduated with an MSc in Demography. Before that, he studied Economics and International Development at the University of Birmingham.

Hannah Haycox is ESRC Postdoctoral Fellow at The University of Manchester where she is researching racial inequalities, refugee resettlement and multi-scalar policy governance. Her previous work as Research Assistant with CoDE at The University of St Andrews provided an intersectional approach to lived experiences of housing policy and practice, including its racialised, classed and gendered impacts. She has been the recipient of several prestigious prizes, including the Presidential Doctoral Scholar Award for future global leaders of research. She has disseminated policy recommendations to high-quality academic journals, UNHCR, media outlets, cross-parliamentary groups and non-governmental organisations.

Emma Hill is Research Fellow in Geography and Sustainable Development at the University of St Andrews, where she is working on an ESRC-funded project on the racialised dynamics of post-pandemic housing practices in the UK. She was previously a Research Fellow on the JPI ERA Net/ Horizon 2020 Governance and Local Integration of Migrants and Europe's Refugees (GLIMER) Project in Sociology at the University of Edinburgh, and completed her PhD in Cultural Research at Heriot-Watt University, for which her doctoral thesis was awarded the 2017 MacFarlane Prize. She is an associate editor for the *Identities: Global Studies in Culture and Power* journal, a steering committee member for the Glasgow Refugee, Asylum and Migration Network (GRAMNet) and a Trustee for the Maryhill Integration Network (Glasgow). Her research interests include the postcolonial dynamics of South-North migration in former colonial centres.

Dharmi Kapadia is Senior Lecturer in Sociology at the University of Manchester and a member of CoDE. She is a mixed-methods researcher with interests in racism, mental health and illness, stigma and older people. She has also conducted research in ethnic inequalities in women's use of mental health services and socioeconomic inequalities in suicide, and has also undertaken work looking at ethnic inequalities in the labour market and the role of social networks in poverty for different ethnic groups.

Angelo Moretti is Assistant Professor in Statistics at the Department of Methodology and Statistics, Utrecht University. He is a survey statistician and an elected member of the International Statistical Institute (ISI). He has conducted research in small area estimation under multivariate generalised mixed models, survey calibration, mean squared error estimation based on bootstrap approaches, and data integration methods (statistical matching and probabilistic record linkage). He is also interested in applications related to understanding geographical differences in social exclusion, crime and public attitude indicators.

James Nazroo is Professor of Sociology at the University of Manchester. His work on ethnic inequalities in health has led the field in demonstrating the importance of both socioeconomic inequalities and experiences of racism and racial discrimination. It has also provided novel findings on early life effects, generational differences, ecological effects and the positive effects of ethnic density. His publications in relation to ageing have advanced our understanding of the patterns and determinants of social and health inequalities, as well as the health and wellbeing outcomes of retirement and later life employment, and he has also developed and tested theoretical models of class that more accurately capture socioeconomic position in later life. He is a Fellow of the British Academy, a Fellow of the Academy of Social Sciences and the founding Director of the ESRC Centre on the Dynamics of Ethnicity.

Nico Ochmann received his PhD in Economics from the University of Manchester in February 2021 with the dissertation title 'Essays in immigration economics'. His areas of interest are immigration, ethnicity, labour, micro-econometrics and causal inference. He has been with CoDE since September 2020. He holds an MSc in Applied Economics from Montana State University, Bozeman, and a BSc in Economics from the University of Washington, Seattle. He has worked as an economist in the US, Canada, Germany and the UK.

Natalie Shlomo is Professor of Social Statistics at the University of Manchester. She is a survey statistician with interests in adaptive survey designs, data linkage and integration, non-probability sampling designs, statistical disclosure control and small area estimation. She has written a diverse range of publications in both survey statistics and the social sciences. She is a Fellow of the Academy of Social Sciences in the UK, an elected member of the ISI and a Fellow of the Royal Statistical Society.

Michaela Šťastná is Research Associate at CoDE. She is a PhD student at the University of St Andrews, researching family complexity and children's outcomes in relation to family resources. Her research focuses on in-depth life-course measures of family complexity using advanced quantitative methods, and on early childhood outcomes, especially mental health. She holds an MSc in Attachment Studies from the University of Roehampton and a BSc Psychology from Birkbeck, University of London.

Harry Taylor is Research Associate in the Department of Global Health and Social Medicine, King's College London, and formerly of CoDE. He received his PhD in Social Statistics from the University of Manchester in 2022. His primary research uses quantitative methods to explore ethnic inequalities in health. He has also conducted research into misinformation and vaccine hesitancy for the Alan Turing Institute. Prior to his doctoral study, he worked in spend analysis and logistics consultancy, investigating applications of AI techniques to business problems, among other projects.

Acknowledgements

We extend sincere thanks to all those who took part in the EVENS Survey. We hope that you see some of your stories in the pages of this book and that the evidence here and in the EVENS dataset will be part of the movement to effect change.

The EVENS researcher team at CoDE were unfailing in their dedication to this project. They worked with exceptional skill, imagination, tenacity and collegiality. Sincere thanks to Andrea Apricio-Castro, Neema Begum, Magda Borkowska, Daniel Ellingworth, Joseph Harrison, Angelo Moretti, Nico Ochmann, Michaela Šťastná and Harry Taylor. You are fine researchers indeed.

We are grateful to our CoDE colleagues for encouragement and for providing such a rich environment for scholarship. Thankyou to Emma Tsoneva and Hazel Burke for keeping the project mechanics running smoothly. Thankyou to CoDE Director Bridget Byrne and Co-Director Claire Alexander for your ongoing support for EVENS.

The EVENS Voluntary and Community Sector partners brought such energy and enthusiasm for this project and reminded us throughout of the fundamental motivation for producing evidence for equality. Thankyou to Black and Ethnic Minority Infrastructure in Scotland (BEMIS), Business in the Community, Ethnic Minorities and Youth Support Team Wales, Friends, Families and Travellers, the Institute for Jewish Policy Research, the Migrants Rights Network, the Muslim Council of Britain, NHS Race and Health Observatory, Operation Black Vote, the Race Equality Foundation, The Runnymede Trust, The Stuart Hall Foundation and The Ubele Initiative.

Words of Colour, led deftly by Joy Francis, produced the superb EVENS design and branding and led the strategic communications through survey recruitment with drive and dexterity. Thankyou.

The Ipsos team who managed the survey implementation were wholly committed to producing high quality data, and with eagerness to develop the innovative aspects of EVENS. It was a pleasure working with you.

Thanks go to the University of Manchester Ethics Committee for their careful consideration of the EVENS project and for their responsiveness to the many amendments to the ethics application.

We thank those who gave comments on drafts of this book particularly Bridget Byrne, Stephen Jivraj and Georgia Haire.

Thank you to Andrea Pazos for the cover design and production of tables and figures and for never hesitating in responding to the many and varied comments from the EVENS team.

We are obliged to Shannon Kneis, Anna Richardson, Annie Rose and colleagues at Policy Press/Bristol University Press and Newgen Publishing for careful work to bring this book to fruition.

We acknowledge the UK Data Service for providing the platform for EVENS data access and for user support.

The EVENS project would not have been possible without funding from the UKRI Economic and Social Research Council (ESRC). EVENS was funded via the CoDE grants 'Exploring racial and ethnic inequality in a time of crisis' (ES/V013475/1) and 'The social, cultural and economic impacts of the pandemic on ethnic and racialised groups in the UK' (ES/W000849/1).

Heartfelt thanks go to all those who promoted the EVENS Survey and have supported the broader project. NRF is grateful for the Riverside hideaway which provided a haven for overseeing the project (as well as a break from home schooling during lockdowns); and to Alan, Freya, Laurie and Xander for always findings ways and enthusiasm for what needed to be done. LBS is thankful for the support and love from Teo, Nuria, Tati, and abuela.

Nissa Finney, James Nazroo, Natalie Shlomo,
Dharmi Kapadia, Laia Bécares
St Andrews, Manchester, London
November 2022

Note on the figures

Table 2.3 and Figures 4.1, 4.3, 6.1 and 7.2 have been published in a font size smaller than our house style. To see full-sized versions of these figures, please visit https://policy.bristoluniversitypress.co.uk/ethnic-inequalities-in-a-time-of-crisis.

To find out more about CoDE, EVENS and how to access the EVENS data see www.ethnicity.ac.uk

Introduction: the need for Evidence for Equality

*Nissa Finney, James Nazroo, Laia Bécares, Dharmi Kapadia
and Natalie Shlomo*

What would a racially just society look like?

How close is Britain to being a racially just society?

Has the COVID-19 pandemic taken Britain further away from racial justice and ethnic equality?

This book's examination of ethnic inequalities in life circumstances and experiences is motivated by these questions of racial justice. Its central premise is that understanding how and why people's experiences differ, and the nature of the disadvantage and inequality underpinning these experiences, is required for racial equality. What distinguishes this book is its use of a unique dataset to conduct a robust investigation of ethnic inequalities in Britain. The analyses in this book go further than previous studies – further in terms of the issues that are investigated and the granularity of ethnic groups that is considered. This has been made possible by the Evidence for Equality National Survey (EVENS) dataset.

This book provides the most comprehensive and up-to-date evidence on ethnic inequalities in Britain. This is highly pertinent to contemporary social and political race debates and policy agendas in the post-pandemic recovery context. The COVID-19 pandemic brought ethnic inequalities to the fore as it became evident that infection and mortality rates were higher among ethnic minorities than the population as a whole (ICNARC, 2020; Nazroo and Bécares, 2020; ONS, 2020; Platt and Warwick, 2020). In May 2020, as the devastating and unequal impacts of the pandemic were being realised, the murder of George Floyd in Minnesota in the US saw a resurgence of Black Lives Matter (BLM) movements globally (Alexander and Byrne, 2020). In response, the UK government published the Sewell Report in 2021 which relayed the conclusions of the Commission on Race and Ethnic Disparities (Commission on Race and Ethnic Disparities, 2021), and, subsequently, the *Inclusive Britain* report in 2022 which laid out policy recommendations (Department for Levelling Up, Housing and Communities, 2022).

A fundamental critique of the Sewell Report is that its conclusion that racial inequalities are not an issue of deep concern for UK society is not borne out by the evidence (Byrne et al, 2020). Furthermore, the *Sewell Report* failed to take account of the considerable and longstanding body of knowledge that demonstrates how structural and institutional racism have shaped ethnic inequalities in the UK and elsewhere (Byrne et al, 2020; Nazroo et al, 2020; Meer, 2022). The impacts of the *Inclusive Britain* recommendations remain to be seen, but, as shown in *The Race Report* from the Stuart Hall Foundation, of the 589 recommendations made by UK race and inequality reports and commissions since the 1980s, many have yet to be implemented (Ashe, 2021).

Among the repeated recommendations of race and inequality reviews over the last 50 years has been the call for 'regular, improved and standardised forms of data collection which measures and monitors the nature of racism, racial inequality and the effectiveness of policy interventions' (Ashe, 2021: 7). The EVENS survey represents a step change in such data collection. As such, this book is a foundation for ideas, initiatives and actions to bring about equality and to ensure that addressing ethnic inequalities is at the fore in policy and practice. It also provides the evidence for this to be done with care, accuracy and robustness.

Ethnicity and ethnic categorisation

Three core concepts bind this book: ethnicity, inequality and racism. Here we elaborate our conceptualisation of ethnicity and the challenges in depicting it quantitatively. We then turn to inequality and racism. Ethnicity can be described as a form of (individual and collective) identity that draws on notions of ancestry, cultural commonality and geographical origins. The boundaries of ethnic groups are symbolic and marked by practices of, for example, language, religion or, more generally, 'culture'. Ethnicity also often incorporates race, which invokes notions of shared physical features, most particularly represented through skin colour.

We understand ethnicity not as something essential, intrinsic or fixed, but as socially constructed; a way of labelling and grouping people that has been devised by society throughout long histories of social disaggregation. Through the discursive generation of racial and ethnic groups, differences are accorded social significance. This identification, rendering of meaning and value, and placement on a hierarchal scale is a process described as racialisation. Racial classification and racialisation have been central to historically determined colonial systems of domination that are ongoing and employ racial hierarchies as a rationale for exploitation, marginalisation and exclusion of those considered to be inferior (Emirbayer and Desmond, 2015; Golash-Boza, 2016; Bhopal, 2018; Meer, 2022).

The recognition of ethnicity as socially constructed and of the potent power of discursive generation of racialised social order to marginalise and exclude brings a tension to this research. We want to take account of the richness of ethnic identities, but also want to make comparisons in order to characterise inequalities. Comparisons require categorisation. As you flick through these pages, you will see that all the evidence presented is based on ethnic categorisation, with ethnic groups represented by neat, delineated bars and dots that suggest cohesion and consistency. This belies what has just been discussed about the social production of categories and their associated meanings.

Categories are part of how we make sense of and are oriented to others, and thus shape our everyday social interactions (Ahmed, 2007). Yet the meanings of categories are often not voiced or directly expressed, and are almost never interrogated. Where categories carry differential value, which they almost always do, this has material consequences for both those included in and those excluded from particular categories. And when a category is stigmatised and has the potential to subsume other elements of a person's identity, the consequences for the individual may reach into all elements of their life in profound ways. In addition, social categories are no more than crude and inaccurate summaries of our personal experience and of a particular dimension of our identity. And this is the case even if the categorisation is relatively refined.

A crucial step is to acknowledge that the ethnic categories that come from attempts to summarise ethnicity are *not the cause* of differential risk between ethnic groups for a particular outcome. Rather, the ways in which the category is racialised, and the material consequences of this, are likely to be the cause. So, we use categories and consequently run the risk of fixing and essentialising the social meanings that drive the inequalities we care about. Thus, we use categories with care, precision and reflection in this book. It is our intention that the discussions that follow can contribute to critical debates about ethnic categorisation (and thus be of interest to critical decolonial scholarship) from the premise that ethnicity is meaningful for people's self-identities and, as a definer of ourselves and others, ethnic categorisation is central to how society is organised and works.

There is a long history of ethnic categorisation in official statistics in Britain (contrary to the approach in other nations - see, for example, Simon, 2008, 2017). This was motivated in the 1970s and 1980s by concerns about racism, discrimination and inequalities which were at the core of the Race Relations Act 1976. Ethnic groups routinely became categorised from the 1991 Census (Peach, 1994). This was the first time that ethnicity had been part of the census questionnaire and the approach – measuring ethnicity and the categories used – quickly became the standard (Finney and Simpson, 2009). The categories used in the 1991 Census were the outcome of extensive

---

• TABLE 1.1: ETHNIC GROUPS IN THE EVENS SURVEY •

White Irish
White Eastern European
Gypsy/Traveller
Roma
Jewish
Any other White background
Indian
Pakistani
Bangladeshi
Mixed White and Asian
Chinese
Any other Asian background
Black Caribbean
Mixed White and Black Caribbean
Black African
Mixed White and Black African
Any other Black background
Arab
Any other mixed/multiple background
Any other ethnic group
White British

---

discussions and consultations, and the ethnic categories used in official statistics have since been revised a number of times by the national statistical agencies.

The Office for National Statistics (ONS) Census 2021 ethnic groups are the basis for the categories in the analyses presented in this book. However, we have somewhat amended the standard list in the categories we use and the way we present (that is, label and order) them. We include two additional groups to the standard ONS categories: Jewish and White Eastern European ethnic groups are specified to enable evidence for groups who have distinct experiences, but are largely invisible in existing surveys. We present ethnic groups, consistently through the book, in the order in Table 1.1; note that the mixed ethnic groups are not grouped consecutively. The ethnic groups in the EVENS survey are discussed further in Chapter 2 and critical reflection on categories of ethnic identification is the focus of Chapter 3. It is important from the outset to note that all those upon whom these analyses are based defined their own ethnicity, though within the limits of the categories that we offered them.

Inequality

Categorisation enables comparison and identification of inequality. We understand inequality as difference that is unjust and preventable. Inequalities can be seen as the inevitable consequence of (imperialist, racist, capitalist and patriarchal) societies (Hooks, 1984) operating on the premise that one's security comes at the expense of other's insecurity; one's power and privilege comes at the expense of others' marginalisation (Harvey, 2017; Dorling, 2019). In presenting evidence for equality we are not arguing for sameness – people are at liberty to choose how they live – but for the identification of inequalities that represent racial injustice.

A common conceptual distinction on inequality with relevance to the contemporary political and policy context is between equality of outcome and equality of opportunity. Policy discussions and recommendations predominantly focus on equality of opportunity; in this book we focus on and emphasise equality of outcome. We do so partly because it is incredibly difficult to measure equality of opportunity, but, more importantly, from the premise that understanding differential outcomes is the starting point for understanding the mechanisms – processes of racial injustice – that cause them. In this book we take indicators of circumstance and experience in key life domains and compare these across ethnic groups. In the interpretations and discussions we consider the drivers and implications of ethnic inequalities.

The main question raised by this book is why we see ethnic inequalities. The book does not directly address this question empirically, but is theoretically motivated by a stance that racism is the key driver of ethnic inequalities in opportunity, circumstance and experience. What this novel evidence enables is questions about how racism produces and sustains ethnic inequalities.

Racism

Racism is central to the discussions in this book; we take the position that racism is the mechanism of racial injustice and a root cause of ethnic inequalities. Inequalities do not arise from the inherent properties of ethnic groupings; rather, they are a result of historically embedded and culturally and politically shaped meanings ascribed to ethnic identities which generate a racialised social order. Thus, the overarching theoretical framing of this book is that ethnic inequalities result from racism and racial injustice driven by historical and ongoing processes of colonialism (Bonnett, 2022; Byrne et al, 2020; Meer, 2022). The central argument is that racism and racialisation underpin the ethnic inequalities that are presented, which most often show disadvantage for ethnic minority groups.

Racism manifests on multiple levels, including structural, institutional and interpersonal levels (Jones, 2000; Nazroo et al, 2020). Structural racism leads to disadvantage in accessing economic, political, physical, social and cultural resources (Essed, 1991). This also has ideological dimensions that involve the denigration of ethnic minority groups, which serves to rationalise this uneven distribution of resources (Emirbayer and Desmond, 2015). Within the UK, there are deep-rooted ethnic inequalities across almost all socioeconomic dimensions: income, employment, residential location, health, housing and education. These have persisted over time and across generations (Modood et al, 1997; Jivraj and Simpson, 2015; Byrne et al, 2020), despite the introduction of equality legislation, which has been in place in the UK for more than 50 years. This persistence of ethnic inequalities illustrates how difficult it is to address the processes associated with racism (Meer, 2022).

Interpersonal racism (ranging from discrimination to everyday slights and to verbal and physical aggression) is a form of violence that emphasises the devalued and fundamentally insecure status of both those who are directly targeted and those who have similarly racialised identities. It is through such interpersonal actions that the denigrated aspects of racialised identities come into being (Emirbayer and Desmond, 2015; Funnell, 2015). A range of studies has acutely demonstrated that interpersonal experiences of racism and discrimination are central to the lives of ethnic minority people, operating across, and impacting upon, their life courses, and resulting in significant harm (Karlsen and Nazroo, 2002a; Karlsen and Nazroo, 2004; Wallace et al, 2016).

Institutional racism refers to how the norms, policies and practices of institutions negatively shape the experiences of members of racialised groups within them (Carmichael and Hamilton, 1967). Institutional settings provide a context within which structural forms of disadvantage and interpersonal racism are concentrated and amplified (Phillips, 2010; Emirbayer and Desmond, 2015; Bailey et al, 2017). The outcomes of institutional racism can be seen in the greater likelihood of ethnic minority people to have more negative pathways through care, poorer access to effective services and interventions, and poorer outcomes. This is present in education (Alexander and Shankley, 2020), health and social care (Chouhan and Nazroo, 2020; Kapadia et al, 2022), housing (Shankley and Finney, 2020), arts and culture (Malik and Shankley, 2020), and politics (Sobolewska and Shankley, 2020). It is most striking in those institutions that have a regulatory or disciplinary function, such as criminal justice (Shankley and Williams, 2020) and mental health (Nazroo et al, 2020).

In this book we capture the outcomes of structural and institutional racism (in Chapters 5, 6, 7, 8 and 9) and present evidence on the everyday experiences of interpersonal racial discrimination (Chapter 4).

The need for EVENS

The story of EVENS – from an innovative starting point to an unrivalled dataset – has its roots in the frustration of the inadequacies of data on ethnicity and a consequent knowledge gap that became intensified during the COVID-19 pandemic. When COVID-19 hit Britain in the early months of 2020 and inequalities across ethnic groups were immediately apparent, researchers at the Centre on the Dynamics of Ethnicity (CoDE) embarked on an intense endeavour to document and understand the experiences of ethnic minority people during this crisis. This programme of work built from CoDE's decade of experience in evidencing, understanding and addressing ethnic inequalities in the UK (Jivraj and Simpson, 2015; Byrne et al, 2020). It aimed to:

1. Document new and changing forms of racial and ethnic inequality in the wake of the COVID-19 pandemic and responses to it.
2. Explore emergent forms of social, political and cultural mobilisation around racism and racial inequality during and following the resurgence of the Black Lives Matter (BLM) movement.
3. Examine responses within particular social arenas and from institutions (education, health, housing, welfare, culture, employment and businesses, and policing) to the COVID-19 pandemic and BLM.
4. Work with community, policy and third sector partners to understand how racial and ethnic inequality was being addressed during the pandemic, and to formulate future plans for addressing racial injustice.

It was clear that what was lacking in the evidence landscape was a robust, large-scale, quantitative dataset focusing on ethnic minorities and their experiences and centring racism as the root cause of the inequalities. Thus, EVENS was established as a core part of CoDE's programme of work. EVENS is the largest and most comprehensive survey to document the lives of ethnic and religious minorities in Britain during the pandemic. Moreover, it employs cutting-edge survey methods to ensure a uniquely robust dataset (see Chapter 2). EVENS has a number of distinctive features that make it a uniquely useful source for understanding contemporary ethnic inequalities:

• recognition and representation of more ethnic minority groups;
• larger samples of ethnic minority groups;
• use and development of innovative and robust survey methods;
• working in partnership with ethnic minority communities to ensure the relevance and quality of the data.

Concern about the ethnicity data gap (and, indeed, the value of producing ethnicity data) is by no means a new development. In a book collaboration in 1980, the Runnymede Trust and the Radical Statistics Race Group published *Britain's Black Population*. Motivated by the same quest for racial justice as this collection and having presented the best available evidence of the time, the book asserted that 'attention be paid to the collection of statistics about the particular circumstances and needs of black people in the areas of health, housing, education, employment and the social services' (Runnymede Trust and the Radical Statistics Race Group, 1980: 129). In some ways the data landscape has improved for understanding the experiences of ethnic minority people: the UK censuses have included an ethnicity question since 1991, there is oversampling of ethnic minority participants in several large-scale social surveys (though this is not without methodological challenges – see Chapter 2) and ethnic monitoring has become routine in administrative data as a result of the 2010 Equalities Act. However, with the exception of Understanding Society (the UK Household Longitudinal Study), there has been a reluctance to design and resource new data about the experiences of ethnic minority people, and, indeed, some data initiatives from the early 2000s, such as the Citizenship Survey, have been jettisoned.

Although in a sense we are awash with ethnicity data and it has become normal to 'tick' ethnicity monitoring questions, there are some severe limitations to existing UK data on ethnicity. Administrative data, while having good coverage of the population, do not usually disaggregate ethnic groups beyond broad categories, which are both difficult to interpret and mask differences between ethnic groups subsumed into broader categories, and are limited in the nature of the information that is collected. In particular, these data do not tell us about experience, perception or opinion, and crucially they do not tell us about the reasons behind inequalities. So, for example, from administrative data we may know how many Bangladeshi people had a General Practitioner (GP) appointment in 2021, but we know nothing of the motivations for or experiences of that appointment, or other details about this person that may be relevant for understanding their health. Census data are unrivalled in their population coverage, geographical detail and (through the Longitudinal Studies) ability to evidence trends over five decades, but are restricted in terms of understanding the details and drivers of ethnic inequalities because of their necessary focus on demographic and socioeconomic indicators.

As for understanding experiences and impacts of the COVID-19 pandemic, existing COVID-19-related data are severely limited for generating adequate understandings of the extent of ethnic inequalities or the mechanisms behind them. Such surveys conducted during the COVID-19 pandemic are often of poor quality (both in terms of topic coverage and sample design) or do not focus on the experiences that are particularly pertinent to ethnic and religious minority people.

EVENS and this book offer a unique and timely intervention to the ethnicity data gap and to debates about inequalities and racism in the post-COVID-19 context. EVENS is an unrivalled data source, as Chapter 2 will elaborate: it offers greater topic coverage than other sources, it is designed specifically to be relevant to the lives of ethnic and religious minority people, it represents a collaboration with 13 leading voluntary, community and social enterprise (VCSE) organisations, and it uses innovative non-probability survey methods. EVENS has a sample of 14,200 participants, of whom 9,700 identify as members of ethnic and religious minority groups, uniquely allowing comparative analyses of their experiences.

The EVENS data, which are freely available for use in research, were collected during the COVID-19 pandemic and the chapters in this book give insight to the experiences of ethnic minority people during this unique period. Yet the potential of the data goes beyond an understanding of the pandemic specifically. The focus on this pivotal historical moment enables discussion about the history and persistence of racism and the resulting ethnic inequalities which have led to differential experiences. Evidencing ethnic inequalities during the pandemic reveals the workings of racism and racial injustice. The pandemic context exposes fragilities, insecurities, disruptions and destabilisation, and encourages reflection that can be a catalyst for regenerative change.

Reading this book

Following this introduction, Chapter 2 relays the methods used to generate the unique data used in this book, emphasising the innovative approaches that were taken. Next, in Chapter 3, we engage critically with ethnic categorisation through analysis of the various questions on ethnic identification that were part of EVENS, drawing out lessons on how people identify and on the measurement of ethnicity. The chapter illustrates the diversity within ethnic categorisations and the ways in which people describe their ethnic identities that are not well captured using current standard categorisations. It also demonstrates the salience of ethnic identification and the strength of belonging to British society across ethnic groups.

Chapters 4 to 9 present findings from EVENS thematically: racism, health, housing, work, socioeconomics and politics. In each of these chapters, the results presented show inequalities between ethnic groups on key indicators. Each chapter has a summary at the start and a measures and methods box describing the analyses. The empirical chapters can be read in any order; the book can be dipped into as well as read sequentially.

Among the highlights of the book, we see the stark prevalence of experiences of racism and the worsening of experiences of racism during the pandemic (for Chinese and Eastern European groups in particular). Ethnic minority people in Britain were more likely to have poor physical health, experience COVID-19-related bereavement and have difficulty accessing health services than White British people. However, based on some indicators (including loneliness and depression), some ethnic minority groups fared better than the White British group. In housing, ethnic minority groups in Britain are subject to material deprivation in residential experience, yet succeed in developing strong attachment to their local neighbourhoods and enriching this during this period of crisis. We see the persistence of ethnic inequalities in the labour market and, during the pandemic, particular risk of job precarity for some ethnic minority groups (notably Jewish and Chinese women). The detrimental financial impact of the pandemic has been greater for ethnic minority people than the White British majority; socioeconomic deprivation is particularly evident for Arab, Roma and Gypsy/Traveller groups, and people from Arab, Bangladeshi and Pakistani backgrounds have notably high levels of worry about financial circumstances. In general, ethnic minority people report relatively high levels of political trust (though greater towards the devolved parliaments than the UK Parliament) and continue to have high levels of political engagement indicated by interest in politics and political party affiliation. Overall, the chapters demonstrate the power of robust and innovative data to evidence ethnic inequalities.

The findings chapters (Chapters 3 to 9) have been written by experts in the thematic field; authors represent disciplines across the social sciences (geography, sociology, economics, demography, social statistics, population health and politics). The book is thus interdisciplinary in offering expert discipline-oriented empirical chapters within a framing that speaks across disciplines to vital questions of racism and ethnic inequality.

2

The making of EVENS

*Natalie Shlomo, James Nazroo, Nissa Finney, Laia Bécares,
Dharmi Kapadia, Andrea Aparicio-Castro, Daniel Ellingworth,
Angelo Moretti and Harry Taylor*

Introduction

During the COVID-19 pandemic in 2020, the Centre on the Dynamics of Ethnicity (CoDE) team along with Ipsos developed and implemented the Evidence for Equality National Survey (EVENS) and collected data between February and November 2021. The aim of the survey was to produce unrivalled high-quality data to document the experiences of ethnic and religious minority people in Britain during the COVID-19 pandemic. EVENS goes far beyond the limited number of ethnic minority groups that are typically reported in many UK national surveys, where surveys with small sample sizes prohibit the release of meaningful estimates and surveys with larger sample sizes typically focus on only five or six ethnic minority groups. Here, we report on the experiences of 20 ethnic minority groups, where appropriate disaggregated by age group, sex and geographical region. Prior to EVENS, no other survey comprehensively captured detailed experiences of ethnic minority groups. Hence, there was high demand for such a survey and support to implement an innovative online survey design.

The ambition of EVENS, to recognise and represent more ethnic minority groups than other surveys, to provide larger samples of ethnic minority groups, to ensure the relevance of the data to ethnic minority communities and to deliver high-quality data, required innovation in survey methods from questionnaire development to data adjustments after fieldwork. At the core of this innovation is an open invitation to ethnic minority people to take part in the survey. While ostensibly straightforward this approach creates challenges for making it possible to use the data in ways that can be said to be representative of ethnic minority people in Britain. This is because the open invitation to participate is contrary to established social science survey methods that, for example, invite people from specific addresses to take part, thus knowing who from their representative pool has and has not responded and allowing adjustments to be made to the dataset accordingly so that it can be confidently used as representative of the target population. These standard probability-based survey approaches cannot be used with an open invitation to participate such as that used in EVENS because the sample cannot be drawn from a known representative pool of the population with an established sampling frame. Thus, EVENS is based on a non-probability survey approach and is one of the first large-scale applications of such a survey methodology in the social sciences.

This chapter outlines how EVENS was made; how the pioneering non-probability approach was implemented, from questionnaire development, recruitment strategies to the nature of the sample, quality assurance and weighting adjustments. We conclude with reflections on the opportunities provided by, and the challenges of, innovative non-probability survey approaches for understanding experiences of ethnic and religious minority people.

EVENS questionnaire development

The questionnaire content was driven by the primary aim of EVENS: to understand the experiences of ethnic and religious minority people in Britain during the COVID-19 pandemic. To develop the questionnaire content, it was important to obtain feedback and advice from EVENS voluntary, community and social enterprise (VCSE) organisation partners who helped shape the questionnaire in terms of content, question order and question wording in order to ensure that it was both relevant for their work and appropriate for the communities they engaged with in the course of their work and provision of services. Concurrently, the questionnaire had to meet the requirements of a non-probability survey, particularly in terms of including some questions common to those found in probability-based samples. This allows for statistical adjustments through survey weights to compensate for selection and coverage biases found in non-probability surveys. These questions should include key socioeconomic and demographic variables, and information on how the respondents are recruited into the survey and their motivation for participating. Typical variables that explain participation in an online survey are related to social involvement and attachment to society (Voogt and Saris, 2003). Other potential participatory variables are internet access, trust in political establishments, voting and volunteering.

The EVENS questionnaire is divided into topic-based modules, shown in Box 2.1. Many of these are adapted from those in established probability-based surveys and others were developed specifically to capture constructs not covered (or not well-covered) in existing surveys, such as the impact of COVID-19 and experiences of racism and racial discrimination. The questionnaire was developed for both online and Computer Assisted Telephone Interviewing (CATI) data collection and was offered in 14 languages: Arabic, Bengali, Chinese, Gujarati, English, Polish, Portuguese, Punjabi (Gurmukhi), Punjabi (Shahmukhi), Romanian, Somali, Turkish, Urdu and Welsh. The questionnaire and its implementation received

---

Box 2.1: Topics in the EVENS questionnaire

1. *Demographic characteristics.* Including date of birth, sex and gender identity.
2. *Household and accommodation.* Including household composition, tenure, type and location of accommodation, access to water and sanitation services, and house value.
3. *Social cohesion and neighbourhood belonging.* Including feelings of belonging to neighbourhood and to local area, and internet access and use.
4. *Ethnicity and migration.* With constructs measuring ethnic and religious identity, country of birth, year of arrival to Britain, nationality and feelings of belonging to England/Scotland/Wales.
5. *Socioeconomic characteristics.* Including educational qualifications, current economic activity, number of hours worked, number of hours worked from home, occupation, impact of COVID-19 on employment, childcare and home-schooling, use of benefits and financial worries.
6. *Racism and racial discrimination.* Including experiences of racism and racial discrimination over time and across domains, vicarious exposure, anticipation of discrimination and coping mechanisms.
7. *Health.* Including general self-rated health, limiting long-term illness, depression (CES-D 8), anxiety (GAD-7), chronic conditions, COVID-19 infection and related symptoms, experiences accessing the NHS, caring and receipt of care, receipt of and attitude towards the COVID-19 vaccine, and experiences of bereavement.
8. *Social isolation.* Including feelings of loneliness and isolation, and ways of connecting with others.
9. *Black Lives Matter (BLM).* Including participation in protests and support of the BLM movement.
10. *Attitudes towards the police.* Including confidence and trust in the police, being stopped by the police since the start of the outbreak of the COVID-19 pandemic, and overall sense of police activity in the community.
11. *Political participation.* Including trust in local and national governments in relation to managing the pandemic, interest in politics and voting intentions.
12. *Additional demographics.* Including marital status, sexual orientation, personal and household income, and immigration status.

---

full ethical approval from the University of Manchester Research Ethics Committee.

Recruitment to the survey

In any non-probability survey, recruitment strategies need to ensure representation of the target population. This was even more important for

EVENS as we aimed to collect data from a wide range of ethnic minority groups across age groups, sex and geographical regions. To facilitate the advertising of the survey, we allocated budget for the branding of the survey, a dedicated website from which the survey could be accessed and the development of a (predominantly online) marketing strategy. We held highly publicised online events to promote the survey, including an online launch event on the day the survey went live (February 2021), which included high-profile speakers from our VCSE partners. In addition, a steady stream of focused traditional and digital media campaigns was launched, particularly in ethnic and religious minority media outlets.

Partnerships with leading VCSE organisations in the race equality sector in Britain were central to the marketing strategy. Partners supported events, distributed recruitment materials via their mailing lists and in-house advertising, hosted events, spoke about EVENS in media coverage and worked with their networks to engage survey participants. Additionally, they advised on specific advertising channels (such as bespoke mailing lists and community media). The VCSE organisations ensured EVENS achieved broad coverage of the target ethnic minority groups and sufficient geographical coverage of Britain.

To ensure that only eligible persons (belonging to an ethnic minority group, 18 and over, and living in Scotland, Wales or England) took part in the main online survey, an open-link registration survey was first set up as a screening instrument and included preliminary questions to determine eligibility. The registration survey also included information about the survey with an opt-in routing question, questions on how the individual was recruited into the survey and the selected language. If the individual was found to be eligible, a unique link was provided to the main online survey. On completion of the survey, the individual received an additional four links to pass on to family and friends (the 'snowball' sample). A dedicated telephone number on the Ipsos website also made it possible to complete the questionnaire via telephone (CATI) instead of online. Participation in the survey was incentivised with the offer of a £10 gift voucher which was provided after completion of the survey.

The EVENS sample

EVENS aims to provide detailed information on the experiences of the COVID-19 pandemic for ethnic minority people and, in addition, to obtain data to enable robust reporting and analysis for more detailed ethnic minority groups than typically appear in probability-based surveys. Overall, results in this book are provided for 21 ethnic groups (including those identifying as Jewish, the White British group, any other White background, any other mixed/multiple background and any other ethnic group). Ethnic minority groups were targeted during data collection for a range of age groups (18–24, 25–34, 35–44, 45–54, 55–64, 65 and over), sex (male, female) and region of the UK (East Midlands, East of England, London, North East, North West, Scotland, South East, South West, Wales, West Midlands, Yorkshire and the Humber). To ensure we recruited enough people in each ethnic minority group for robust statistical analysis, we carried out data collection monitoring. For this we calculated desired sample sizes (quotas) for each age-specific, regional ethnic minority group. Due to small sample sizes, we combined Black African Sub-Saharan and Other Black African for a final 17 ethnic minority groups, as shown in Table 2.1. Ethnic minority groups not specially monitored were White British, Any other White, Any other mixed and Any other ethnic group. In addition, religious groups were not specifically monitored in the data collection (except for Jewish people) as we anticipated that they would be sufficiently captured within the ethnic minority samples. We aimed for a sample covering the 17 ethnic minority groups of approximately 12,000 individuals.

To specify the desired sample sizes (quotas), we first needed to obtain the British population totals for each monitored ethnic minority group by age group, sex and region. One important source of data for estimated counts of ethnic minority groups between national censuses is produced by the 'ETHPOP' project (Wohland et al, 2018, extracted for year 2020). Data are provided in two-year age groups, by sex and by region, and include the following ethnic groups: Bangladeshi, Black African, Black Caribbean, Chinese, Indian, Mixed, Other Asian, Other Black, Other ethnic groups, Pakistani, White British and White other.

Next, the ETHPOP distributions were adjusted to current population benchmarks. The population benchmarks were obtained from weighted survey counts of the 2019 UK Annual Population Survey where the survey weights are calibrated to official 2019 mid-year population estimates released by the Office for National Statistics (ONS). We applied a multivariate method (Structure Preserving Estimation [SPREE] [Purcell and Kish, 1980]) of calibrating the ETHPOP distributions of ethnic minority group by region, sex and age group to the population benchmarks. This procedure preserves the existing structure and proportions of the ethnic minority groups in the ETHPOP database and ensures that the totals by region, sex and age group equal the population benchmarks. For ethnic minority groups that did not have projected population totals in the ETHPOP data, we pro-rated from the derived proportions from the 2011 UK Census.

The updated estimates for the population by ethnic minority groups, age group, sex and region were used to allocate our target total sample size of 12,000 across ethnic groups (Table 2.1). For some ethnic minority groups that are traditionally under-represented in probability -based surveys, the target quota represented an oversampling relative to their proportion in the population, to give a minimum target sample of 375. This meant that other ethnic minority groups were undersampled. The final desired sample sizes (quotas) for the data collection monitoring and the achieved sample size for all ethnic minority groups are shown in Table 2.1. There is high variability in the achieved sample sizes compared to the proportional sample sizes due to the undersampling and oversampling, and a relatively small sample collected for the White British group, and this had implications for the variability of the final survey weights and width of confidence intervals.

Data collection and monitoring

The final sample of EVENS included data collected via a variety of pathways: the main survey from the online data collection (supplemented with CATI and some face-to-face interviews), established web panels from Ipsos and the commercial Prolific panel, as well as some face-to-face interviews with people from Gypsy/Traveller and Roma groups (to be discussed later). The final sample sizes of the different sample components of EVENS are in Table 2.2. The sex, age and regional characteristics of the survey weighted (to be discussed later) ethnic groups in the EVENS sample are shown in Table 2.3 (a and b). The final sample size was 14,221 participants.

Targeted data collection was carried out mainly through focused mainstream and social media campaigns and working with partner VCSEs to develop and implement recruitment strategies for those under-represented groups. To increase sample sizes, we were able to include ethnic minority panel members from the established 'Custom Panel' of Ipsos as well as their probability-based online panel, 'Knowledge Panel'. We also drew ethnic minority sample members from a commercial panel, Prolific (see https://www.prolific.co/). Efforts to improve the data collection with respect to the desired sample sizes (quotas) were filtered through the panels – for example, panel members were oversampled if they belonged to ethnic minority groups or lived in Scotland or Wales.

Daily monitoring of the responses to EVENS was essential for ongoing quality checks and ensuring that the desired sample sizes (quotas) were being met. In the spirit of responsive survey designs from the probability-based survey literature (Groves et al, 2006; Schouten and Shlomo, 2017), we reviewed all univariate and bivariate cross-tabulations of the ethnic minority groups by age group, sex and region on a daily basis to identify specific groups which were in need of targeted recruitment. We also assessed the representativeness of the collected sample data using a Representativity (R-) Indicator (Bianchi et al, 2019). The R-Indicator provides a single quantitative measure to assess the variability of subgroup response rates, in this case for the cross-classified variables of ethnic minority group, age group, sex and region. If the response rates are all the same in each subgroup, the maximal

TABLE 2.1: ALLOCATION OF THE PROPORTIONAL SAMPLE, THE DESIRED SAMPLE SIZE AFTER OVERSAMPLING OF ETHNIC MINORITY GROUPS AND ACHIEVED SAMPLE SIZE OF THE EVENS SURVEY

Ethnic group	Adjusted sample size by proportion in population		Desired sample size (quota)		Achieved sample size	
	N	%	N	%	N	%
In quotas						
White Irish	757.50	6.31	750	6.25	118	1.41
White Eastern European	1,682.25	14.02	975	8.13	363	4.34
Gypsy/Traveller	41.25	0.34	375	3.13	251	3.00
Roma	41.25	0.34	375	3.13	73	0.87
Jewish	316.50	2.64	750	6.25	674	8.06
Indian	1,965.00	16.38	1,350	11.25	1,288	15.40
Pakistani	1,337.25	11.14	975	8.13	866	10.36
Bangladeshi	469.25	3.91	900	7.50	406	4.86
Mixed White and Asian	329.25	2.74	375	3.13	525	6.28
Chinese	801.00	6.68	750	6.25	664	7.94
Any other Asian background	1,173.00	9.78	750	6.25	673	8.05
Black Caribbean	663.00	5.53	900	7.50	566	6.77
Mixed White and Black Caribbean	411.75	3.43	375	3.13	355	4.25
Black African	1,246.50	10.39	1,275	10.63	1,049	12.54
Mixed White and Black African	160.50	1.34	375	3.13	159	1.90
Any other Black back ground	283.50	2.36	375	3.13	180	2.15
Arab	321.00	2.68	375	3.13	152	1.82
Total	12000.00	100.00	12000	100.00	8362	100.00
No quotas						
Any other White background					698	
Any other mixed/multiple background					378	
Any other ethnic group					270	
White British					4,513	
Total					5,859	
Overall total					14,221	

● TABLE 2.2: FINAL SAMPLE SIZE OF THE EVENS SURVEY, BY SAMPLE COMPONENTS ●

Component	Sample size		
	Ethnic minority groups	White British	Total
Main Survey	3,292	114	3,406
Panels	3,554	4,114	7,668
Prolific	2,862	285	3,147
Total	9,708	4,513	14,221

value of the R-Indicator would be 1. The final R-Indicator of the EVENS sample was 0.434, a relatively low value from the maximal representativeness that is indicative of the achieved sample sizes having large differences from their proportional sample sizes (see Table 2.1). This results in high variability in the final survey weights.

An example of a responsive design intervention to EVENS data collection as a result of sample monitoring was the introduction of face-to-face interviews with Roma and Gypsy Traveller people. Monitoring of responses revealed that fewer people than were needed from these ethnic groups were taking part in the survey and thus there was a need for targeted recruitment. In close collaboration with EVENS partner organisation Friends, Families and Travellers (FFT), two key barriers to participation were identified: lack of trust based on concerns that taking part in the survey could be detrimental to individuals (and that anonymity could not be assured); and lack of motivation emanating from a sense that the survey would not produce any benefit for the communities. In response, the EVENS team together with FFT and with support from Ipsos developed a community interviewer approach to Roma and Gypsy Traveller participation. Seven community interviewers were trained to support people in completing EVENS online by conducting interviews face to face within Roma and Gypsy Traveller communities. The approach was successful, recruiting 324 participants who identified as Roma or Gypsy Traveller and uniquely enabling the documentation of their experiences and inequalities in relation to other ethnic groups.

Ensuring data quality

Early in the fieldwork period, quality checks through daily monitoring by the EVENS team and Ipsos identified abnormalities in data indicating potential sample quality concerns. The survey was paused for a period of weeks to allow additional quality checks to be embedded in order to ensure that only legitimate responses to the survey were recorded. Additional quality checks included a weekly Bespoke Data Quality Monitoring process, undertaken collaboratively by the EVENS team and Ipsos. This included the introduction of stronger 'digital fingerprinting', a computational process that can identify and track internet users and devices online and ensure single responses from IP addresses. For the EVENS open-link design, this meant that any 'snowball' links that were given to participants to pass on to family and friends would be deemed problematic if they were using the same IP address as the link participant. Therefore, an identical survey platform was built for family members with the same IP address to access EVENS. Other additional checks included a 'reCAPTCHA'-type question, posting out the vouchers following an email verification instead of sending electronic vouchers by email automatically on completion of the survey, monitoring

TABLE 2.3: THE EVENS SAMPLE: A) ETHNIC GROUPS BY

Weighted

Ethnic group	Sex		Age group				
	F	M	18–24	25–34	35–44	45–54	55+
White Irish	50.50	49.50	7.40	13.00	24.60	19.50	35.50
White Eastern European	48.60	51.40	14.20	44.30	26.40	8.80	6.30
Gypsy/Traveller	49.60	50.40	18.10	19.50	30.90	18.00	13.40
Roma	49.00	51.00	18.50	20.90	31.30	23.30	6.00
Jewish	51.90	48.10	10.20	15.70	15.20	15.30	43.60
Any other White background	51.90	48.10	12.50	28.20	33.80	14.40	11.10
Indian	48.70	51.30	11.10	24.10	24.80	15.20	24.80
Pakistani	48.70	51.30	17.70	24.90	24.80	16.00	16.60
Bangladeshi	48.20	51.80	19.60	24.20	25.00	16.70	14.50
Mixed White and Asian	47.90	52.10	24.50	28.20	19.50	13.30	14.50
Chinese	53.30	46.70	17.90	42.20	16.00	9.30	14.60
Any other Asian background	50.70	49.30	13.70	24.60	23.40	19.70	18.60
Black Caribbean	54.60	45.40	10.00	14.20	14.00	20.80	41.00
Mixed White and Black Caribbean	50.90	49.10	28.10	26.60	18.30	13.80	13.10
Black African	50.40	49.60	16.00	23.80	23.40	20.90	16.00
Mixed White and Black African	50.40	49.60	20.30	29.30	22.20	15.20	13.00
Any other Black background	49.50	50.50	19.90	20.80	18.70	20.40	20.10
Arab	39.80	60.20	16.10	27.20	25.80	16.00	14.90
Any other mixed/multiple background	52.70	47.30	19.60	31.00	20.40	13.30	15.70
Any other ethnic group	46.40	53.60	12.00	25.30	25.30	17.80	19.60
White British	51.30	48.70	9.50	14.50	13.80	17.10	45.10
Total	51.10	48.90	10.60	17.00	16.10	16.90	39.40

the email addresses of the respondent, and quality checks on the duration of completing the questionnaire and the quality of write-in text.

In addition, a series of logic checks on the weekly collected sample were carried out by the EVENS team to verify participants. These included the following checks: the language used for the survey and the ethnic group identification of the participant was not incongruous; participants' ages compared with the ages they provided separately for members of the household (including themselves); a very high number of people in the household (n > 15); whether the ethnic group was consistent with the VCSE partner through which they heard about the survey; the number of people in the household compared with the number of people who contributed to household finances; highest level of qualification and whether this was consistent

AGE AND SEX AND B) ETHNIC GROUPS BY REGION OF BRITAIN •

Region

North East	North West	Yorkshire and Humber	West Mid-lands	East Mid-lands	East of England	South West	South East	London	Wales	Scotland	N (weighted)
2.80	2.10	2.10	9.90	7.10	5.40	4.70	9.30	30.90	4.90	13.10	158.60
1.70	4.90	4.90	7.90	8.90	10.50	5.50	13.20	25.10	3.00	12.40	225.70
2.00	2.00	2.00	8.20	5.80	27.90	3.70	21.50	15.30	2.80	0.60	45.70
0.00	0.00	0.00	3.20	36.20	11.30	7.80	0.00	32.40	0.00	0.00	45.00
0.70	3.20	3.20	3.10	1.20	13.60	2.40	7.60	54.10	0.40	2.50	63.30
1.10	3.90	3.90	3.60	4.60	11.20	5.80	17.40	40.00	1.80	5.30	491.00
0.90	4.80	4.80	15.20	11.50	6.40	2.60	11.00	36.10	1.50	2.40	394.90
1.50	18.70	18.70	20.10	3.90	5.60	0.90	7.90	19.60	0.70	5.60	274.20
1.80	4.60	4.60	11.80	2.00	7.60	2.00	6.70	47.00	5.50	0.90	99.40
1.40	8.40	8.40	7.70	5.20	10.30	6.40	16.60	29.90	2.80	1.60	64.30
2.50	6.30	6.30	8.90	5.70	7.60	4.00	13.50	29.10	2.40	7.90	151.00
0.80	4.50	4.50	8.40	5.60	7.00	3.10	14.80	43.20	3.00	2.80	245.90
0.10	4.10	4.10	14.50	5.00	7.10	2.30	7.70	53.10	0.80	0.70	139.20
1.80	9.40	9.40	15.90	11.20	6.50	6.00	11.00	25.10	2.20	1.10	83.50
1.20	4.40	4.40	6.80	4.50	8.20	2.60	9.50	52.20	1.30	2.70	263.00
0.70	7.50	7.50	3.50	3.70	10.80	3.90	12.00	35.10	1.80	1.00	30.20
0.70	0.80	0.80	13.50	2.50	5.20	2.00	13.10	56.60	0.30	1.30	59.20
0.70	2.60	2.60	6.50	4.10	5.70	4.40	6.50	34.60	14.50	14.80	62.30
1.20	6.20	6.20	6.20	4.70	10.00	6.80	12.70	38.60	3.60	1.30	61.50
1.00	6.20	6.20	8.10	3.80	6.90	4.00	9.90	48.20	3.70	2.20	95.50
4.80	9.00	9.00	8.90	7.90	9.90	10.10	14.60	7.10	5.70	9.80	11,167.70
4.00	8.30	8.30	9.10	7.60	9.60	8.70	14.00	13.60	5.00	8.70	14,221.00

with their age; or for multiple IP addresses, whether there was consistent reporting of the number of people in the household, the age structure of the household and the geographical location.

Data adjustments after fieldwork: imputation

Following the completion of data collection, a number of adjustments were made to the EVENS data. First, we ensured that the survey responses were as complete as possible. Out of the 14,221 participants in EVENS, there were 121 cases where the respondent abandoned the online questionnaire after completing more than half of the questions; these cases were retained in the sample. To ensure the data from these respondents were as complete as possible, information was calculated (or imputed) for missing variables based on what was already known about the respondents.

A nearest-neighbour random hot deck imputation approach (Kalton and Kasprzyk, 1986) was used to identify a single donor (another participant in the sample) for imputing the missing values of the abandoned case. In this method, we looked for a 'nearest neighbour' for the abandoned case out of all potential donors by calculating a (Gower's) distance metric (Gower, 1971) on all previous completed questions that had a full response. In order to minimise the number of comparisons between each abandoned case and all potential donors, we only looked for donors if they matched exactly on: sex, age group, ethnic group, region, education and employment. If there was more than one donor for an abandoned case, we selected one donor randomly. Furthermore, once a donor was used for imputation, it was taken out of the selection pool for the next abandoned case, so a donor was only used once. All imputed cases have a flag so that they can be identified in the EVENS dataset.

Data adjustments after fieldwork: survey weights

Work was undertaken to account for potential biases in the sample. Biases are inherent to all data. However, in order to enable EVENS to be used in ways that can be said to be representative of ethnic minority people in Britain, it was necessary to understand the biases and create correction factors (survey weights). As EVENS is a non-probability sample, it was necessary to produce weights to account for biases in population characteristics (coverage biases) and biases in terms of data being from people who were more likely than others to take part in the survey, and to answer in particular ways (selection bias). So, the complex data processing and statistical techniques used to produce survey weights were imperative to make the EVENS sample mirror the characteristics of the British population. The weights are correction factors assigned to each respondent in the survey that, when applied during data analysis and reporting, make the responses of some (categories of) people (who are under-represented in the data) count for more than others (who are appropriately or over-represented in the data).

The EVENS weights were calculated based on a quasi-randomisation approach that uses propensity scores estimated through a statistical model on an integrated dataset which contains both the non-probability EVENS sample and a probability-based reference sample. Based on the propensity scores, a pseudo-design weight was estimated for each respondent in EVENS. This was followed by a calibration step to ensure that the final survey weights in EVENS totalled the population benchmarks within weighting classes (defined below). This approach introduces 'randomisation' into the non-probability sample which will allow for statistical modelling and generalisation to the target population (in a similar way in which probability-based surveys can be used).

The four weighting variables that were used to calibrate the pseudo-design weights in EVENS were region, age group, sex and ethnic group. The calculations required data on these variables for all respondents. This necessitated some imputation of weighting variables within the EVENS dataset for 254 missing values on age group, 43 missing on sex, 32 missing on ethnic group and 8 missing on region. Similar to the method used for imputations of the abandoned cases, a nearest neighbour hot deck donor imputation using the Gower's distance metric was used. We implemented a simulation study to assess the best strategy for imputing missing weighting variables and the most successful approach was to find the donor with the smallest Gower's Distance on 37 matching variables. All imputed cases have an appropriate flag and can be identified in the EVENS dataset.

Preparing population benchmarks for survey weights

Similar to the calculation of the desired sampled sizes (quotas), we needed to calculate 2020 population benchmarks by ethnic group, age group, sex and region to be used in the calibration of the EVENS weights. Again, we used the ETHPOP database with projections to 2020 (and featuring a 'Brexit' scenario) with further disaggregation of ethnic minority groups according to proportions derived from the 2011 UK Census. We then updated the ETHPOP estimates using the official 2020 mid-year population estimates by age group, sex and region released by the ONS according to the SPREE method.

In some cases, we also used external considerations to obtain updated information about the population size of an ethnic minority group. For example, it was considered that the Roma and Gypsy/Traveller ethnic groups were substantially under-represented in the UK 2011 Census and hence do not appear in the official 2020 mid-year estimates. We therefore used external information for these populations (see, for example, Brown et al, 2013) for estimates of the Roma population according to geographical location and applied growth factors where relevant. We hope to recalculate population benchmarks using the 2021 UK Census in the future (the data were not available at the time of writing).

At the end of the process, we obtained updated population benchmarks for the cross-classified weighting variables for a total of 2,310 weighting classes (11 regions × 2 sex × 5 age groups × 21 ethnic groups). The definition of the weighting variables is shown in Box 2.2.

Due to small sample sizes for older people in EVENS, we had to combine the 55–64 age group with the 65 and over age group. It was also found that

---

Box 2.2: EVENS weighting variables

Region – London/South East/South West/East of England/East Midlands/West Midlands/
Yorkshire and Humber/North West/North East/Scotland/Wales
Sex – Male/Female
Age Group – 18–24/25–34/35–44/45–54/55+
Ethnicity – White: British (English/Scottish/Welsh [excluding Northern Ireland]/White:
Irish/White: Eastern European/White: Gypsy/Traveller/White: Roma/White: Any other
White background/Jewish/Asian: Indian/Asian: Pakistani/Asian: Bangladeshi/Mixed:
White and Asian/Asian: Chinese/Asian: Any other Asian background/Black: Caribbean/
Mixed: White and Black Caribbean/Black: African/Mixed: White and Black African/
Black: Any other Black/African/Caribbean background/Other: Arab/Other: Any other
ethnic group/Mixed: Any other mixed/multiple background

---

605 out of the 2,310 weighting classes had a zero sample size in EVENS. We therefore had to combine weighting classes by collapsing the region variable for those sparse ethnic minority groups. The final number of weighting classes was 1,705.

Preparing the probability reference sample

We used the Annual Population Survey (APS) 2019 and 2020 data (ONS, Social Survey Division, 2020, 2021) and the European Social Survey (ESS) rounds 8 and 9 (European Social Survey, 2016, 2018) to create a probability reference sample for those aged 18 and over in England, Wales and Scotland. The APS had 378,716 respondents and the ESS had 3,916 respondents. The APS provides information on key socioeconomic variables that overlap with those collected in EVENS, and the ESS collects data on attitudes and social participation which can explain selectivity mechanisms for participating in an online non-probability survey.

The first step was to statistically match the ESS to the APS (D'Orazio et al, 2006) where we assumed that the APS is the base file. The aim was to bring the participation variables from the ESS over to the APS dataset. Using the Gower's Distance, we identified the nearest neighbour for each ESS respondent in the APS according to common sociodemographic variables shown in Table 2.4 and attached the ESS participation variables (shown in Table 2.5) to the APS. To reduce computation time, we required an exact match on a two-year band of age. In Table 2.6 we show summary statistics of the Gower's distances in the statistical matching stage of the ESS to the APS.

────── • TABLE 2.4: MATCHING VARIABLES COMMON TO THE ANNUAL • ──────
POPULATION SURVEY (APS) AND THE EUROPEAN SOCIAL SURVEY (ESS)

Variable	APS	ESS	Harmonised measurement
Age	AGE	agea	Single year age
Economic status	INECAC05	mnactic	1 Employed 2 Unemployed 3 Retired 4 Sick/Disabled 5 Student 6 Other
Education	HIQUL15D	eduagb2	1 Degree or equivalent 2 Higher Education 3 GCE, A level, GCSE or equivalent 4 Other/no qualifications. 5 Over 70
Ethnicity	ETHGBEUL	anctry1	1 British 2 Other White 3 Black/African/Caribbean 4 Other Asian 5 Pakistani/Bangladeshi/Indian 6 Chinese 7 Other
First digit of occupation	SC10MMJ	isco08	First digit of the occupation
Gender	SEX	gndr	1 Male 2 Female
Marital status	MARSTA	maritalb	1 Married 2 Civil 3 Separated 4 Divorced/Dissolved 5 Widowed/Partner died 6 Other
Region	GOR9D	region	Government office regions

The next step was to mass-impute the ESS participation variables in the statistically matched APS/ESS dataset for all remaining records. We used a method called fractional hot-deck imputation (FHDI), which creates a single complete dataset with 'fractional weights' for each potential imputed value (Kalton and Kish, 1984; Kim and Fuller, 2004; Kim, 2011; Im et al, 2018). The imputation approach uses a two-stage process as follows: first, imputation cells are formed by cross-classifying predictor variables (ethnic group, marital status, education, broad occupation, economic status, sex and age) in order to be able to match potential donors to recipients. The units

• TABLE 2.5: EUROPEAN SOCIAL SURVEY (ESS) PARTICIPATION VARIABLES •

Variable	ESS	Measurement	Short question
Vote	vote	1 Yes, 2 No, 3 Not Eligible	Voted last national election
Interest in politics	polintr	1 Very ... 4 Not at all	How interested in politics
Subjective general health	health	1 Very good, 2 Good, 3 Fair, 4 Bad, 5 Very bad	Subjective general health
Religious events	Rlgatnd	1 Every day ... 7 Never	How often attend religious services apart from special occasions
Religiosity	Rlgdgr	0 Not at all ... 10 Very	How religious are you
Citizen of the country	Ctzcntr	1 Yes, 2 No	Citizen of country
Trust in parliament	Trstprl	0 No trust ... 10 Complete trust	Trust in country's parliament
Trust in the police	Trstplc	0 No trust ... 10 Complete trust	Trust in the police
Member of a discriminated group	Dscrgrp	1 Yes, 2 No	Member of a group discriminated against in this country

TABLE 2.6: SUMMARY STATISTICS OF GOWER'S DISTANCES IN THE MATCHING OF THE ANNUAL POPULATION SURVEY (APS) AND THE EUROPEAN SOCIAL SURVEY (ESS)

TABLE 2.6: SUMMARY STATISTICS OF GOWER'S DISTANCES IN THE MATCHING OF THE ANNUAL POPULATION SURVEY (APS) AND THE EUROPEAN SOCIAL SURVEY (ESS)

Summary statistics	Value
Min.	0.000
1st Quartile	0.000
Median	0.003
Mean	0.000
3rd Quartile	0.000
Max.	0.140

with complete data serve as donors, and units with at least one missing item serve as recipients. In the second stage, each possible value for the missing item is assigned a 'fractional weight' representing the likelihood of being the true value. Since our variables were all categorical, the final imputed value we chose was the one with the highest fractional weight. In case of equal fractional weights, we drew a value at random.

Calculating the probabilities of participation and pseudo-design weights

Stacking the EVENS sample with the APS/ESS reference sample, we used a statistical model to estimate propensity scores where the dependent variable takes a value of 1 if the individual responded to EVENS, otherwise the dependent variable takes a value of 0. The independent variables in the model are: age group, sex, region, ethnic minority group, economic status, education, marital status, occupation, trust in Parliament, trust in police, interest in politics, subjective general health, member of a discriminated group and an interaction term of the subjective general health variable with broad ethnic group. Note that these independent variables included both key sociodemographic variables and participation variables. We implemented the method proposed in Chen, Li and Wu (2019) to estimate the propensity scores where we carried out the estimation separately for White British and All other ethnic groups.

Following the estimation of the propensity scores, we obtained the pseudo-design weight by sorting the EVENS dataset by the estimated propensity score and producing 20 groupings of equal sizes. Within each group, we calculated the average propensity score and took its inverse to obtain the pseudo-design weight for all individuals in EVENS in that group. The

• TABLE 2.7. DISTRIBUTIONS OF ALTERNATIVE WEIGHTING SCHEMES OF EVENS •

Weights	Minimum	Maximum	Median	Mean	Standard deviation	Coefficient of variation	Increase in variance
Calibration only	36.4	24,549	1,230.1	3,632.9	4,187.2	1.15	1.33
Propensity score stratification and calibration	1.0	66,852	1,072.4	3,632.9	6,067.3	1.67	2.79

propensity score stratification method allows for smoother pseudo-design weights compared to taking the inverse of the propensity score.

Calibration to population totals

To calibrate the pseudo-design weighted EVENS to population benchmarks, we carried out an iterative proportional fitting procedure (raking ratio adjustment) (Kalton and Kasprzyk, 1986) using all two-way interactions of the weighting variables: region, age group, sex and ethnic group. This ensures that all survey weighted estimates from EVENS sum to the population benchmarks on these four weighting variables. We trimmed the smaller weights to a minimum value of 1.

We also calculated a survey weight for EVENS without the pseudo-design weights and only applying the calibration step, thus allowing for a comparison of the methods and an understanding on the variability of the survey weights. The summary results of the final weighting procedure are in Table 2.7. As expected, we obtained a large variation in the final survey weights largely due to the oversampling of small ethnic minority groups and the undersampling of large ethnic minority groups. In addition, the White British sample is small relative to their proportion of the population and therefore they have large survey weights.

Conclusion

EVENS represents methodological innovation primarily in the use of a non-probability survey design for a large national survey. Importantly, our experience with EVENS shows that this type of survey design can be particularly advantageous for recruiting minoritised and marginalised populations. By making the invitation to participate open to all, partnering with key race equality organisations for questionnaire design and recruitment, having a large number of ethnic minority groups represented, responsively adapting our fieldwork methods (particularly procedures for data collection, data monitoring and quality assurance) and implementing comprehensive post-fieldwork data adjustments to ensure a complete, robust dataset, we have shown how data generated with our innovative methods can be used as representative of ethnic minority people in Britain. As a successful example of a non-traditional, non-probability approach to social surveys, EVENS presents a challenge to data producers and data users to better represent ethnic minority populations. There are many lessons to be learnt from the EVENS methodology and we hope that the novel and important findings presented in the chapters of this book will encourage others in pursuing new approaches to collecting social science data.

3

Ethnic identities

Magda Borkowska, James Nazroo, Nissa Finney and Joseph Harrison

---

Key findings

Ethnic identity is important to people alongside a strong sense of belonging to British society but standardised measures of ethnicity do not fully capture the complex ways that people describe their ethnicity.

- The free-text ethnic identity responses demonstrate that the standardised ethnic categories do not allow people to accurately express complex ethnic origins and migration experiences; they exclude identities from certain parts of the world and subnational, place-based identities.
- Ethnic identity is important for most people from minority backgrounds. This is especially true for those from Black African, Black Caribbean, Pakistani, White Irish and Jewish backgrounds. Ethnic identity is the least important for White British people, followed by people from White Eastern European, White Other, and Mixed White and Asian backgrounds.
- Religious belonging varies considerably across ethnic groups. People from Bangladeshi, Pakistani, Black African, Arab and Indian backgrounds most frequently report having a religion. Those from White British, Mixed White and Asian, and Mixed White and Black Caribbean backgrounds most frequently declare having no religious affiliation.
- Strong religious attachment is more common when people identify with minority religions and when there tends to be a consistency between ethnic identity and religious affiliation.
- Most people from ethnic minority backgrounds participate in practices linked to their ethnicity or religion. White British are the least likely to report participation in such practices, followed by White Irish and White Eastern Europeans. Eating food associated with one's ethnic or religious background is the most popular practice across ethnic groups.
- A sense of belonging to British society is very high across all groups. A particularly high sense of belonging is reported by those from Bangladeshi, Indian, Pakistani, Black African, Black Other, Arab, Jewish and White British backgrounds. A strong sense of belonging to English, Scottish and Welsh societies is somewhat less common among people from ethnic minority backgrounds compared to those from a White British background.

Introduction

In the UK, we have become used to filling in ethnicity classification forms for a range of administrative purposes and are commonly offered a standardised set of categories derived from the census. The use of a common set of categories has the advantage of tracking ethnic and racial inequalities over time, offers consistency across datasets and enables comparisons with the population census. However, there is a risk that much is missed by the standardisation of ethnic categories. For example, we cannot accurately capture the increasingly diverse, changing population using the limited number of standardised ethnic categories. We also do not know how strongly people identify with their ethnic, racial, national or religious groups and what these identities mean for them in everyday life.

This chapter explores articulations of and attachment to ethnic and religious identities. Additionally, the sense of belonging to British, English, Scottish and Welsh societies is examined across ethnic groups. This is possible with the Evidence for Equality National Survey (EVENS) data because, in addition to including standardised ethnic categories, EVENS enabled people to describe their ethnic identity in their own words and to indicate how significant ethnic, religious, national and subnational identities were to them. The survey also asked them about their everyday practices related to ethnic and religious identifications. By examining responses on ethnic identification, we can reflect upon what is (and is not) captured by standardised ethnic group categorisation.

Theoretical conceptualisations of ethnicity acknowledge that ethnic identities are socially constructed and shaped by many factors, including ancestry or country of origin, skin colour, religious beliefs, culture and language (Aspinall, 1997). Most importantly, however, ethnic identity also refers to a subjective sense of belonging to a particular ethnic community. Similar to other group identities, the sense of belonging to an ethnic group is a dynamic and fluid process rather than a fixed construct. Just like other group identities, it is also highly context-dependent and relative to a frame of reference as outlined by social identity theory (Tajfel and Turner, 1979).

Over time, there has been a growing recognition among researchers that ethnic identity is a complex and multidimensional phenomenon that extends beyond simple self-identification with a particular ethnic identity label. To measure such a complex construct across different ethnic groups, Phinney (1992) developed a widely used multidimensional psychological scale, the Multigroup Ethnic Identity Measure, which comprises three main subscales: (1) self-identification and the extent of positive feelings towards one's group; (2) the extent of having a developed, secure ethnic identity; and (3) participation in activities associated with one's ethnic identity. The questions included in EVENS tap into domains (1) and (3).

Having positive ethnic and/or religious identities might be associated with many practical and emotional benefits. There is a general agreement that positive attachment to ethnic identity is likely to increase psychosocial functioning, that is, it might positively affect psychological wellbeing and self-esteem, and can protect members of ethnic minority groups from the negative consequences of experiencing racial discrimination (Roberts et al, 1999; Umaña-Taylor, 2011). For minority groups, participating in ethnicity- and/or religion-related practices might provide a safe space for people to interact with others, build a positive sense of self and foster a sense of belonging. Furthermore, religious institutions have long served as hubs of social and civic life as well as places offering practical advice and charitable activities. As noted by Nicholson (2018), for migrant communities, churches, mosques, gurdwaras, temples and synagogues play a particularly important role for connection and practical support in a new country.

Ethnic and religious identities not only constitute building blocks of self-concept but are also used as social markers (Kapadia and Bradby, 2021), which affect how group boundaries are defined and used in a society. For example, in the UK, the ethnicity classifications have been introduced with the intention of better understanding and monitoring social inequalities among different social groups that share common origin/ancestry (Williams and Husk, 2013). However, it is important to acknowledge that such ethnicity categorisations are defined and to some extent imposed by the more powerful 'majority' on the less powerful 'minority' (Nazroo and Karlsen, 2003). This means that, in part, minority ethnic identities become constructed in response to externally defined ethnic groupings. The use of such categorisations can in turn marginalise certain ethnic minority groups.

The process of categorisation makes groups more or less visible and situates them within debates on integration, social cohesion and British values. Every few years, the debates on the national identity crisis resurface, especially in the context of growing ethnic and religious diversity and immigration (Finney and Simpson, 2009). Feelings of belonging to the national community are generally believed to have many positive consequences, including greater social cohesion and a sense of solidarity. Focus on cohesion and solidarity has characterised government reports on diversity in recent years (see, for example, Casey Review, 2016). Such discussions led to the turn against policies of multiculturalism and the emphasis on shared national values as underpinning integration. This has resulted in policies such as more demanding citizenship tests and mandatory citizenship ceremonies, with the aim of ensuring the 'successful integration' of naturalised citizens. The ideology behind and the success of such practices have been contested (Byrne, 2017), but the appetite for practices that intend to facilitate a common sense of British identity and belonging have remained popular in political discourse. For example, since 2014, schools in the UK have been required to introduce the active promotion of British values into their curricula (Department for Education, 2014).

Despite concerns about a low sense of national belonging among ethnic minority groups in political and media discourses, academic studies have consistently shown that ethnic minority people feel strongly attached to British society and do not perceive incompatibility between their ethnic and religious identities and British values (Nazroo and Karlsen, 2003; Finney and Simpson, 2009; Maxwell, 2009; Manning and Roy, 2010; Demireva and Heath, 2014; Nandi and Platt, 2014; Karlsen and Nazroo, 2015). Research has also found strong sense of belonging among ethnic minority groups to local areas (see Chapter 6). These findings suggest that people do not tend to perceive their national, ethnic and religious identities as mutually exclusive, but rather as complementary.

Given the inevitable limitations of the standardised ethnic identity classifications for accurately reflecting how people understand their ethnic identities, in this chapter, we reflect on key ways of describing ethnicity used by respondents outside the predefined ethnic categories. By doing this, we aim to better understand which aspects of ethnic identity are missing in the existing classifications and what additional ethnicity categories should be considered in the future to better reflect the diversity of the UK population.

The first empirical section of this chapter gives an overview of the common types of ethnic identity articulations expressed by EVENS participants in the free text responses. It also reflects on the consequences of growing ethnic diversity on the existing standardised classifications. The second section focuses on the questions concerning the subjective importance of group identities. In particular, it asks the following questions: how important are ethnic and religious identities to people? Are there substantive differences in the strength of attachment to ethnic identity among people from different ethnic and religious backgrounds? How much do people engage in practices related to their ethnic backgrounds? Finally, the last section explores sense of belonging to British society across different ethnic groups and compares it to the sense of belonging to English, Scottish and Welsh societies.

How do people describe their ethnic background?

This section provides a snapshot of the ways in which respondents described their ethnicity in response to an open-ended write-in question which asked: 'How would you describe your ethnic background in your own words?' All answers were classified into one of three categories: 'standardised ethnicity articulation', 'non-standardised ethnicity articulation' or 'non-engagement'. 'Standardised ethnicity articulation' category includes people who described their ethnicity using the same words that are used in the standardised ONS ethnicity categories. 'Non-standardised ethnicity articulation' includes people who expressed their identities using either non-standardised conceptualisations of ethnicity (that is, they referred to concepts other than race, ethnicity, religion or nationality) or used different language from the language used in standardised ethnicity categories. Finally, the 'non-engagement' category refers to respondents who did not engage at all with the open-ended question.

Figure 3.1 shows the distribution of the types of ethnicity articulations for the 21 standardised ethnic groups used in the EVENS. First, it can be noted that the majority of respondents in most ethnic groups did engage with the open-ended ethnicity question and provided at least a short, written description of their ethnic identity. Second, for most ethnic groups, those respondents who provided an answer were likely to use standardised concepts and language to describe their ethnic identity. This relatively high consistency between the write-in ethnicity articulations and the standardised ethnicity categories – shown in the 'standardised' segments in Figure 3.1 – is likely to reflect that most people in the UK are very familiar with administrative ethnicity categories, which are conventionally used for monitoring purposes in almost all public service settings (including health, education and employment). However, a substantial proportion in each ethnic group expressed their ethnic identity in a non-standardised way. The highest proportion of non-standardised articulations was found among people from Jewish, White Eastern European, White Gypsy/Traveller and Chinese backgrounds, and those who classified themselves as belonging to various 'Other' ethnic groups (Figure 3.1).

The common complexities expressed by those who used non-standardised articulations often reflected their complex ethno-racial origin and/or migration journey(s). As expected, the complexities of ethno-racial origin were particularly highlighted by those who chose different variations of 'Other' ethnicity categories. Some of those who chose 'Any other ethnic group' pointed out that their ethnic origin was simply missing from the ONS classification. For example, as illustrated by the first two responses in Table 3.1, people from the Americas currently do not have more specific ethnicity categories to choose from. Other responses indicated that the 'Any other' standardised ethnicity category often includes people with complex ethno-racial origins who think of themselves as British. Similar reasoning might be applied to other examples presented for 'Other Arab', 'Other Asian' and 'Other Black' categories, where the respondents refer to their complex (usually non-White) ethnic origins, but also highlight that they generally see themselves as British. The two responses shown in Table 3.1 from respondents who selected the 'Other White' category demonstrate different types of commonly mentioned complexities: (1) the fact that people's migration journeys and, in particular, the experiences of forced migration and persecution are important reference points for ethnic identity

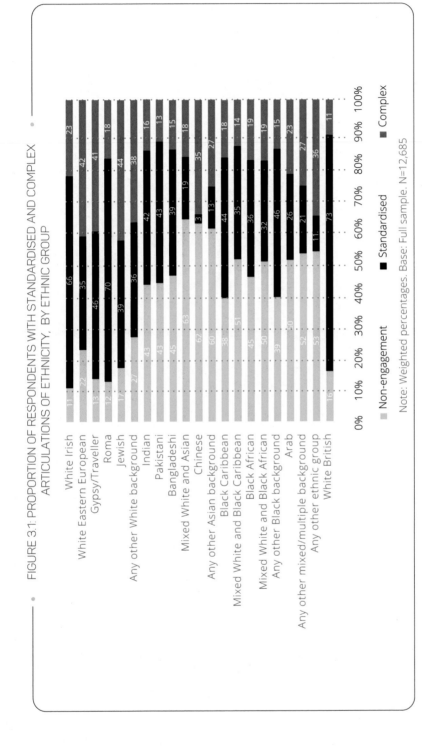

FIGURE 3.1: PROPORTION OF RESPONDENTS WITH STANDARDISED AND COMPLEX ARTICULATIONS OF ETHNICITY, BY ETHNIC GROUP

Note: Weighted percentages. Base: Full sample. N=12,685

■ Non-engagement   ■ Standardised   ■ Complex

TABLE 3.1: EXAMPLES OF COMPLEX ARTICULATIONS OF ETHNICITY, BY ETHNIC GROUP

Any other ethnic group	• I would describe my ethnic background as "Latina", which personally, I think of it as a mixture between South American and European people. Usually I don't see any option that I feel describe my ethnic background when I am asked to record my ethnicity, it seems like they forget of the people from the American continent.
	• I am a member of the confederated tribes of the Siletz Indians. What some describe as a Native American. I am not an "other-other" as described on this survey, or on NHS forms. Natives from N. America, S. America, and Australia are completely ignored by the NHS.
	• I am Turkish, but my mother is of Tatar descent and my father immigrated to Turkey from Greece where he was part of a Turkish speaking Muslim ethnic minority.
	• I am born in Kenya, great great grand parents from India, brown skinned but of African origin. However I consider myself British.
Other ethnic group: Arab	• I am Middle Eastern. I came from an Arabic speaking country located in Africa and I am Muslim.
	• I'm ethnically Iraqi. Both of my parents are Iraqi and I was born there. I came to the UK at age 1 so I also identify as British.
Other ethnic group: White	• My ethnic background is complex due to political persecution and exile of some of my family members from previous generations from their native country.
	• Cornish, not British not English.
Other ethnic group: Asian	• My parents are Sri Lankan and me and my brothers we were born in Italy so we are Italian. Before 5 years my mum applied for Italian passport and we are Italian officially now.
Other ethnic group: Black	• My ethnic background is Sierra Leonian and Jamaican.
	• Black British of African Caribbean, Arab and Irish heritage.
Other ethnic group: Mixed	• Indian Pakistani mixed
	• Black British of African Caribbean, Arab and Irish heritage
	• South Asian and Iranian heritage
	• I am half white, my other half is Malagasy, however I come from the Merina tribe, which is from Indonesia
	• Mix European and native Brazilian

36

formation; and (2) the importance of subnational, place-based identities. The quotes presented for the 'Other mixed' category remind us that the standardised 'Mixed' categories solely focus on a mix with 'White'.

These examples already provide a hint that those who classify themselves into different variants of 'Other' ethnic groups have parents and grandparents born in different parts of the world. Country of family origin is often used in the construction of standardised ethnicity categories (for example, Pakistani, Bangladeshi and Indian are used in the ONS classification), but they do not incorporate multiple origin countries. The EVENS sample provides a very good illustration that even in a single country context, such as the UK, people identifying with a particular ethnic group can originate from a wide range of countries (see Figure 3.2). The EVENS sample comprises individuals originating from 155 countries, which highlights the diversity of the UK ethnic minority population.

How attached do people feel to their ethnic and religious identities?

The importance of ethnic identity

Despite the difficulties and complexities of defining ethnicity, many people feel that their ethnic background is an important part of their self-definition. EVENS asked respondents to assess on a scale from 1 (very important) to 4 (not at all important): 'How important is your ethnic background to your sense of who you are?' Previous literature suggests that both gender and age are likely to shape how strongly people identify with their ethnic and national identities (Warikoo, 2005; Huddy and Khatib, 2007; Ali and Heath, 2013; Karlsen and Nazroo, 2015; Nandi and Platt, 2020). Given this, all the results presented in this chapter adjust for the age and sex of respondents (unless otherwise specified).

In line with the existing literature, we find that all ethnic minority groups have a stronger attachment to their ethnic identities compared to the majority, White British population (as illustrated in Figure 3.3). Black African, Black Caribbean, Pakistani, Irish and Jewish people report the highest attachment to their ethnic identity: over 90% say that their ethnic background is very or fairly important to their sense of self. Lower percentages of people who classify themselves as belonging to different Mixed groups (58–79%), in comparison to the Black (85–91%), Asian (77–91%) and Arab (81%) groups, report a strong attachment to ethnic identity. Among White groups, the Jewish (94%) and White Irish (92%) groups have the highest percentage that feel that their ethnic identity is important to their sense of self, followed by those from Gypsy (90%) and Roma (70%) backgrounds. Only around 58–59% of those from the White Eastern European and White Other backgrounds share that view.

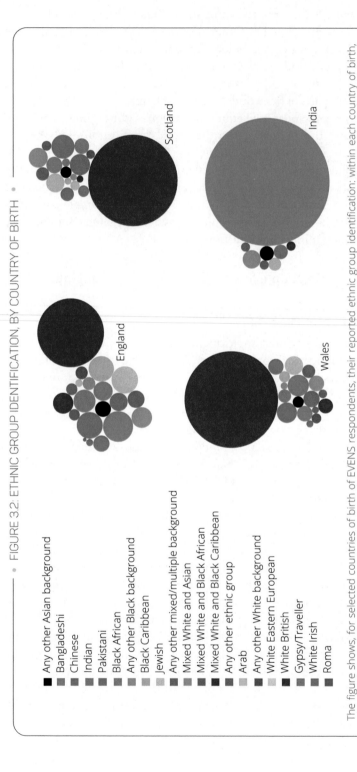

● FIGURE 3.2: ETHNIC GROUP IDENTIFICATION, BY COUNTRY OF BIRTH ●

Any other Asian background
Bangladeshi
Chinese
Indian
Pakistani
Black African
Any other Black background
Black Caribbean
Jewish
Any other mixed/multiple background
Mixed White and Asian
Mixed White and Black African
Mixed White and Black Caribbean
Any other ethnic group
Arab
Any other White background
White Eastern European
White British
Gypsy/Traveller
White Irish
Roma

The figure shows, for selected countries of birth of EVENS respondents, their reported ethnic group identification: within each country of birth, circles showing ethnic group identification are proportionately sized. The figure represents 8,384 respondents born in England, 718 born in Scotland, 517 in Wales, 412 in India, 263 in Nigeria, 188 in China, 186 in Poland, 156 in the USA, 87 in France, 75 in South Africa, 75 in France, 48 in Northern Ireland, 43 in Australia and 39 born in Brazil.

FIGURE 3.2: ETHNIC GROUP IDENTIFICATION, BY COUNTRY OF BIRTH (continued)

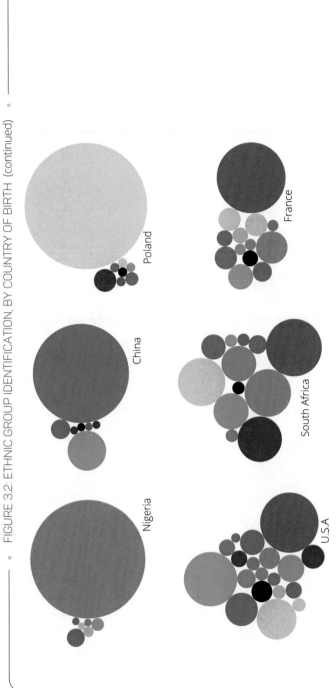

The figure shows, for selected countries of birth of EVENS respondents, their reported ethnic group identification: within each country of birth, circles showing ethnic group identification are proportionately sized. The figure represents 8,384 respondents born in England, 718 born in Scotland, 517 in Wales, 412 in India, 263 in Nigeria, 188 in China, 186 in Poland, 156 in the USA, 87 in South Africa, 75 in France, 48 in Northern Ireland, 43 in Australia and 39 born in Brazil.

(continued)

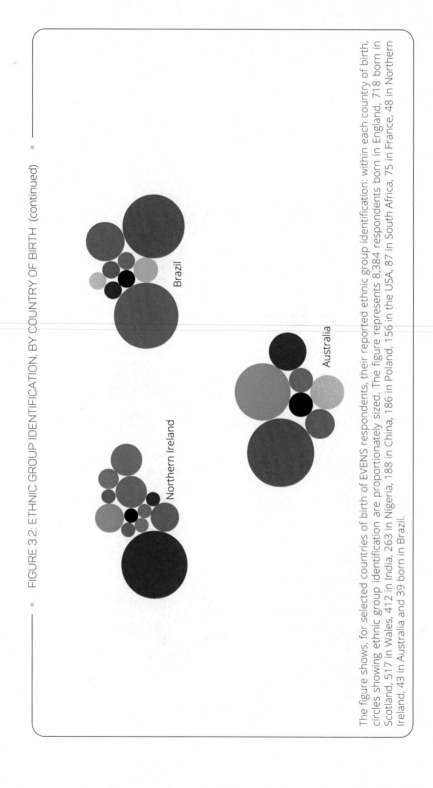

FIGURE 3.2: ETHNIC GROUP IDENTIFICATION, BY COUNTRY OF BIRTH (continued)

The figure shows, for selected countries of birth of EVENS respondents, their reported ethnic group identification: within each country of birth, circles showing ethnic group identification are proportionately sized. The figure represents 8,384 respondents born in England, 718 born in Scotland, 517 in Wales, 412 in India, 263 in Nigeria, 188 in China, 186 in Poland, 156 in the USA, 87 in South Africa, 75 in France, 48 in Northern Ireland, 43 in Australia and 39 born in Brazil.

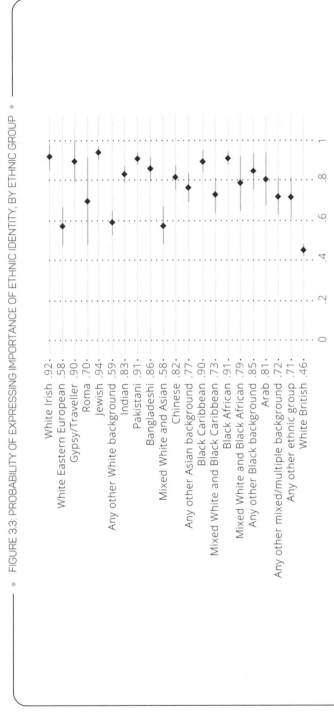

FIGURE 3.3: PROBABILITY OF EXPRESSING IMPORTANCE OF ETHNIC IDENTITY, BY ETHNIC GROUP

Note: Chart shows predicted probabilities of responding 'Very or fairly important' to the question 'How important is your ethnic background to your sense of who you are?', adjusted for age, age squared and sex. 95% confidence intervals shown. N=12,816

Interestingly, British and foreign-born individuals report similar levels of attachment to ethnic identities (the results are not shown here), suggesting that the importance of one's ethnic background is not something that is only felt by the foreign born, but is a significant part of self-definition regardless of migrant generation.

The importance of religious identity

In EVENS, religious attachment is measured by the following question: 'How important is your religion to your sense of who you are?' Four options are provided to choose from (very important, fairly important, not very important and not at all important). The results show a large variation in the levels of religious affiliation among ethnic groups. As shown in Figure 3.4, people from Mixed, White British, Other White and Chinese backgrounds most frequently report having no religious affiliation. Within other ethnic groups, there tends to be a consistency between religious affiliation and ethnic identity. For example, over 80% of Pakistani, Bangladeshi and Arab people in EVENS identify as Muslim, while nearly 80% of the Black African, nearly 70% of the Black Caribbean and nearly 70% of the Black Other groups identify as Christian. As mentioned earlier, Jewish people are treated as a separate ethnic group in the EVENS classification.

We observe that those who identify with minority (non-Christian) religions, especially when there tends to be a consistency between religious affiliation and ethnic identity, tend to be more likely to report having a strong attachment to their religion. Figure 3.5 shows that those who identify as Muslim and Jewish are the most likely to report strong attachment, followed by those who identify as Sikh, Hindu and Other: more than 7 in 10 people who identify with these religions feel strongly attached to their religion. In comparison, about 5 in 10 Christians and 6 in 10 Buddhists report a strong attachment to their religion. Figure 3.6 shows that a strong religious attachment is reported by over 80% of people from Pakistani, Bangladeshi, Arab, Black African, Other Black, Jewish, Gypsy/ Traveller and Roma groups, and over 70% of those from Black Caribbean and Other Asian groups. This is likely to be associated with a stronger consistency between religious affiliation and ethnic identity among these groups and with the more prominent social role of Black churches in the case of Black communities.

How much do people engage in practices associated with their ethnic and/or religious background?

EVENS included three questions assessing how much people engage in practices that are linked to their ethnic and/or religious identities: 'How

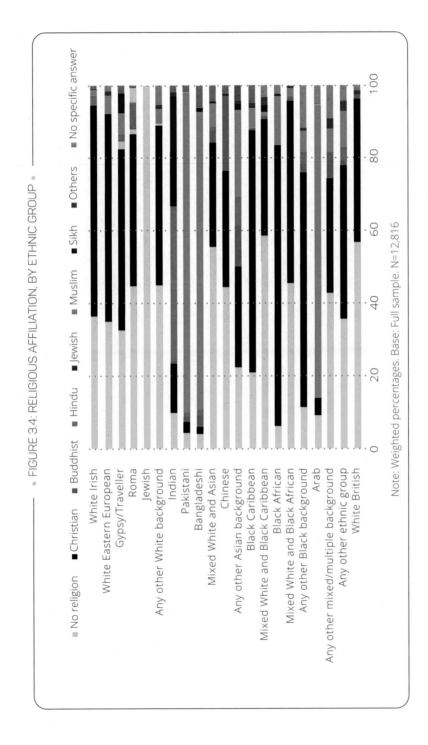

● FIGURE 3.4: RELIGIOUS AFFILIATION, BY ETHNIC GROUP ●

Note: Weighted percentages. Base: Full sample. N=12,816

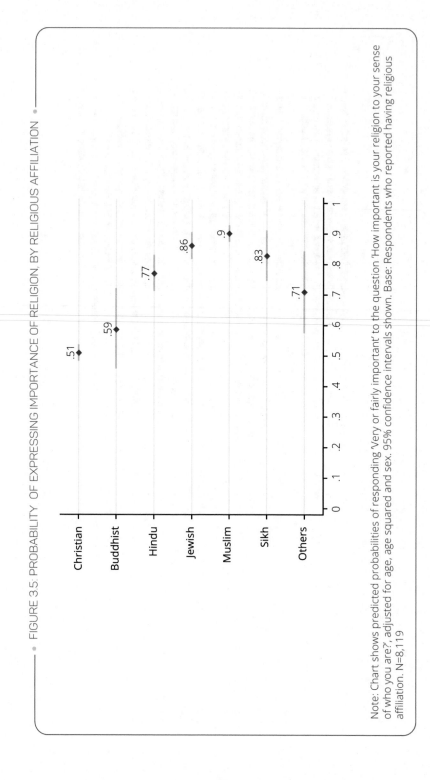

FIGURE 3.5: PROBABILITY OF EXPRESSING IMPORTANCE OF RELIGION, BY RELIGIOUS AFFILIATION

Note: Chart shows predicted probabilities of responding 'Very or fairly important' to the question 'How important is your religion to your sense of who you are?', adjusted for age, age squared and sex. 95% confidence intervals shown. Base: Respondents who reported having religious affiliation. N=8,119

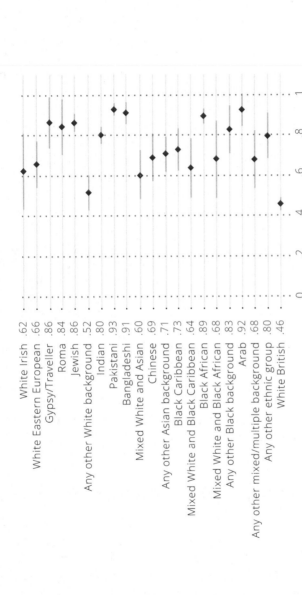

• FIGURE 3.6: PROBABILITY OF EXPRESSING IMPORTANCE OF RELIGION, BY ETHNIC GROUP •

White Irish .62
White Eastern European .66
Gypsy/Traveller .86
Roma .84
Jewish .86
Any other White background .52
Indian .80
Pakistani .93
Bangladeshi .91
Mixed White and Asian .60
Chinese .69
Any other Asian background .71
Black Caribbean .73
Mixed White and Black Caribbean .64
Black African .89
Mixed White and Black African .68
Any other Black background .83
Arab .92
Any other mixed/multiple background .68
Any other ethnic group .80
White British .46

Note: Chart shows predicted probabilities of responding 'Very or fairly important' to the question 'How important is your religion to your sense of who you are?', adjusted for age, age squared and sex. 95% confidence intervals shown. Base: Respondents who reported having religious affiliation. N=8,119

45

often, if at all, do you wear clothes or something that shows a connection with your ethnic identity or religion?' 'How often do you participate in activities that are connected with your ethnicity or religion?' 'How often do you eat food that is associated with your ethnic background or religion?' Eating food linked to one's ethnic or religious background was the most prevalent practice across ethnic groups – on average, 40% of respondents reported that they regularly eat specific types of food linked to their ethnicity or religion. Only 10% reported they regularly wear specific clothes and 14% regularly participate in activities, related to their ethnicity or religion. Due to the high prevalence of food-related practices, we classified responses into 'participation in any practices (including food)' and 'participation in practices other than food'.

As shown in Figure 3.7, regular participation in any form of practice connected with ethnicity or religion varies considerably across ethnic groups. People from certain White ethnic groups, such as White British (35%), White Irish (35%) and White Eastern European (42%), tend to participate at lower rates than people from non-White minority groups. Interestingly, White British people are the least likely to report participation in any type of activities, including food, which suggests that engagement in ethnically specific practices is less relevant for those who are not members of a minoritised, or racialised, group. Ethnic groups for whom we observed strong religious attachments are also among those most likely to participate in non-food-related activities associated with their ethnic background or religion (Bangladeshi: 69%, Pakistani: 68%, Jewish: 64%, Black African: 57%, Arab: 55%, Gypsy: 56% and Roma: 49%). Although the EVENS does not explicitly ask what kind of practices people participate in, it might be that many respondents thought of activities associated with practising their religion. In contrast, people who identify as Other White (14%), White Irish (17%), Mixed White and Black Caribbean (20%), and White Eastern European (20%) were the least likely among ethnic minority groups to engage in ethnicity or religion-related practices other than food.

How strongly do people feel a sense of belonging to British, English, Scottish, Welsh society?

EVENS asked people to assess, on a scale from 1 (strongly agree) to 4 (strongly disagree), 'to what extent do you agree or disagree that you personally feel a part of British society?'. The respondents living in different constituent countries were also asked equivalent questions about their sense of belonging to English, Scottish and Welsh societies depending on their place of residence. We find that the vast majority of people (between 72% and 95%) from all ethnic backgrounds (with the exception of

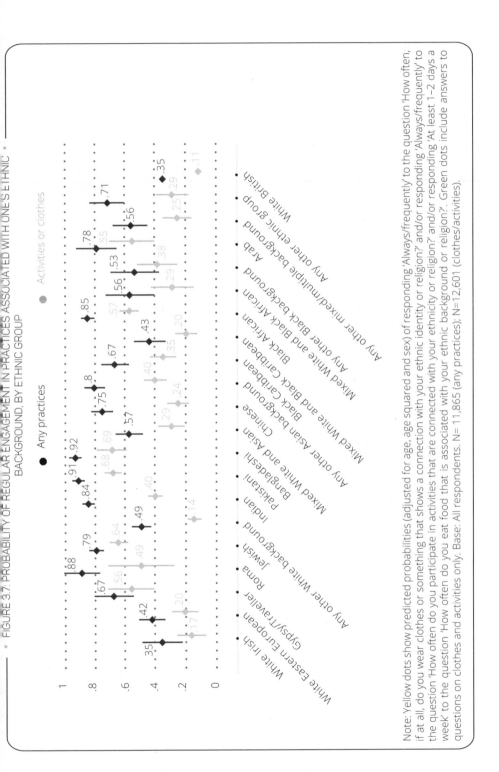

• FIGURE 3.7: PROBABILITY OF REGULAR ENGAGEMENT IN PRACTICES ASSOCIATED WITH ONE'S ETHNIC BACKGROUND, BY ETHNIC GROUP

Note: Yellow dots show predicted probabilities (adjusted for age, age squared and sex) of responding 'Always/frequently' to the question 'How often, if at all, do you wear clothes or something that shows a connection with your ethnic identity or religion?' and/or responding 'Always/frequently' to the question 'How often do you participate in activities that are connected with your ethnicity or religion?' and/or responding 'At least 1–2 days a week' to the question 'How often do you eat food that is associated with your ethnic background or religion?'. Green dots include answers to questions on clothes and activities only. Base: All respondents. N= 11,865 (any practices); N=12,601 (clothes/activities).

Roma – 33%) report having a strong sense of belonging to British society (as illustrated in Figure 3.8). Interestingly, the likelihood of reporting positive belonging to British society was highest for some of the groups who were also most likely to express strong sense of attachment to their ethnic identity, including the Arab (95%), Jewish (93%), Indian (92%), Pakistani (92%), Bangladeshi (92%), Black African (90%), and Black Other (89%) ethnic groups. For people from Black Caribbean (78%), Gypsy (79%) and White Irish (76%) ethnic groups, the likelihood of reporting positive belonging to British society was slightly lower compared to the likelihood of having a strong sense of attachment to their ethnic identity. On the contrary, White Eastern European (86%) and White Other (77%) people, for whom we observed a relatively low sense of ethnic identity, reported a strong sense of belonging to the British society.

Across all ethnic minority groups (with the exception of Gypsy and Roma), the likelihood of having a strong sense of belonging to English, Scottish and Welsh societies was lower than the likelihood of having a strong sense of belonging to British society (Figure 3.8). However, the patterns of attachment to the constituent nations were not uniform across all minority groups. The most pronounced differences between the likelihood of having positive attachment to British and to English societies were noted for the Black Caribbean, Bangladesh, Indian, Pakistani, Other White and Arab groups. Among ethnic minority groups, the smallest difference between affiliation to a British or an English identity was observed for the Eastern European, Chinese, Gypsy/Traveller and Roma groups, and the likelihood of having a positive sense of belonging to British and to English society was essentially the same for the White British group. Nevertheless, the differences between belonging to British and to English society were relatively small and the majority within each ethnic group felt that they were part of British and part of English society, with the exception of the Roma group. Similar patterns were found in relation to the sense of belonging to Scottish and Welsh societies (these are not shown here).

Discussion

The detailed questions on multiple aspects of people's ethnic, religious and national identities included in EVENS allow us to better understand the importance of different types of ethnic, religious and national identities. The inclusion of an open-ended write-in ethnic identity question illustrates how people tend to think about their ethnicity when they are not bound by predefined categories.

As shown by the analysis of the free text responses, the majority of people articulate their ethnic identity using phrases and expressions typically used in the standardised ethnicity classifications. This can be attributed to the

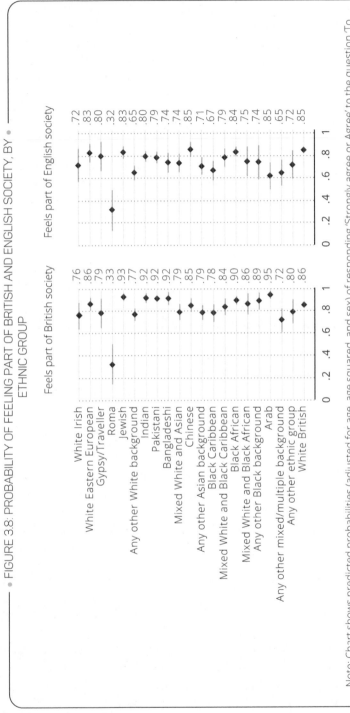

• FIGURE 3.8: PROBABILITY OF FEELING PART OF BRITISH AND ENGLISH SOCIETY, BY •
ETHNIC GROUP

Feels part of British society   Feels part of English society

	Feels part of British society	Feels part of English society
White Irish	.76	.72
White Eastern European	.86	.83
Gypsy/Traveller	.79	.80
Roma	.33	.32
Jewish	.93	.83
Any other White background	.77	.65
Indian	.92	.80
Pakistani	.92	.79
Bangladeshi	.92	.74
Mixed White and Asian	.79	.74
Chinese	.85	.85
Any other Asian background	.79	.71
Black Caribbean	.78	.67
Mixed White and Black Caribbean	.84	.79
Black African	.90	.84
Mixed White and Black African	.86	.75
Any other Black background	.89	.74
Arab	.95	.85
Any other mixed/multiple background	.72	.65
Any other ethnic group	.80	.72
White British	.86	.85

Note: Chart shows predicted probabilities (adjusted for age, age squared, and sex) of responding 'Strongly agree or Agree' to the question 'To what extent do you agree or disagree that you personally feel a part of British society?' and to the question 'To what extent do you agree or disagree that you personally feel a part of English society?'. Base: All respondents. N=12,266 (British Society); N=10,304 (English Society)

49

widespread use of such classifications, which in turn affects how people conceptualise ethnicity. Nevertheless, a significant proportion of the sample used non-standardised ethnicity articulations that included references to the complex migration journeys and multicountry and multiracial origins that are not possible to capture in existing classifications. Such articulations of ethnic identity are often present among those who classify themselves into various 'Other' standardised ethnicity categories. The growing diversity of the UK population, which in turn results in increasingly complex patterns of family and migration backgrounds, is likely to make existing standardised ethnicity categories less able to accurately capture meaningful ethnic identities over time. Changing migration patterns means that new, sizeable groups from non-traditional origin countries are not accurately represented in the official ethnicity classifications. Another limitation of standardised ethnicity categories highlighted by textual responses is the lack of non-White Mixed ethnicities. The nature of standardised classifications also limits people's ability to express their identity in non-racialised terms or to use subnational definitions of ethnic identity. The focus on demographic heritage of standardised ethnicity classifications, although useful for monitoring purposes, limits individuals' ability to express subjective ethnic identities. Such rigid categorisation can sometimes create frustration among those who do not feel comfortable with putting themselves into predefined ethnicity categories.

This chapter has also shown that despite the challenges of defining ethnic identities, especially in standardised, fixed terms, most people report strong attachment to their ethnic and religious backgrounds. Ethnic identity is particularly important for those from the Black African, Black Caribbean, Pakistani, White Irish and Jewish backgrounds, and the least important for those from White British, White Eastern European and White Other groups. Religious identity is important for higher proportions of people who identify with minority religions and for people for whom there tends to be a consistency in religious affiliation and ethnic identity – for example, for people from Pakistani, Bangladeshi, Black African, Arab and Jewish groups.

Although an explanatory analysis of why the importance of ethnic identity is more prevalent among certain groups is beyond the scope of this chapter, we can speculate about some of the possible explanations based on the past literature. Some of the commonly identified determinants of the strength of ethnic identity include: prevalence of ethnic discrimination (Gilroy, 2013; Rumbaut, 2005), cultural distance (Nesdale and Mak, 2003), community involvement (Maehler, 2022) and parental socialisation (Phinney and Chavira, 1995; Xu et al, 2004). Experience of ethnic discrimination, in line with social identity theory, is likely to increase the salience of ethnicity to one's self-concept. Non-White groups are particularly at risk of experiencing racism, which in turn structures how they view their own identity and how having such an identity shapes their interactions with others (Karlsen and Nazroo, 2002b). Greater perceived cultural distance to the ethnic majority might affect the development of a strong ethnic and/or religious identity through positive and negative mechanisms. Positive mechanisms include increased motivation to preserve one's own cultural heritage and the development of a positive distinctiveness based on group belonging (Turner, 2010), whereas negative mechanisms might be associated with experience of greater prejudice from the majority group (Ford, 2011). Greater involvement in ethnicity and/or religion-related practices has also been shown to be correlated with ethnic identity development during adolescence and adulthood (Hardy et al, 2011).

People from those ethnic minority groups that have a high prevalence of strong attachment to their ethnic identity are also highly likely to report a strong sense of belonging to British society. This is the case for those from the Bangladeshi, Pakistani, Indian, Chinese, Black African, Black Other, Arab and Jewish groups. For some of these groups, these patterns are in line with the existing evidence (Demireva and Heath, 2014; Karlsen and Nazroo, 2015; Nandi and Platt, 2014). However, for others, such as the Arab and Jewish groups, EVENS provides the first large-scale evidence on their subjective sense of attachment to ethnic and national communities.

EVENS also provides the first evidence on the patterns of ethnic, religious and national belonging among a nationally representative sample of White Eastern European people. We have learned that people from the White Eastern European group tend to express a strong sense of belonging to British society, but less so to their ethnic identity. Interestingly, they are also among a few groups who are almost equally likely to report a strong sense of belonging to a British as well as an English national community. These patterns are likely to reflect the role of whiteness in the construction of British and English identities, as well as lower levels of ethnic discrimination among most of the White minority groups (see Chapter 4).

We also note that people from the White Roma, Gypsy, White Irish and Black Caribbean ethnic groups are less likely than other ethnic groups to have a strong sense of belonging to British society compared to their strength of attachment to their ethnic identity. Some of these patterns might be associated with ethnicity-related discrimination, although a formal analysis on the impact of discrimination on the strength of ethnic and national attachments is beyond the scope of this chapter. However, previous literature did find that perceived discrimination is a major factor affecting the strength of British identity among ethnic minority individuals (Maxwell, 2009; Karlsen and Nazroo, 2015).

The lower likelihood of having a positive sense of belonging to English rather than British society among people from ethnic minority backgrounds, particularly those at higher risk of experiencing racial discrimination, might be explained by the difference in the racialisation and inclusiveness of these two national identities. The construction of Englishness is based more on the 'ethnic' than the 'civic' concept of identity (Leddy-Owen, 2014). As a consequence, Englishness is more likely to be defined in terms of ancestry and Whiteness, whereas Britishness is more linked with political community boundaries and citizenship.

In sum, despite some differences in the strength of belonging to British society, the overall picture coming from the analysis of the EVENS data is a positive one. We see that the overwhelming majority of people across (almost) all ethnic groups feel a strong sense of belonging to the national community. Furthermore, it seems that having a strong attachment to one's ethnic identity often goes hand in hand with the strong sense of belonging to British society.

Box 3.1: Ethnic identities: measures and methods

All the results presented in this chapter are weighted by the propensity weights available in the EVENS dataset. The sample includes all EVENS respondents aged 18–65.

Predicted probabilities are based on logistic regression models adjusted for age (measured in years), square term of age, and sex. Predicted probability can be interpreted as the likelihood that person x gave answer y, while taking into account that men and women and people of different ages have different likelihoods of giving answer y.

Variable coding:

Write-in ethnic identity: All textual responses are coded based on the words used by the respondent into one of three categories: non-engagement (lack of valid response); standardised ethnicity articulation (all words used by the respondent correspond to words used in standardised ethnicity classifications) and non-standardised ethnicity articulation (at least some words used by the respondent differ from those used in standardised classifications).

Strong/fairly strong attachment to ethnic (/religious) background includes people who said they ethnic (/religious) background is very or fairly important to their sense of who they are.

Strong/fairly strong sense of belonging to British (English/Scottish/Welsh) societies includes those who said they strongly agree or tend to agree that they feel part of British (English/Scottish/Welsh) society.

Regular participation in practices (including food) refers to people who said that they regularly participate in activities or wear clothes (always or frequently) or eat food (every day or most of the days) associated with their ethnic background.

Regular participation in practices (excluding food) refers to people who said that they regularly participate in activities or wear clothes (always or frequently) associated with their ethnic background.

4

Racism and racial discrimination

Daniel Ellingworth, Laia Bécares, Michaela Šťastná and James Nazroo

Key findings

Racism and racial discrimination shape the lives of ethnic minority groups in the UK: there are persistent experiences of racial discrimination both before and during the pandemic, across a wide range of settings.

- The Evidence for Equality National Survey (EVENS) enables an assessment of racism and racial discrimination experienced in the period before the start of the pandemic, and during its first year.
- Almost one in six ethnic minority people reported having experienced a racist physical assault. Over half of respondents from the Gypsy/Traveller, Jewish and Other Black ethnic groups reported such an experience.
- Close to a third of ethnic minority people reported experiencing racial discrimination in education, with a similar proportion reporting racial discrimination in employment.
- Around a fifth of ethnic minority people (19%) reported experiences of racial discrimination when seeking housing.
- The prevalence of experienced racial discrimination from the police prior to the pandemic is particularly high for some ethnic groups. For example, 42.7% of Black Caribbean, 42% of Any other Black, 36.4% of Roma and 34.6% of Gypsy/Traveller people reported racial discrimination from the police.
- On average, close to a third of ethnic minority people reported experiencing racial discrimination in public settings prior to the pandemic. Gypsy/Traveller people reported the highest prevalence (49.4%). People in the Black Caribbean (49.3%), Any Other Black (44.4%) and White and Black Caribbean (40.7%) ethnic groups also reported a very high prevalence of racial discrimination experienced in public settings.
- 47% of ethnic minority people have experienced racial discrimination in at least one setting. Over 10% have experienced racial discrimination in five or more different settings. People from Roma, Mixed White and Black African, Gypsy/Traveller, Any Other Black and Arab ethnic groups reported the highest number of different forms of racial discrimination in the pre-pandemic period.
- During the first year of the pandemic, on average 14% of ethnic minority people reported a racist assault (verbal, physical and damage to property), with several ethnic

minority groups having a prevalence figure of over 15%. The Gypsy/Traveller (41%) and Jewish (31%) groups had the highest figures. High prevalence of assault was also reported by people from the Black Caribbean group and the Mixed White and Black African groups (both 19%), and people from the Any Other Black group and White and Black Caribbean groups (both 18%).

- Men generally experienced a higher prevalence of different forms of racial discrimination than women. However, in some settings, and for some ethnic minority groups, the prevalence for women was higher than that for men. For example, in relation to unfair treatment in education and employment, women from the Black Caribbean and the White and Black African ethnic groups reported a higher prevalence of discrimination in the pre-pandemic period than men in the same ethnic group.
- Comparing the experiences of the period before the pandemic and the pandemic year, Chinese, Other Asian and Eastern European people experienced increases in experiences of racial discrimination relative to other ethnic minority groups during the pandemic year.
- During the pandemic, people from Roma, Gypsy/Traveller and Chinese ethnic groups reported the highest perception of increased police activity, and the highest rate of stops by the police.

Introduction

Racism is a complex system of structuring opportunity and assigning relative value based on phenotypic characteristics, unfairly disadvantaging ethnic minority groups and unfairly advantaging white people (Jones, 2000). Racism manifests on multiple levels, including structural, institutional, interpersonal and internalised (Jones, 2000; Nazroo et al, 2020).

One of the challenges of studying experiences of racism and racial discrimination, and their association with ethnic inequities, has been its conceptualisation and measurement (Williams, 1996; Karlsen and Nazroo, 2006; Landrine et al, 2006; Brondolo et al, 2009; Williams and Mohammed, 2009), with studies of interpersonal experience of racism and racial discrimination receiving the most empirical attention. Extensive efforts have been dedicated to quantifying these experiences in order to understand their prevalence, how this varies across groups, contexts and time, and whether (and how) such encounters shape the social, economic and health outcomes of ethnic minority people.

There is extensive evidence documenting both the prevalence of racism and racial discrimination in the UK, as well as the association between these experiences and adverse social, economic and health outcomes. For example, using the UK Household Longitudinal Study, Wallace et al (2016) found that 8.8% of ethnic minority people reported experiencing racial discrimination a single time in their lives and that 9.2% reported repeated experiences. They also report a cumulative effect of racism on mental health, whereby ethnic minority people who experience interpersonal racism repeatedly over time and across settings of their lives (for example, in both education and in employment) have poorer mental health compared to ethnic minority people who report experiencing racism only once, and only in one setting of their lives. Studies have shown that the prevalence of racism and racial discrimination has remained constant over time. Karlsen and Nazroo (2002b) compared data from two surveys to measure levels of exposure to racist discrimination in 2000 and 2008/9, and found that Muslim groups had experienced increased levels of racist or religiously motivated violence over a period characterised by an increasingly hostile rhetoric against Muslim people in the UK. In 2000, 13% of Muslim Indian people, 13% of Pakistani Muslim people and 18% of Bangladeshi Muslim respondents reported having experienced racist abuse, assault or vandalism in the past year. By 2008/9, the same ethnic and religious groups reported an increased prevalence of 18%, 19% and 19% respectively, while over the same period, the prevalence of racism experienced by Black Caribbean people changed slightly from 14% to 12%. Consistent with this, evidence from the British Social Attitudes survey suggests barely changing levels of racial prejudice among the general population in the UK over the period from 1983 to 2013 (Nazroo, 2021). Recent studies have also documented an association between structural and institutional racism, and increased levels of vaccine hesitancy among ethnic minority groups in the UK (Bécares et al, 2022).

These studies have been crucial in confirming the existence of racism and racial discrimination in the UK, and in assessing associations between racism and economic, social and health outcomes, many of which are explored in this book. However, their measurement of racism and racial discrimination suffers from important limitations. Most measures ask about experiences that have happened either in the respondent's lifetime (ever) or within a shorter timeframe (from the past week up to the past five years) (Utsey, 1998; Kressin et al, 2008; Bastos et al, 2010). This focus on short-term or vague (ever) timeframes obstructs a thorough analysis of how racial discrimination is associated with adverse outcomes over people's lives. Although a few measures ask about experiences that occur at specific times in the life course, these are restricted to broad time periods, such as childhood/adolescence (Krieger et al, 2005; Dominguez et al, 2008; Adam et al, 2015) or adulthood (Dominguez et al, 2008). This hinders our knowledge of the chronicity and accumulation of exposures to racism and racial discrimination (Blank et al, 2004), and of the key periods in people's lives when racism and racial discrimination may pattern inequalities in economic, social and health outcomes and the pathways through which this may operate.

Explicit attention to the timing of experienced racism and racial discrimination, especially the continuity of exposure to racist events, and the timing of these events, is critical for a greater theoretical and empirical understanding of how racism and racial discrimination lead to inequalities. Recognising these conceptual and methodological deficiencies and building on recent scholarship on the life course provides a theoretical foundation for developing measures that may more adequately capture experiences of racism and racial discrimination. The measure of racism and racial discrimination included in EVENS emerges from the theoretical propositions described earlier in order to capture the timing of events, the domains of life in which they occur, and to cover a wider timeframe (see Box 4.1). It is the first time that such a measure has been used in the UK.

However, for the purposes of this book, we focus on experiences of racial discrimination prior to the pandemic and compare them with experiences of racial discrimination during the pandemic. We consider experiences of racist assault (physical or verbal attack, or damage to property) and experiences of racial discrimination within a range of institutional settings and social settings.

The analyses in this chapter aim to document the experiences of racism and racial discrimination – of different forms and across different contexts – that ethnic minority people have experienced before the pandemic and during the first year of the pandemic. We comment on the prevalence of racism and racial discrimination, describing the percentage of people in each ethnic minority group that report experiences of racism and racial discrimination. The prevalence figures are compared across different ethnic minority groups, gender and age groups. Given that racism is a system of oppression that disadvantages ethnic minority groups, we focus here on the experiences of ethnic minority people only (that is, people who self-identify as an ethnic group other than White English, Welsh, Scottish or British).

We also discuss change in prevalence of racial discrimination during the pandemic compared to experiences prior to that. The pandemic may be expected to impact on these experiences in a number of ways; the experience of lockdown may have been expected to reduce interactions and so the possibility of experiencing racial discrimination. However, it may also be the case that some people, such as those with public-facing employment, may have been increasingly vulnerable to such assaults due to increased exposure to the public. A further possibility is that the popular and media discourse around the causes of the COVID-19 pandemic may have resulted in some ethnic groups being targeted, with Chinese and other Asian ethnic groups perhaps experiencing a heightened risk.

Results

First, we focus on the most salient experiences of interpersonal racism, which we term 'racist assault': insults, property damage and physical attack. Table 4.1 presents the prevalence of experiencing a racist assault at any time prior to the COVID-19 pandemic. The 'Overall' row shows that over a third of the respondents had experienced a racist assault of some kind. The ethnic minority groups with the highest reports of experiencing any racist assault were Gypsy/Traveller (61.9%), Any Other Black (60.9%) and Jewish (56.7%) people.

Of the three categories of racist assault, insults were the most prevalent, with 26.1% of ethnic minority people reporting a verbal insult because of their ethnicity, race or colour. A total of 17.3% of ethnic minority people reported experiencing property damage, and 15.5% reported experiences of physical assaults – that is, almost one in six of the ethnic minority sample reported having experienced a racist physical assault. Racist insults were particularly prevalent among people self-identifying as Any Other Black (44.6%).

Table 4.2 presents the prevalence of experiences of racial discrimination prior to the pandemic within institutions. These domains capture the context of the experiences rather than the precise nature of the incidents. These could encompass a range of types of racial discrimination within the one domain: for example, a respondent answering that they had experienced racial discrimination within education could have experienced a direct racist assault, or could have been denied particular educational opportunities, or could have received unfair treatment in determining outcomes, or all of these.

Close to a third of ethnic minority people (29.2%) report experiencing racial discrimination in education. People who self-identify as Roma (52.5%), Any Other Black (48.6%), Black Caribbean (46.3%), White and Caribbean (45.8%) and Gypsy/Traveller (44.2%) reported the highest levels of racial discrimination in education.

A similar proportion of ethnic minority people (29.4%) reported experiencing racial discrimination in employment prior to the pandemic. This is particularly high for Black Caribbean people (55.1%) and for Gypsy/Traveller people (40.7%).

Around a fifth of ethnic minority people (19%) reported experiences of racial discrimination when seeking housing prior to the pandemic. Prevalence is higher for people from Roma (37.5%), Any Other Black (32.9%), Black African (27.7%), Black Caribbean (25.3%), White and Black Caribbean (27.2%), Gypsy/Traveller (31.5%) and Arab (26.8%) ethnic groups.

Racial discrimination experienced from the police is clearly a particularly important area, given the concerns around discriminatory policing and the documentation of specific incidents in the UK, the US and elsewhere that gave rise to the resurgence of the Black Lives Matter movement. The

• TABLE 4.1: EXPERIENCE OF RACIST ASSAULT PRIOR TO THE COVID-19 PANDEMIC, BY ETHNIC GROUP •

Weighted percentages

	Insult	Property damage	Physical attack	Any racist assault (one or more experience of any of the three)	N
	%	%	%	%	
White Irish	30.7	21.4	18.4	42.0	97
White Eastern European	15.8	5.3	6.9	19.6	360
Gypsy/Traveller	40.0	28.9	33.3	61.9	227
Roma	31.3	14.5	35.1	47.4	73
Jewish	43.9	26.2	22.2	56.7	476
Any other White background	13.5	6.4	4.7	16.0	650
Indian	23.0	18.1	13.0	31.5	1255
Pakistani	27.6	21.6	16.2	36.8	849
Bangladeshi	31.7	23.6	19.7	39.3	406
Mixed White and Asian	18.8	10.1	14.1	27.5	520
Chinese	23.5	14.1	15.3	30.0	662
Any other Asian background	17.5	14.6	10.9	25.4	663
Black Caribbean	36.3	22.9	21.7	47.0	557
Mixed White and Black Caribbean	37.8	19.3	18.1	48.1	354
Black African	23.5	18.1	16.2	33.0	1040
Mixed White and Black African	43.4	25.0	20.3	48.1	155
Any other Black background	44.6	37.3	37.8	60.9	176
Arab	21.3	13.6	12.8	22.5	152
Any other mixed/multiple background	25.3	12.3	11.1	31.7	363
Any other ethnic group	21.8	10.6	8.2	24.2	252
Overall	26.1	17.3	15.5	34.5	9287

● TABLE 4.2: EXPERIENCE OF RACIAL DISCRIMINATION IN INSTITUTIONAL SETTINGS PRIOR TO THE COVID-19 PANDEMIC ●

Weighted percentages

	Education %	Employment %	Seeking housing %	By the police %	N
White Irish	18.6	31.35	18.0	17.8	406
White Eastern European	13.2	16.98	15.2	12.6	662
Gypsy/Traveller	44.2	40.74	31.5	34.6	1255
Roma	52.5	17.85	37.5	36.4	849
Jewish	33.8	29.51	11.8	20.8	663
Any other White background	9.4	14.88	9.1	9.3	1040
Indian	27.9	31.97	16.0	18.7	557
Pakistani	28.4	28.6	15.6	22.5	176
Bangladeshi	31.5	41.88	17.9	25.3	520
Mied White and Asian	24.6	18	12.5	16.5	155
Chinese	25.4	23.55	18.8	17.1	354
Any other Asian background	21.8	25.95	15.4	16.8	363
Black Caribbean	46.3	55.12	25.3	42.7	360
Mixed White and Black Caribbean	45.8	35.26	27.2	33.8	227
Black African	33.2	29.57	27.7	28.2	97
Mixed White and Black African	36.8	34.62	15.6	34.5	73
Any other Black background	48.6	39.6	32.9	42.0	650
Arab	26.1	21.09	26.8	17.5	152
Any other mixed/multiple background	35.1	27.55	17.8	21.2	252
Any other ethnic group	21.9	25.95	18.2	16.7	476
Overall	29.2	29.4	18.7	22.5	9287

prevalence of experienced racial discrimination from the police prior to the pandemic is very high for some ethnic groups. For example, 42.7% of Black Caribbean, 42% of Any Other Black, 36.4% of Roma and 34.6% of Gypsy/Traveller people reported police-related racial discrimination.

Table 4.3 presents the prevalence of experiences of racial discrimination prior to the pandemic within social settings, in public, from neighbours and from family, partner and friends. As for the questions covering institutional settings, these domains capture the context of the experiences rather than the precise nature of the incidents.

On average, close to a third of ethnic minority people reported experiencing racial discrimination in public prior to the pandemic. The Any Other White group had the lowest rate (10.6%), while the Gypsy/Traveller group had the highest rate (49.4%). People in the Black Caribbean (49.3%), Any Other Black (44.4%) and White and Black Caribbean (40.7%) groups also reported a very high prevalence of racial discrimination experienced in public settings.

Almost one in six ethnic minority people (15.5%) report experiencing racial discrimination from neighbours, with some groups reporting a much higher prevalence. For example, 46.6% of Other Black people and 38.7% of Gypsy/Traveller people reported experiencing racial discrimination from their neighbours prior to the pandemic.

Finally, 16.6% of ethnic minority people reported experiencing racial discrimination from family, partner or friends prior to the pandemic, with rates ranging from 6.8% for the Any Other White group to 33.4% for the Gypsy/Traveller group and 33.5% for the Any Other Black group.

Experiences of racial discrimination by gender

The prevalence of experience of racial discrimination differs by gender across ethnic minority groups. Overall, reports of racial discrimination experienced by men are generally higher than those experienced by women, though this masks a great deal of variation across different ethnic groups. Comparing the prevalence figures for women and men across the various contexts in which discrimination was experienced highlights some differences to the general pattern.

Figure 4.1 looks at pre-pandemic experiences of racist assaults, comparing the different experiences of men and women. In general, men reported a higher prevalence of racist assaults than women, although this pattern is reversed among Black Caribbean (women 51.5%, men 41.7%), Gypsy/Traveller (women 64.6%, men 59.2%) and Roma (women 58.2%, men 37.1%) ethnic groups.

Prior to the pandemic, Gypsy/Traveller women experienced a considerably higher prevalence of racial discrimination compared to Gypsy/Traveller men

TABLE 4.3: EXPERIENCE OF RACIAL DISCRIMINATION IN SOCIAL SETTINGS PRIOR TO THE COVID-19 PANDEMIC

Weighted percentages

	In public	From neighbours	From family, partner or friends	N
	%	%	%	
White Irish	28.8	21.2	11.8	406
White Eastern European	12.4	12.1	8.4	662
Gypsy/Traveller	49.4	38.7	33.4	1255
Roma	17.8	19.1	18.2	849
Jewish	29.7	20.5	13.5	663
Any other White background	10.6	7.9	6.8	1040
Indian	30.0	14.6	15.0	557
Pakistani	32.9	23.6	18.1	176
Bangladeshi	34.1	24.0	16.0	520
Mixed White and Asian	20.6	14.5	19.7	155
Chinese	24.5	21.0	18.7	354
Any other Asian background	25.8	16.5	12.8	363
Black Caribbean	49.3	21.4	15.3	360
Mixed White and Black Caribbean	40.7	30.0	25.8	227
Black African	34.0	20.7	16.9	97
Mixed White and Black African	39.9	28.0	28.1	73
Any other Black background	44.4	46.6	33.5	650
Arab	18.3	24.0	11.4	152
Any other mixed/multiple background	34.1	18.4	15.8	252
Any other ethnic group	27.6	19.8	22.3	476
Overall	29.9	15.5	16.6	9287

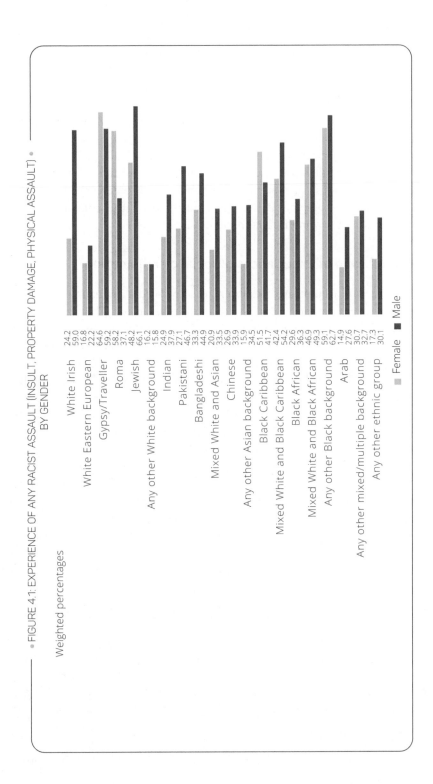

● FIGURE 4.1: EXPERIENCE OF ANY RACIST ASSAULT (INSULT, PROPERTY DAMAGE, PHYSICAL ASSAULT) ●
BY GENDER

Weighted percentages

	Female	Male
White Irish	24.2	59.0
White Eastern European	16.8	22.2
Gypsy/Traveller	64.6	59.2
Roma	58.2	37.1
Jewish	48.2	66.1
Any other White background	15.8	16.2
Indian	24.9	37.9
Pakistani	27.1	46.7
Bangladeshi	33.3	44.9
Mixed White and Asian	20.9	33.5
Chinese	26.9	33.9
Any other Asian background	15.9	34.5
Black Caribbean	51.5	41.7
Mixed White and Black Caribbean	42.4	54.2
Black African	29.6	36.3
Mixed White and Black African	46.9	49.3
Any other Black background	59.1	62.7
Arab	14.9	27.6
Any other mixed/multiple background	30.7	32.7
Any other ethnic group	17.3	30.1

in relation to property damage (42% women, 16% men). In educational settings, more women from the Black Caribbean group (53% women, 38% men) and from White and Black African group (51% women, 23% men) experienced racial discrimination. In relation to education, more women from Black Caribbean (53% women, 38% men) and White and Black African groups (51% women, 23% men) experienced racial discrimination. Women from those same ethnic groups reported a higher prevalence of unfair treatment in employment compared to men (Black Caribbean 61% women, 47% men; White and Black African 40% women, 30% men). In the context of housing, there are noticeable gender differences for people from Roma (55% women, 21% men) and from Any other mixed/Multiple background (24% women, 10% men) ethnic groups.

Accumulation of experiences of racial discrimination

The impact of accumulated experiences of racial discrimination reinforces positions of vulnerability and disadvantage over time. The bar chart in Figure 4.2 shows the average number of different settings within which racial discrimination has been experienced (including both the four institutional settings covered in Table 4.2 and the three social settings covered in Table 4.3). It also gives the distribution of each ethnic group according to the number of settings within which racial discrimination has been experienced, with the distribution for all ethnic minority people shown below the figure. The overall figures show that 47% of ethnic minority people have experienced racial discrimination in at least one setting. Over 10% have experienced racial discrimination in five or more different settings. Figure 4.2 shows that the ethnic groups with the highest accumulation of experienced racial discrimination (captured by the average number of settings within which they have experienced racial discrimination) are Roma (3.2 settings), White and Black African (1.61 settings), Gypsy/Traveller (1.36 settings), Any Other Black (1.59 settings) and Arab (1.03 settings). Each of these ethnic groups has an average of more than one setting per respondent in the period before the pandemic.

Experiences of racial discrimination during the first year of the pandemic

Having established the patterns of experiences of racist assault and racial discrimination in the period prior to the pandemic, this section now considers the experiences of racial discrimination that took place in the first year of the COVID-19 pandemic. As noted earlier, racist assaults (verbal insults, damage to property and physical attack) are considered first.

Table 4.4 presents the prevalence of experiencing a racist assault by respondents at any time during the first year of the COVID-19 pandemic.

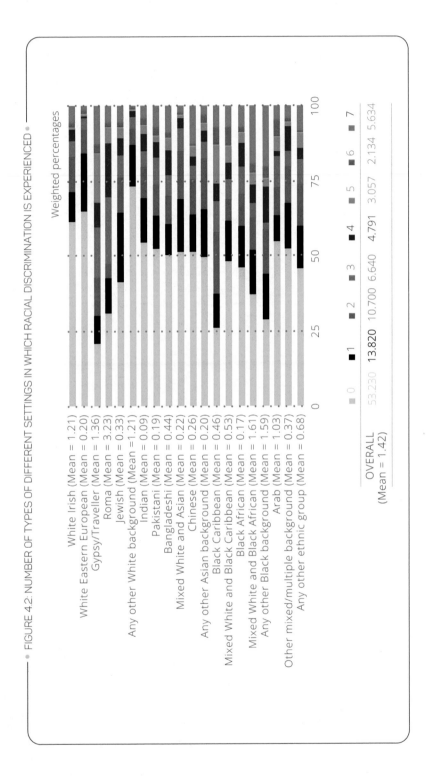

FIGURE 4.2: NUMBER OF TYPES OF DIFFERENT SETTINGS IN WHICH RACIAL DISCRIMINATION IS EXPERIENCED

Weighted percentages

White Irish (Mean = 1.21)
White Eastern European (Mean = 0.20)
Gypsy/Traveller (Mean = 1.36)
Roma (Mean = 3.23)
Jewish (Mean = 0.33)
Any other White background (Mean =1.21)
Indian (Mean = 0.09)
Pakistani (Mean = 0.19)
Bangladeshi (Mean = 0.44)
Mixed White and Asian (Mean = 0.22)
Chinese (Mean = 0.26)
Any other Asian background (Mean = 0.20)
Black Caribbean (Mean = 0.46)
Mixed White and Black Caribbean (Mean = 0.53)
Black African (Mean = 0.17)
Mixed White and Black African (Mean = 1.61)
Any other Black background (Mean = 1.59)
Arab (Mean = 1.03)
Other mixed/multiple background (Mean = 0.37)
Any other ethnic group (Mean = 0.68)

OVERALL
(Mean = 1.42)

0	1	2	3	4	5	6	7
53.230	13.820	10.700	6.640	4.791	3.057	2.134	5.634

• TABLE 4.4: EXPERIENCE OF RACIST ASSAULT DURING THE COVID-19 PANDEMIC •

Weighted percentages

	Insult	Property damage	Physical attack	Any racist assault (one or more experience of any of the three)	N
White Irish	8.1	3.2	0.3	11.2	97
White Eastern European	5.3	1.3	1.8	5.3	360
Gypsy/Traveller	37.8	16.3	7.4	41.2	227
Roma	4.7	13.4	4.4	16.2	73
Jewish	27.9	4.5	6.2	30.7	476
Any other White background	3.0	0.5	1.3	3.9	650
Indian	9.6	2.4	2.0	10.6	1255
Pakistani	10.8	3.1	2.3	12.8	849
Bangladeshi	11.9	3.3	2.3	12.4	406
Mixed White and Asian	5.2	0.8	1.4	6.5	520
Chinese	11.1	9.5	5.8	16.9	662
Any other Asian background	10.2	2.4	3.3	13.1	663
Black Caribbean	14.9	4.3	5.5	19.1	557
Mixed White and Black Caribbean	16.7	4.6	3.6	18.1	354
Black African	12.5	3.1	2.6	13.8	1040
Mixed White and Black African	17.3	10.2	7.3	18.9	155
Any other Black background	13.0	8.9	7.8	18.5	176
Arab	5.4	2.2	1.7	5.9	152
Any other mixed/multiple background	9.1	4.1	5.1	16.6	363
Any other ethnic group	11.0	5.8	5.3	14.5	252
Overall	11.7	4.0	3.4	14.1	9287

The prevalence levels are lower than the pre-pandemic levels, which is to be expected as the data here refer to a single year, whereas the pre-pandemic levels refer to lifetime experience. The specific experience of lockdown could also have limited the exposure to risks of assault, or at least in public. On average, 14% of ethnic minority people reported such an assault, with several ethnic minority groups experienced a prevalence figure of over 15% for experiencing any of the assaults in the pandemic year. Gypsy/Traveller (41%) and Jewish (31%) ethnic groups experienced the highest prevalence of assaults. A high prevalence of assaults were also reported by people from the Black Caribbean and the Mixed White and Black African group (both 19%), and people from the Any Other Black, and White and Black Caribbean ethnic groups.

As before the pandemic, racist insults were the most prevalent (11.7% overall had experienced such an assault) with prevalence of property damage (4%) and physical assaults (3.4%) at a broadly similar level to each other. The highest levels of experiencing racist insults were found for people from the Gypsy/Traveller ethnic group (38%), who also reported the highest rates of racist property damage (16.3%) and the second highest rate of physical assault (7.4%) – people in the Any Other Black group had the highest rate of experiencing a racist physical assault during the pandemic (7.8%). Property damage was also most commonly experienced by the Roma group (13.4%) and the White and Black African group (10.2%). Physical assaults were most commonly reported by the White and Black African (7.3%), Jewish (6.2%), Chinese (5.8%), Black Caribbean (5.5%), Other (5.3%) and Other mixed/multiple (5.1%) ethnic groups.

Looking across experiences of racial discrimination in institutional settings during the pandemic, presented in Table 4.5, the highest reports of racial discrimination are within employment, followed by racial discrimination in education. People from the Gypsy/Traveller ethnic group reported the highest prevalence in two of the four of the domains (education, 12.6% and employment 14%), while Roma people reported the highest prevalence in relation to the housing (13%) and police (27.6%) settings. Gypsy/Traveller people also reported the second highest percentage of experience of racial discrimination by the police (18.3%), more than three times the overall rate (5.7%).

Table 4.6 shows the prevalence of experiencing racial discrimination in a range of social settings. About 11% of ethnic minority people reported experiences of racial discrimination in public settings, with variation across ethnic groups. Roma respondents reported nearly four times the average prevalence (at 39.2%), and Gypsy/Traveller respondents also reported high figures (32.5%). Roma respondents reported a high prevalence of racial discrimination from neighbours (17.6%).

In general, over the first year of the pandemic, men reported higher levels of racial discrimination than women, but these differences were not

TABLE 4.5: EXPERIENCE OF RACIAL DISCRIMINATION IN INSTITUTIONAL SETTINGS DURING THE COVID-19 PANDEMIC

Weighted percentages

	Experience of racism during the pandemic				
	Education	Employment	Seeking housing	By the police	N
White Irish	3.6	2.5	1.4	1.2	406
White Eastern European	2.6	6.3	8.3	3.6	662
Gypsy/Traveller	12.6	14.0	9.5	18.3	1255
Roma	0.1	11.1	13.0	27.6	849
Jewish	2.5	5.5	4.2	3.7	663
Any other White background	3.3	3.0	2.1	2.1	1040
Indian	3.0	6.2	2.8	4.4	557
Pakistani	5.0	7.1	4.4	6.1	176
Bangladeshi	3.6	8.5	5.3	4.7	520
Mixed White and Asian	4.0	8.7	5.5	5.6	155
Chinese	9.8	9.6	8.3	6.7	354
Any other Asian background	9.1	10.1	5.7	6.0	363
Black Caribbean	4.8	9.9	3.5	10.0	360
Mixed White and Black Caribbean	6.2	3.7	3.2	7.2	227
Black African	4.9	9.4	4.4	4.6	97
Mixed White and Black African	5.0	11.3	12.6	4.2	73
Any other Black background	5.9	11.1	8.7	5.7	650
Arab	3.7	4.5	3.1	3.9	152
Any other mixed/multiple background	0.7	6.2	3.1	2.3	252
Any other ethnic group	3.3	11.7	6.2	9.9	476
Overall	6.8	7.8	4.9	5.7	8881

• TABLE 4.6: EXPERIENCE OF RACIAL DISCRIMINATION IN PUBLIC SETTINGS DURING THE COVID-19 PANDEMIC •

Weighted percentages

	Experience of racism during the pandemic			
	In public	Neighbours	Family, partner or friends	N
White Irish	4.5	0.0	4.4	97
White Eastern European	3.4	1.9	2.2	360
Gypsy/Traveller	32.5	7.1	3.3	227
Roma	39.2	17.6	8.6	73
Jewish	16.0	7.9	8.7	476
Any other White background	2.1	2.1	1.8	650
Indian	8.5	3.5	2.8	1255
Pakistani	8.5	4.8	2.2	849
Bangladeshi	14.5	5.3	5.2	406
Mixed White and Asian	8.4	4.1	5.7	520
Chinese	12.6	9.4	6.7	662
Any other Asian background	9.1	5.1	6.3	663
Black Caribbean	20.0	6.7	8.6	557
Mixed White and Black Caribbean	13.4	1.9	3.8	354
Black African	11.2	5.4	4.0	1040
Mixed White and Black African	12.3	11.5	10.9	155
Any other Black background	13.7	10.9	8.5	176
Arab	7.7	5.8	2.1	152
Any other mixed/multiple background	3.5	2.8	3.6	363
Any other ethnic group	13.0	6.5	3.3	252
Overall	10.9	5.2	4.6	9287

substantial. However, Roma men reported a significantly higher prevalence of experiencing racist assaults than Roma women (1.3% women, 30.5% men) and in relation to unfair treatment in education (0.1% women, 10.3% men) and racial discrimination from neighbours (8.3% women, 26.5% men). In contrast, Roma women reported higher rates of racial discrimination from the police (37% women, 19.0% men).

Changes in experiences of racial discrimination from the pre-pandemic to the pandemic periods

The task of comparing the prevalence of racist assault and racial discrimination experienced in the pre-pandemic and pandemic periods is not straightforward, primarily because the periods of time considered in this chapter are of different lengths. In order to overcome this, the groups are ranked according to the prevalence of racist assault and racial discrimination. An increase in rank for a particular ethnic group, for example, would indicate that, relative to other ethnic groups, their experience has worsened.

Looking across the findings of the change in the ranking of ethnic groups for the ten different experiences of racist assault and racial discrimination covered by the EVENS between the pre-pandemic and pandemic periods, the change for three ethnic groups is marked. Chinese respondents have experienced a relative increase in experienced racial discrimination in comparison to other ethnic groups almost all settings (nine out of ten), as have the Other Asian and Eastern European groups.

Anticipation of experiencing racial discrimination

EVENS also asked respondents about how worried they were about experiencing racial discrimination. The findings presented in Figure 4.3 show that more than half of the Jewish, Chinese and the Gypsy/Traveller groups, and 40% of the Black 'Other' and the Pakistani ethnic groups were worried about experiencing racist assaults or racial discrimination.

Experiences with the police

Figure 4.4 shows how experiences with police activity during the pandemic differed across ethnic minority groups. Roma (47.9%), Gypsy/Traveller (30.1%) and Chinese (29.1%) ethnic groups reported the highest prevalence of changes in police activity over the pandemic. Figure 4.4 also shows that people in these groups also had the highest prevalence of having been stopped by the police (33.8% of Gypsy/Traveller, 21.4% of Roma and 19.4% of Chinese ethnic groups reporting this).

FIGURE 4.3: WORRIES ABOUT EXPERIENCING RACIAL ASSAULT OR DISCRIMINATION

Weighted percentages

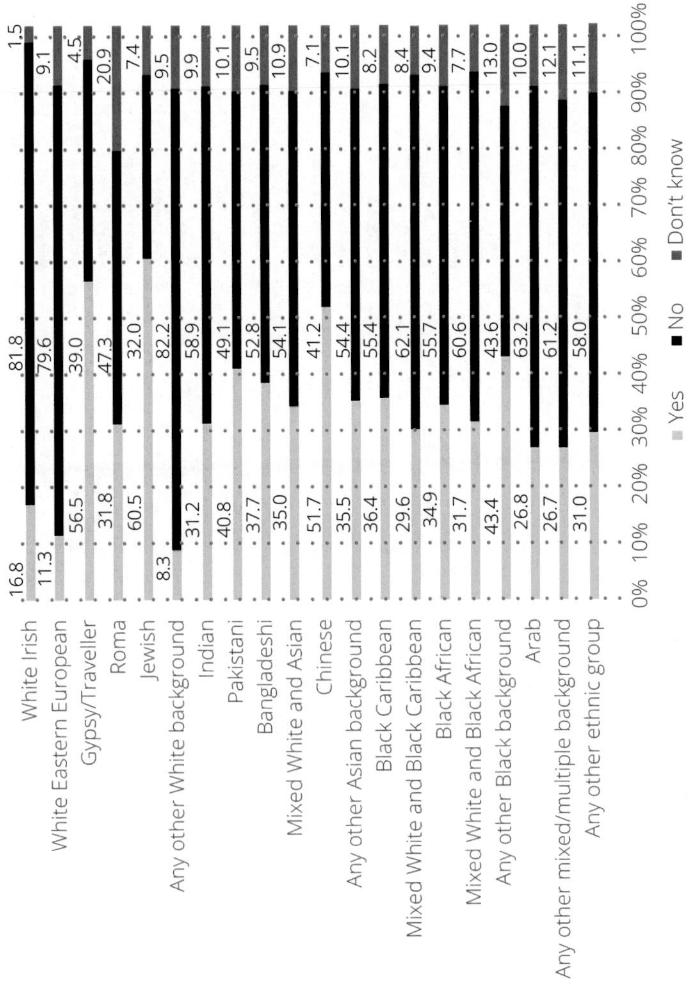

Ethnic group	Yes	No	Don't know
White Irish	16.8	81.8	1.5
White Eastern European	11.3	79.6	9.1
Gypsy/Traveller	56.5	39.0	4.5
Roma	31.8	47.3	20.9
Jewish	60.5	32.0	7.4
Any other White background	8.3	82.2	9.5
Indian	31.2	58.9	9.9
Pakistani	40.8	49.1	10.1
Bangladeshi	37.7	52.8	9.5
Mixed White and Asian	35.0	54.1	10.9
Chinese	51.7	41.2	7.1
Any other Asian background	35.5	54.4	10.1
Black Caribbean	36.4	55.4	8.2
Mixed White and Black Caribbean	29.6	62.1	8.4
Black African	34.9	55.7	9.4
Mixed White and Black African	31.7	60.6	7.7
Any other Black background	43.4	43.6	13.0
Arab	26.8	63.2	10.0
Any other mixed/multiple background	26.7	61.2	12.1
Any other ethnic group	31.0	58.0	11.1

0%   10%   20%   30%   40%   50%   60%   70%   80%   90%   100%

■ Yes   ■ No   ■ Don't know

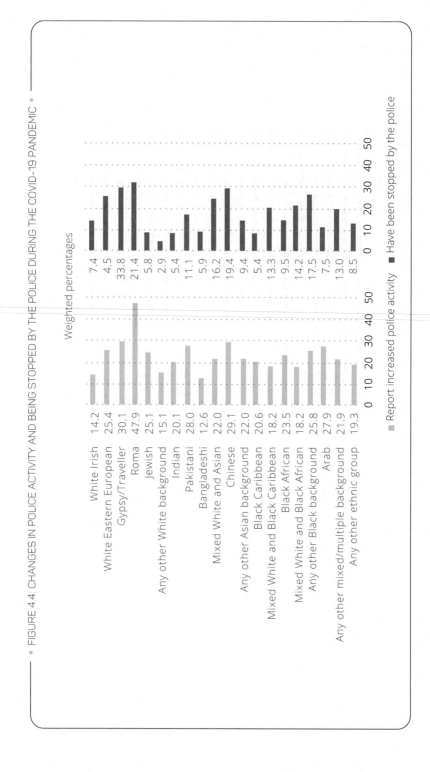

Discussion

The measures of racial discrimination included in EVENS enabled us to capture the insidiousness and persistence of interpersonal racism and racial discrimination that ethnic minority people experience over time and across settings.

We find clear evidence that racism and racial discrimination are prevalent in the UK. Over a third of respondents reported experiences of racist assault (verbal, physical or damage to property) prior to the pandemic, with over half the respondents from the Gypsy/Traveller, Jewish and Any Other Black ethnic groups reporting such experiences. Over a fifth of ethnic minority people reported experiences of racial discrimination in institutional settings and by the police, close to a third reported experiences of racial discrimination in public settings, and almost one in six ethnic minority people reported experiencing racial discrimination from neighbours. During the pandemic year, these figures were lower because they capture a much shorter period of time, but still show that around 14% of ethnic minority people reported experiencing some form of racist assault and over 10% experienced racial discrimination in public settings.

Racism is a system that disadvantages the lives of all ethnic minority people, but how racial discrimination is experienced may differ across ethnic minority groups. We found differences across ethnic groups in reported prevalence across time and settings, and we also found gender differences within ethnic groups. For example, we found that people from Any Other Black, Roma, Black Caribbean, Gypsy/Traveller, and Mixed White and Black Caribbean ethnic groups reported high rates of racial discrimination in education. Men tended to report higher levels of interpersonal discrimination than women, but that is far from a universal finding: this pattern is reversed among the Gypsy/Traveller, Roma and Black Caribbean ethnic groups, where the prevalence for women is higher than that for men. We found that Chinese, Other Asian and Eastern European people reported considerable increases in experiences of racial discrimination during the pandemic year relative to other ethnic minority groups compared to experiences prior to the pandemic.

Our findings show that experiences of racial discrimination are not isolated to a single setting; rather, accumulation of experiences of racial discrimination across different settings is common. For example, Roma respondents report having experienced discrimination in an average of over three different settings, and Gypsy/Traveller, White and Black African, Other Black, and Arab respondents reported experiences of racial discrimination in more than one setting on average.

We also examined respondents' levels of worry about experiencing racial discrimination. Our findings show that the ethnic groups with the greatest levels of worry (the Jewish, Chinese, Gypsy/Traveller and Any Other Black ethnic groups) are also among the groups with the highest prevalence of assault during the pandemic year.

We considered experiences of racial discrimination relating to police activity, and found that the Black Caribbean, Roma and Gypsy/Traveller ethnic groups reported the highest prevalence before the pandemic. During the pandemic, Roma, Gypsy/Traveller and Chinese ethnic groups reported the highest perception of increased police activity and the highest rate of stops by the police.

Conclusion

The EVENS survey provides robust evidence of the existence of racism and racial discrimination in the UK. We show persistent and extensive experiences of racial discrimination over time and across a multitude of settings. Racism and racial discrimination have strong implications for the economic, social and health outcomes of ethnic minority people, producing and maintaining ethnic inequalities over time. The chapters that follow provide evidence of ethnic inequalities across these outcomes, and although their methodological approach precludes us from making explicit empirical links from the ethnic inequalities reported in those chapters to the racism and racial discrimination we report here, other studies have clearly documented the fundamental role of racism and racial discrimination in leading to ethnic inequalities (Williams, 1996; Karlsen and Nazroo, 2002b; Landrine et al, 2006; Brondolo et al, 2009; Williams and Mohammed, 2009; Wallace et al, 2016; Stopforth et al, 2022). As policy and practice efforts are targeted towards recovering from the pandemic, commitment and action to eliminate racism and racial discrimination are paramount in addressing ethnic inequities in the UK.

Box 4.1: Racism and racial discrimination: measures and methods

All analysis reported in this chapter was produced using Stata 16.1 (StataCorp, 2019). All analyses are adjusted for benchmarking and propensity weights. Due to insufficient response rates among older age groups, the data are censored at 65 years of age for respondent age.

Experiences of racism and of racial discrimination

In this chapter we use data from the core module of the EVENS survey that asks respondents about their experiences of racism and racial discrimination over various time periods. The areas addressed were as follows.

Domain	Question
Physical assault	Has anyone physically attacked you for reasons to do with your ethnicity, race, colour or religion? If yes, when did this happen?
Property damage	Has anyone deliberately damaged any property that belonged to you for reasons to do with your ethnicity, race, colour or religion?
Insults	Has anyone insulted you for reasons to do with your ethnicity, race, colour or religion? By insulted, I mean verbally abused, threatened or been a nuisance to you?
Education	In education, have you ever been treated unfairly because of your ethnicity, race, colour or religion?
Employment	In your job, have you ever been treated unfairly because of your ethnicity, race, colour or religion?
Housing	When seeking housing, have you ever been treated unfairly because of your ethnicity, race, colour or religion?
Police	Have you ever been treated unfairly because of your ethnicity, race, colour or religion by the police?
In public	When you were in public settings, such as out shopping, in parks, cafes or restaurants, or on public transport, have you ever been treated unfairly because of your ethnicity, race, colour or religion?
Neighbours	Did neighbours ever make life difficult for you or your family because of your ethnicity, race, colour or religion?
Family, partner or friends	Did those close to you (such as partner, friends or family) ever treat you unfairly because of your ethnicity, race, colour or religion?

For each area, respondents were able to select any of the following options to indicate the timing of their experience:

- In the past year
- Within the past five years
- Within the past ten years
- Over ten years ago
- Don't know
- This hasn't happened to me.

For this chapter, the prevalence of the different forms and settings of racial discrimination are operationalised as dichotomies (occurred/did not occur). We split our analyses between experiences of racial discrimination before and during the pandemic. We count experiences of racial discrimination during the pandemic as those that occurred within the past year. Experiences of racial discrimination before the pandemic account for all the time periods prior to the past year (within the past five years, within the past ten years, over ten years ago or don't know). In the rates of experiencing racial discrimination prior to the pandemic, we include responses of people who selected 'Don't know', assuming that these respondents have had a certain experience in the past, but were unsure about the exact timing.

We report the prevalence of racial discrimination across three broad categories: experiences of a racist assault, experiences of racial discrimination in institutional settings, and experiences of racial discrimination in social settings. We also examine changes in police activity during the pandemic.

We report the number of settings in which people have experienced racial discrimination to capture the accumulation of experienced racial discrimination across ethnic minority people's lives. We also examine gender differences in experiences of racial discrimination within ethnic groups.

Racist assault

We use the term 'racist assault' to jointly look at the experience of insults, property damage or physical attacks due to people's ethnicity, race, colour or religion. In our results, we present the rates of experiencing these events separately as well as combined together (Tables 4.1 and 4.4). Further, we report the rates of experiencing any form of such racist assault by gender (Figure 4.1).

Racial discrimination in institutional settings

Similarly, we look at the experience of racial discrimination in the context of education, employment, policing and seeking housing. We report the rates separately as well as jointly to capture the proportion of people experiencing this type of racial discrimination in at least one of the settings (Tables 4.2 and 4.5).

Racial discrimination in social settings

Further, adopting the same approach, we look at racial discrimination in the context of social settings. Here, we focus on events experienced in public, from neighbours, or from family, partner or friends. We report the prevalence of experiences separately (Tables 4.3 and 4.6).

The accumulation of experienced racial discrimination across settings

To capture the accumulation of experiences of racial discrimination across people's lives settings, we measure the number of settings in which racial discrimination was experienced across time. We capture seven settings, including racial discrimination in education, employment, in public, policing, seeking housing, from neighbours, or from family, partner or friends. We report the sum of settings in which people have experienced racial discrimination, as well as the mean number of settings in which ethnic racial discrimination has been experienced (Figure 4.2).

Worry about experiencing racial discrimination

Respondents were also asked about their levels of worry about experiencing racial discrimination, using the following question: 'Do you worry about being harassed because of your ethnicity, race, colour or religion? By harassed, we mean being insulted, or physically attacked, or having your property damaged.' We report the rates of people indicating they are worried about being racially discriminated (Figure 4.3).

Policing

Lastly, we focus on the experiences of policing during the pandemic. We report two sets of results. First, we look at perceived changes in the levels of policing activity, including visibility, arrests and interventions. We focus on the rates of reporting that the police activity has increased, combining 'Increased a lot' and 'Increased a little' responses (Figure 4.4). Second, we report the levels of people reporting they were stopped by the police during the COVID-19 pandemic (also Figure 4.4).

5

Health and wellbeing

Harry Taylor, Dharmi Kapadia, Laia Bécares, Michaela Šťastná and James Nazroo

Key findings

People from ethnic minority groups in the UK face poorer physical health outcomes, including greater risk of COVID-19 infection and COVID-related bereavement; however, people from ethnic minority groups fared better than the White majority in relation to mental health.

- We found a higher risk of COVID-19 infection among people from many ethnic minority groups compared with the White British group; COVID-19 related bereavement was also more likely among most ethnic minority groups.
- There was a higher risk of physical multimorbidity among Bangladeshi and Black Caribbean women, and Gypsy/Traveller and Roma men, compared with their White British counterparts.
- A higher risk of depression and anxiety was found for the Arab group. A higher risk of anxiety was also seen for people in the Any other Black background and White Irish groups. The White Irish group had a higher risk of experiencing an increase in loneliness during the pandemic. The risk of loneliness was also higher for people from the Mixed White and Black Caribbean group, and those from any other ethnic group.
- People from the Roma and Chinese groups reported more difficulty in accessing health services, compared with the White British group.
- However, there were some outcomes for which ethnic minority groups fared better than the White British group:
  - Levels of anxiety and depression were lower among people in the Black African, Chinese, White Eastern European and Any other Asian groups compared with the White British group.
  - People from Gypsy/Traveller, Roma, Chinese and Black African ethnic groups were less likely to experience loneliness during the pandemic than the White British group, and those from the Roma, Bangladeshi, Black African, Pakistani and Indian groups

had a lower risk of their loneliness increasing compared to before the pandemic than the White British group.

○ People from the White Irish and Black African groups were able to access health services during the pandemic more readily than the White British group.

Introduction

There is a considerable body of evidence demonstrating ethnic inequalities in health in the UK (Nazroo, 1997; Erens et al, 2000; Sproston and Nazroo 2002; Sproston and Mindell, 2006; Bécares, 2015; Darlington et al, 2015; Stopforth et al, 2021a). When the first measures to tackle COVID-19 appeared in the UK in March 2020, the initial messaging from the government and beyond was that the virus does not discriminate. However, people from ethnic minority groups suffered greater levels of infection, hospitalisation and death during the pandemic compared with the White British majority (Pan et al, 2020; Public Health England, 2020; Mathur et al, 2021). This chapter explores ethnic inequalities in health and health-related outcomes in the UK during the COVID-19 pandemic, as well as inequalities in experiences of loneliness and bereavement. It also examines whether people from ethnic minority groups were able to access health services as readily as the White British majority during the pandemic.

Past research has shown the persistence of ethnic inequalities in health in the UK over a number of decades. Additionally, there is considerable evidence to show that racism is a fundamental cause of poor physical and mental health in ethnic minority groups (Karlsen and Nazroo, 2002; Williams et al, 2003; Williams, Neighbours and Jackson, 2003; Wallace et al, 2016; Nazroo et al, 2020 – see also Chapter 4 for a further discussion of the Evidence for Equality National Survey [EVENS] findings regarding racism). Most recently, data from the 2015/17 wave of the UK Household Longitudinal Study (also known as 'Understanding Society') show that the chances of having a limiting long-term illness (LLTI) are increased among Black Caribbean, Black African, Indian, Pakistani and Bangladeshi groups compared with the White British group (Stopforth et al, 2021a). Similarly, data from three pooled years (2009, 2010 and 2011) of the Health Survey for England showed that Pakistani or Bangladeshi people had higher age-adjusted rates of limiting long-term illness compared to the White British majority, whereas those in Black ethnic groups showed lower LLTI rates (Darlington et al, 2015). There is also evidence that ethnic inequalities in health are worse in later life due to the disadvantage that has accumulated for ethnic minority people across the life course (Dannefer, 2003; Stopforth et al, 2021b). For example, in the UK, data from the 2011 Census show that ethnic inequalities in LLTI are most pronounced in older age (65 and over), especially among people from Bangladeshi, Pakistani and Gypsy/Traveller ethnic groups (Bécares, 2015). There is also evidence of unequal access to healthcare in the UK, which points to reduced access to many health services (for example, mental healthcare, dental care and hospital services) for people in some ethnic minority groups (Nazroo et al, 2009; Harwood et al, 2021), as well as worse treatment within health services, compared with the White British majority group (Barnett et al, 2019; Kapadia et al, 2022). Further, people from ethnic minority groups with multiple long-term conditions suffer from suboptimal disease management for those conditions (Hayanga et al, 2021).

The effect of COVID-19 upon the health of the UK's ethnic minority groups has been well documented. Evidence showing increased rates of COVID-19 infection among ethnic minority groups was published only a few months into the pandemic (Pan et al, 2020). Repeated studies have found higher levels of infection among people from ethnic minority groups (Public Health England, 2020). These higher levels of infection translated into higher rates of mortality among ethnic minority groups; for example, people from the Bangladeshi ethnic group had a mortality rate around five times higher than the White British group in the period from December 2020 to December 2021 (Mathur et al, 2021; ONS, 2022). The impact of COVID-19, and the resulting restrictions, also impacted on the mental health of people from ethnic minority groups in the UK. Levels of psychological distress were higher among non-White respondents to the Understanding Society COVID-19 survey (Understanding Society, 2022), and remained steady between Wave 8 (31.1%) and Wave 9 (30.7%) for the non-White group, but psychological distress levels reduced for the White group (24.2% in Wave 8 reducing to 20.3% in Wave 9). The UCL COVID-19 Study also reported higher rates of depression, anxiety, unemployment stress and financial stress among people from ethnic minority groups (Fancourt et al, 2020). In addition to the direct effect of COVID-19 infection on health, the effect of lockdowns and the government's wider response to the pandemic greatly reduced people's access to healthcare services (Mansfield et al, 2021). Furthermore, disruption to hospital admissions was greatest in areas with the largest proportions of ethnic minority people (Warner et al, 2021).

This chapter adds new evidence to the literature on ethnic inequalities of health in the UK, beginning with an investigation of ethnic inequalities in COVID-19 infection, before moving on to limiting long-term illness, mental health, loneliness and access to health services. This chapter will address to what extent the well-documented inequalities in COVID-19 infection are mirrored in other health outcomes, in terms of both physical and mental health.

Results

In this chapter, we present the findings from a selection of the health measures collected in the EVENS data. All results presented here are the outcomes of logistic regression modelling, which was used to adjust for differences in the underlying age and sex structure of the different ethnic groups in the UK. More details can be found in Box 5.1 at the end of this chapter. The results of the logistic regression modelling are presented in charts, each of which compares outcomes for ethnic minority groups with the White British group. The red dotted line in each chart represents the White British group. Each ethnic minority group has a point estimate (represented by a dot) reported in an 'Odds Ratio' (OR) scale. Taking COVID-19 infection as an example, an OR of 2 means that the ethnic group in question experienced twice the levels of infection of the White British group, while an OR of 0.5 means that the ethnic group experienced half the levels of infection of the White British group. The horizontal lines either side of the dots on the chart represent the 95% confidence interval (CI), or the certainty of the estimate. Where these horizontal lines cross the red dotted line, it is unclear whether there is any difference between the ethnic minority group and the White British group.

COVID-19 infection

EVENS participants were asked if they had ever received a positive COVID-19 test. Given the increased likelihood of COVID-19 infection among older people and among men, the results presented here control for age and sex, as well as a squared age term to represent the non-linear effects of age, thereby accounting for the possibility that infection risk grew at an increasing rate with higher ages. Incorporating this adjustment means that we can be confident that any differences observed between ethnic groups are not simply due to differences in the age and sex structure of the population of each ethnic group. Higher levels of COVID-19 infection were seen among people from the Gypsy/Traveller, Bangladeshi, Mixed White and Black African, Pakistani, Black African, White Eastern European, White Irish and Indian groups (see Figure 5.1). The largest inequalities were seen for the Gypsy/Traveller group (OR 2.82, 95% CI 1.31–6.07) and the Bangladeshi group (OR 2.80, 95% CI 1.67-4.70).

Bereavement

In the EVENS survey, respondents were asked if they experienced the bereavement of someone close to them (for example, a partner, family member or close friend) since the start of the pandemic, and whether that

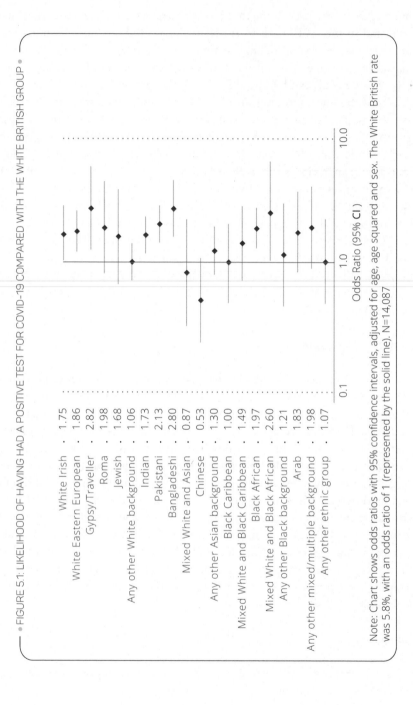

FIGURE 5.1: LIKELIHOOD OF HAVING HAD A POSITIVE TEST FOR COVID-19 COMPARED WITH THE WHITE BRITISH GROUP

White Irish	1.75
White Eastern European	1.86
Gypsy/Traveller	2.82
Roma	1.98
Jewish	1.68
Any other White background	1.06
Indian	1.73
Pakistani	2.13
Bangladeshi	2.80
Mixed White and Asian	0.87
Chinese	0.53
Any other Asian background	1.30
Black Caribbean	1.00
Mixed White and Black Caribbean	1.49
Black African	1.97
Mixed White and Black African	2.60
Any other Black background	1.21
Arab	1.83
Any other mixed/multiple background	1.98
Any other ethnic group	1.07

Odds Ratio (95% CI)

Note: Chart shows odds ratios with 95% confidence intervals, adjusted for age, age squared and sex. The White British rate was 5.8%, with an odds ratio of 1 (represented by the solid line). N=14,087

person died with COVID-19. Figure 5.2 shows two diagrams: (1) being bereaved due to COVID-19; and (2) being bereaved due to any reason (including COVID-19). Higher levels of COVID-related bereavement were seen in all ethnic minority groups, with the exception of the White Eastern European, Roma, Chinese, Mixed White and Black Caribbean, and Any other mixed/multiple background groups. Bereavement due to any reason showed a similar pattern, albeit with slightly fewer differences between ethnic minority groups and the White British group. These results are similar to those seen for risk of infection, although some ethnic minority groups had significantly higher odds of bereavement but not infection, when compared with the White British group. The group suffering the highest levels of bereavement (in both outcomes) compared with the White British group were those from Any other Black background, who had an odds ratio of 5.70 (95% CI 3.05–10.64) for COVID-related bereavement, and an OR of 2.98 (95% CI 1.69–5.25) of any kind of bereavement, compared to the White British group. A noteworthy result is that the Jewish group were more likely to be bereaved due to COVID-19 than the White British group (OR 3.13, 95% CI 1.69–5.82); this is an observation unique to the EVENS data.

Physical multimorbidity

EVENS participants were asked if they had any physical health conditions, drawing from a list of five conditions (high blood pressure, diabetes, heart disease, lung disease and cancer) and were given the opportunity to specify if they had a health condition not included in the list. Here, we define 'multimorbidity' as having two or more physical conditions. Given the reported sex differences in LLTI (Bécares, 2015), separate analytical models were run for men and women. This analysis controlled for age, age squared and sex in order to account for the way in which physical multimorbidity becomes increasingly more prevalent in the most elderly (Barnett et al, 2012). Several ethnic minority groups had higher odds of having physical multimorbidity than the White British group (see Figure 5.3), namely Bangladeshi women (OR 4.91, 95% CI 2.40-10.05), Black Caribbean women (OR 2.54, 95% CI 1.47-4.39), Gypsy/Traveller men (OR 12.42, 95% CI 4.98-30.94) and Roma men (OR 5.08, 95% CI 1.75-14.77). White Eastern European men were less likely to have physical multimorbidity (OR 0.09, 95% CI 0.01-0.84).

Mental health

The EVENS questionnaire contained measures of depression (the Centre for Epidemiological Studies Depression Scale, 8 item version [CES-D 8]; Radloff, 1977) and anxiety (the Generalised Anxiety and Depression Scale 7

FIGURE 5.2: EXPERIENCE OF COVID-19-RELATED
BEREAVEMENT AND BEREAVEMENT OF ANY KIND
COMPARED WITH THE WHITE BRITISH GROUP

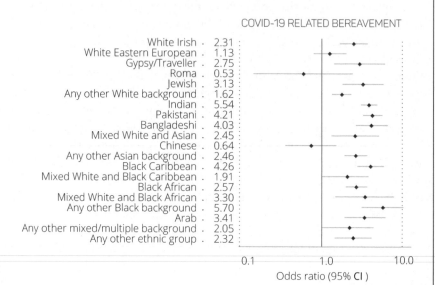

COVID-19 RELATED BEREAVEMENT

White Irish	2.31
White Eastern European	1.13
Gypsy/Traveller	2.75
Roma	0.53
Jewish	3.13
Any other White background	1.62
Indian	5.54
Pakistani	4.21
Bangladeshi	4.03
Mixed White and Asian	2.45
Chinese	0.64
Any other Asian background	2.46
Black Caribbean	4.26
Mixed White and Black Caribbean	1.91
Black African	2.57
Mixed White and Black African	3.30
Any other Black background	5.70
Arab	3.41
Any other mixed/multiple background	2.05
Any other ethnic group	2.32

Odds ratio (95% CI)

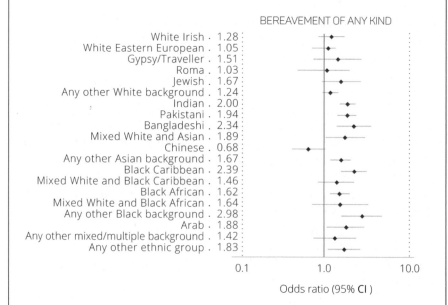

BEREAVEMENT OF ANY KIND

White Irish	1.28
White Eastern European	1.05
Gypsy/Traveller	1.51
Roma	1.03
Jewish	1.67
Any other White background	1.24
Indian	2.00
Pakistani	1.94
Bangladeshi	2.34
Mixed White and Asian	1.89
Chinese	0.68
Any other Asian background	1.67
Black Caribbean	2.39
Mixed White and Black Caribbean	1.46
Black African	1.62
Mixed White and Black African	1.64
Any other Black background	2.98
Arab	1.88
Any other mixed/multiple background	1.42
Any other ethnic group	1.83

Odds ratio (95% CI)

Note: Chart shows odds ratios with 95% confidence intervals, adjusted for age,
age squared, and sex. The White British rates were 8.1% (N=13,389) for COVID-19
related bereavement and 22.7% (N=13,675) for bereavement of any kind, both
with an odds ratio of 1 (represented by the solid line).

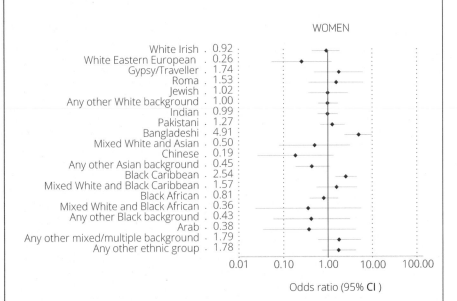

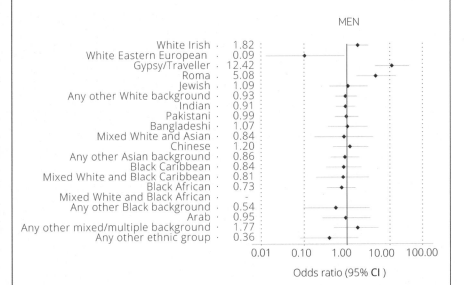

Note: Chart shows odds ratios with 95% confidence intervals, adjusted for age, age squared and sex. The White British rates were 13.8% for women (N=7,996) and 16.2% for men (N=6,219), both with an odds ratio of 1 (represented by the solid line)

item version [GAD-7]; Spitzer et al, 2006). To account for potential changes in levels of mental health difficulties across the pandemic, the regression models presented here correct for the month in which the survey was taken, as well as for age and sex.

Figure 5.4 shows that the Arab group had higher odds of both depression (OR 2.18, 95% CI 1.22–3.90) and anxiety (OR 3.19, 95% CI 1.80–5.66) compared to the White British group. The odds of having anxiety were also higher in the Any Other Black background and White Irish groups. To further explore these observations, we created additional separate models for men and women, and found that Arab women, but not Arab men were at higher risk of depression. Furthermore, only women from the Any Other Black background group had higher odds of anxiety compared with the White British group.

People from the Chinese, Any Other Asian, Black African and White Eastern European groups had lower odds of both anxiety and depression when compared with the White British group. Some ethnic minority groups, namely the Mixed White and Asian, and Roma groups, as well as Indian women, had lower odds of depression than the White British group, but had odds of anxiety that were not significantly different from the White British group.

As previously detailed, the UCL COVID-19 Study found higher rates of depression, anxiety, unemployment stress and financial stress among people from ethnic minority groups during the pandemic. This was generally not reflected in the age and sex-adjusted EVENS analysis. However, it should be noted that the UCL Social Survey results do not adjust for age and that when controlling for age, these ethnic differences are reduced. Indeed, when observing EVENS data that do not adjust for age and sex, there are higher levels of anxiety among people from the Arab, Any Other Black background, White Irish, Mixed White and Black Caribbean, Pakistani and Any Other White background groups compared with the White British group. The reason for this is that anxiety and depression appear to be more common in younger people, and the age structure of the UK's ethnic minority groups is generally younger than the White British group

Social isolation and loneliness

In EVENS, respondents were asked a series of questions on loneliness (the 3-item UCLA scale; Hughes et al, 2004) and also whether their levels of loneliness had increased during the pandemic. Here, we report ethnic differences in being lonely during the pandemic, and whether there were ethnic differences in the extent to which people's feelings of loneliness or isolation increased during the pandemic. There were not significant differences in loneliness across our sample; however, some ethnic minority groups (Gypsy/Traveller, Roma,

● FIGURE 5.4: RISK OF DEPRESSION AND ANXIETY ●
COMPARED WITH THE WHITE BRITISH GROUP

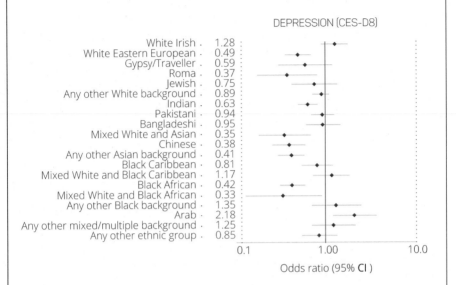

DEPRESSION (CES-D8)

White Irish ·	1.28
White Eastern European ·	0.49
Gypsy/Traveller ·	0.59
Roma ·	0.37
Jewish ·	0.75
Any other White background ·	0.89
Indian ·	0.63
Pakistani ·	0.94
Bangladeshi ·	0.95
Mixed White and Asian ·	0.35
Chinese ·	0.38
Any other Asian background ·	0.41
Black Caribbean ·	0.81
Mixed White and Black Caribbean ·	1.17
Black African ·	0.42
Mixed White and Black African ·	0.33
Any other Black background ·	1.35
Arab ·	2.18
Any other mixed/multiple background ·	1.25
Any other ethnic group ·	0.85

Odds ratio (95% CI)

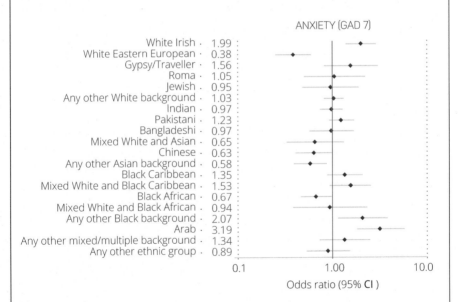

ANXIETY (GAD 7)

White Irish ·	1.99
White Eastern European ·	0.38
Gypsy/Traveller ·	1.56
Roma ·	1.05
Jewish ·	0.95
Any other White background ·	1.03
Indian ·	0.97
Pakistani ·	1.23
Bangladeshi ·	0.97
Mixed White and Asian ·	0.65
Chinese ·	0.63
Any other Asian background ·	0.58
Black Caribbean ·	1.35
Mixed White and Black Caribbean ·	1.53
Black African ·	0.67
Mixed White and Black African ·	0.94
Any other Black background ·	2.07
Arab ·	3.19
Any other mixed/multiple background ·	1.34
Any other ethnic group ·	0.89

Odds ratio (95% CI)

Note: Chart shows odds ratios with 95% confidence intervals, adjusted for age,
age squared and sex. The White British rates were 32.1% (N=12,565) for
depression and 18.2% (N=13,334) for anxiety, both with an odds ratio
of 1 (represented by the solid line)

Chinese and Black African people) appeared to be less likely to be lonely than the White British group, with the Gypsy/Traveller and Roma groups having roughly half the odds of loneliness of the White British group (see Figure 5.5). The Roma, Bangladeshi, Black African, Pakistani and Indian groups were all less likely to have reported an increase in feelings of loneliness during the pandemic compared with the White British group. Some groups were more likely to be lonely compared with the White British group, specifically the Mixed White and Black Caribbean group, the Any Other ethnic group and the Arab group. The White Irish and White Eastern European groups were also more likely than the White British group to report an increase in feelings of loneliness during the pandemic.

Access to services

EVENS participants were asked about how readily they were able to access health and social care services during the pandemic. Here, we report the OR of being able to access required services 'never' or 'hardly ever', or not trying to access services despite having a need to do so. The results given in Figure 5.6 show that access was poorer for people from Roma (OR 2.45, 95% CI 1.31-4.58) and Chinese (OR 1.71, 95% CI 1.18-2.46) ethnic groups compared with the White British group. Conversely, the White Irish (OR 0.57, 95% CI 0.37-0.87) and Black African (OR 0.72, 95% CI 0.53-0.97) groups appeared to be able to more readily access services than the White British group.

Discussion

The results from the EVENS data give a comprehensive picture of the health of people from ethnic minority groups in Britain during the COVID-19 pandemic, with ethnic inequalities being present for physical health outcomes, coupled with mixed findings around inequalities in mental health outcomes. ONS data showed higher levels of COVID-19 infection and mortality for people from many ethnic minority groups, an observation mirrored in the EVENS data on coronavirus infection, and this is also suggested by the EVENS data on experiences of bereavement. Additionally, people from some ethnic minority groups were more likely to have physical multimorbidity compared with the White British group. However, while certain ethnic minority groups, including the Arab, Any other Black background, and White Irish groups, had increased odds of poorer mental health outcomes, the EVENS data shows lower odds of depression, anxiety and loneliness among people from several ethnic minority groups. Finally, there was evidence of inequitable access to services for people from Roma and Chinese groups during the COVID-19 pandemic.

FIGURE 5.5: LIKELIHOOD OF REPORTING LONELINESS AND REPORTING AN INCREASE IN FEELINGS OF LONELINESS DURING THE COVID-19 PANDEMIC COMPARED WITH THE WHITE BRITISH GROUP

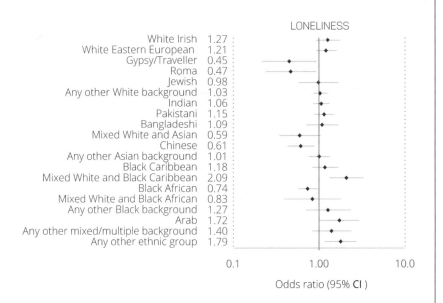

LONELINESS

White Irish	1.27
White Eastern European	1.21
Gypsy/Traveller	0.45
Roma	0.47
Jewish	0.98
Any other White background	1.03
Indian	1.06
Pakistani	1.15
Bangladeshi	1.09
Mixed White and Asian	0.59
Chinese	0.61
Any other Asian background	1.01
Black Caribbean	1.18
Mixed White and Black Caribbean	2.09
Black African	0.74
Mixed White and Black African	0.83
Any other Black background	1.27
Arab	1.72
Any other mixed/multiple background	1.40
Any other ethnic group	1.79

0.1   1.00   10.0

Odds ratio (95% CI)

INCREASE IN LONELINESS

White Irish	1.53
White Eastern European	1.34
Gypsy/Traveller	1.03
Roma	0.39
Jewish	1.05
Any other White background	1.15
Indian	0.80
Pakistani	0.70
Bangladeshi	0.55
Mixed White and Asian	0.99
Chinese	0.83
Any other Asian background	0.87
Black Caribbean	0.91
Mixed White and Black Caribbean	0.99
Black African	0.58
Mixed White and Black African	0.57
Any other Black background	0.69
Arab	1.00
Any other mixed/multiple background	1.24
Any other ethnic group	0.86

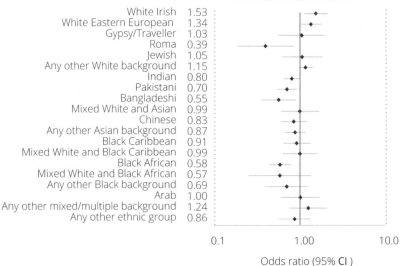

0.1   1.00   10.0

Odds ratio (95% CI)

Note: Chart shows odds ratios with 95% confidence intervals, adjusted for age, age squared and sex. The White British rates were 35.3% (N=13,660) for reporting loneliness and 32.6% (N=14,215) for reporting an increase in loneliness, both with an odds ratio of 1 (represented by the solid line)

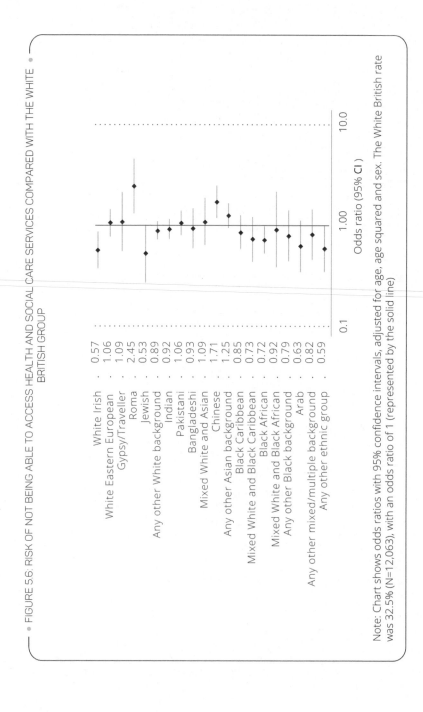

FIGURE 5.6: RISK OF NOT BEING ABLE TO ACCESS HEALTH AND SOCIAL CARE SERVICES COMPARED WITH THE WHITE BRITISH GROUP

	Odds ratio
White Irish	0.57
White Eastern European	1.06
Gypsy/Traveller	1.09
Roma	2.45
Jewish	0.53
Any other White background	0.89
Indian	0.92
Pakistani	1.06
Bangladeshi	0.93
Mixed White and Asian	1.09
Chinese	1.71
Any other Asian background	1.25
Black Caribbean	0.85
Mixed White and Black Caribbean	0.73
Black African	0.72
Mixed White and Black African	0.92
Any other Black background	0.79
Arab	0.63
Any other mixed/multiple background	0.82
Any other ethnic group	0.59

Note: Chart shows odds ratios with 95% confidence intervals, adjusted for age, age squared and sex. The White British rate was 32.5% (N=12,063), with an odds ratio of 1 (represented by the solid line)

COVID-related outcomes

The odds of COVID-19 infection were higher among EVENS participants from the Gypsy/Traveller, Bangladeshi, Mixed White and Black African, Pakistani, Black African, White Eastern European, White Irish and Indian groups, mirroring official statistics during the second wave of the pandemic (September 2020 to May 2021) (ONS, 2021b). Multiple reasons have been proposed for these ethnic inequalities including differential exposure to COVID-19 (for example, through occupation or working conditions), increased vulnerability to infection (for example, due to pre-existing health problems) and differential consequences of control measures (for example, employment insecurity and lack of sick pay) (Katikireddi et al, 2021).

The higher levels of COVID-related bereavement found among many ethnic minority groups, when compared with the White British group, mirror the higher rates of mortality seen in many of these groups according to the official statistics (ONS, 2021d). It should be noted, of course, that a person's networks are likely to stretch beyond their own ethnic group. The detailed ethnic group categorisation used in EVENS facilitated the observation of COVID-related outcomes for ethnic groups that are not usually covered in national surveys. For example, the EVENS data showed that people from the White Eastern European group had higher rates of infection than the White British group, and also showed a higher level of COVID-related bereavement in the Jewish group compared with the White British group, in line with ONS analysis from the pandemic period (ONS, 2021c).

Physical health

Pre-pandemic literature points to poorer health among certain ethnic minority groups in the UK (Nazroo, 1997; Erens et al, 2000; Sproston and Nazroo, 2002; Sproston and Mindell, 2006; Bécares, 2015; Darlington et al, 2015; Stopforth et al, 2021b), and our sample shows this trend continuing, with evidence of ethnic inequalities in COVID-19 infection, COVID-related bereavement and physical multimorbidity. It should be noted that EVENS is the first to have sufficient data to identify poor health among Roma men.

There are some considerations around the use of the EVENS data when looking at physical health. First, existing evidence shows that ethnic inequalities in rates of LLTI are highest among older people (Bécares, 2015), whereas the EVENS data have relatively few participants aged 65 or older. Additionally, it is necessary to consider the timeline of the recruitment of the EVENS sample. The White British sample was recruited mainly through survey panels, three waves of which were conducted at the start of the EVENS data collection (during the second lockdown, in early 2021), with an additional panel being conducted at the end of the data collection, in late 2021. This is in contrast to the ethnic minority sample, which was recruited in various different ways, at a fairly even rate from February to November 2021. The result of this is that the health and wellbeing of the White British sample may have been negatively affected by the context in the UK at the time of the data collection – specifically, during a lockdown that, in addition to the risk of COVID-related illness, is known to have had deleterious effects on mental health, as well as having affected care for those with existing chronic illnesses due to cancelled surgical or medical appointments (Topriceanu et al, 2021).

Mental health and loneliness

Although on the whole, people from ethnic minority groups in the EVENS data had relatively good mental health outcomes compared with the White British group, some ethnic minority groups had poor mental health outcomes. The Arab group had higher odds of anxiety and depression than the White British group. There are very little data on the mental health of the UK Arab population, so this represents a novel finding. In addition, the White Irish group had higher levels of anxiety and higher odds of having experienced an increase in loneliness during the pandemic period than the White British group. This observation is consistent with other literature showing poorer mental health outcomes for Irish people living in England (Delaney et al, 2013).

There were not large differences in loneliness across the ethnic groups included in our sample; however, certain groups (Gypsy/Traveller, Roma, Chinese and Black African people) appeared to be less lonely than the White British group. These results were in contrast to those seen in the July 2020 findings from the UCL COVID-19 Study, where people from ethnic minority groups were more likely to have experienced loneliness since the beginning of the pandemic (Fancourt et al, 2020). In the EVENS data, the Roma, Bangladeshi, Black African, Pakistani and Indian groups were all less likely to have reported an increase in feelings of loneliness compared with the White British group. One potential explanation is that people living in multigenerational housing may have been less susceptible to loneliness when compared with those living alone or with one other person. This may be particularly relevant to the Gypsy/Traveller and Roma groups; in the EVENS data, people in both of these groups were less likely to be lonely than people in the White British group. As the Roma group are often excluded from social research, this represents a novel finding from EVENS.

Access to services

Among EVENS participants, there was some evidence of ethnic inequalities in access to health and social care services during the pandemic, with access to services being more limited for people from Roma and Chinese ethnic groups compared with the White British group. The NHS Race and Health Observatory's rapid review into ethnic inequalities in access to health services (Kapadia et al, 2022) made specific comment regarding a lack of evidence on the experiences of these two groups, indicating a valuable contribution on the part of the EVENS data. Stakeholder engagement conducted as part of that review suggested that the Roma community often struggle to access services due to difficulty accessing GPs combined with language barriers (Kapadia et al, 2022). The review also identified language barriers as an issue for some Chinese women in accessing services (Kapadia et al, 2022); similarly, people of Chinese ethnicity have been found to be less likely to use the NHS Direct telephone service than the White British population (Cook et al, 2014).

It should also be noted that in the EVENS data, those from White Irish and Black African groups appeared to be able to access services more readily during the pandemic. The reasons for this are unclear and would benefit from additional research to understand what factors may be influencing these positive outcomes.

Conclusion

The long-term effects of COVID-19 on the health of the British population, and on ethnic health inequalities, are as yet unknown. In addition to the direct effects of COVID-19 on health, it is also important to consider the consequences of the measures taken to manage the pandemic and the emerging economic downturn. What is generally known is that periods of financial insecurity often affect the most socioeconomically deprived in society most acutely, and that socioeconomic deprivation, racial minority status and poor health are tightly interwoven. Additionally, the widespread levels of bereavement experienced by people from ethnic minority groups reflected in the EVENS data, termed the silent 'pandemic of grief', may have long-term mental health consequences which may not yet be fully apparent.

Box 5.1: Health and wellbeing: measures and methods

All figures reported in this chapter were created using logistic regression models. Data were analysed using R version 4.2.0 (R Core Team, 2022). Analyses adjusted for benchmarking and propensity weights, which were implemented using a weights argument specified in the R glm library. Each model corrected for age (expressed as an integer) and sex. Some models also included an age squared term to account for the non-linearity of the effects of age, whereby its effects on health are often amplified at the oldest ages. The main variables used for each question were taken from the EVENS Health module and the Social Isolation module:

COVID-19 infection: The COVID-19 infection results draw upon the EVENS question HLTH13. 'Have you ever received a positive result for a coronavirus (COVID-19) test?'; we considered the participants who responded 'Yes'.

Bereavement: To explore bereavement, we utilised two questions from the EVENS survey: (i) HLTH16. 'Have you experienced any bereavement of someone close to you (for example, a partner, family member or close friend) since February 2020? (Yes/No/Prefer not to say)'; and (ii) 'HLTH17. Did the person, or any of the people, you lost die with coronavirus? (Yes/No/Don't know/Prefer not to say)'

Physical multimorbidity: Physical multimorbidity was defined according to respondents' answers to question HLTH06: 'Do you currently have or have you ever had any of the following medical conditions? (Please select all that apply): 1. High blood pressure, 2. Diabetes, 3. Heart disease, 4. Lung disease (e.g., asthma or COPD), 5. Cancer, 6. Another clinically-diagnosed chronic physical health condition (please specify).' Physical multimorbidity was defined as those respondents who responded 'Yes' to two or more of these conditions.

Mental health: The measure of depression was calculated using EVENS question HLTH04: 'Now think about the past week and the feelings you have experienced. Please tell me if each of the following was true for you much of the time during the past week.' Participants were then invited to respond (Yes/No/Prefer not to say) according to eight measures. A score was calculated by giving 1 point for 'yes' and 0 points for 'no'. Two scale items (4 and 6) asked about positive symptoms (being happy or enjoying life) so were reverse-coded, whereby a 'no' response received 1 point and a 'yes' response received 0 points. In the analyses presented here, participants were said to have symptoms of depression if they scored 3 or more points. The measure of anxiety was calculated using EVENS question HLTH05: 'Over the last two weeks, how often have you been bothered by any of the following problems?' Participants were asked to respond (Not at all/Several days/More than half the day/Nearly every day/Prefer not to say) to seven separate measures aimed at evaluating symptoms of anxiety, such as trouble relaxing, or not being able to stop or control worrying. For each measure, participants were given a score, with 'Not at all' receiving a score of 0 and 'Nearly every day' receiving a score of 3. The score was summed; participants with a total score of 10 or more indicated symptoms of anxiety.

Social isolation and loneliness: The results on loneliness presented here refer to EVENS question ISOL01L: 'The next questions are about how you feel about different aspects of your life. For each one, please say how often you feel that way at the moment.' Participants were then invited to respond (Hardly ever or never/Some of the time/Often/Prefer not to say) to three questions regarding loneliness and isolation. Each question was scored, with 'Hardly ever or never' receiving a score of 1 and 'Often' receiving a score of 3. Participants with a total score of 6 or more were deemed to be exhibiting symptoms of loneliness. The results on change in levels of loneliness refer to question ISOL03: 'Have your feelings of loneliness and isolation changed since the coronavirus outbreak began in February 2020?' (they have: increased/decreased/ stopped/stayed the same).

Access to services: The results pertaining to access to services consider responses to EVENS question HLTH07: 'Since the coronavirus outbreak began in February 2020, have you always been able to access the community health and social care services and support you need, for instance your GP, a dentist, podiatrist, nurse, counselling for depression or anxiety or personal care?' Participants responded on a scale ranging from 'Yes, always' to 'No, never'. The following results consider those who responded 'No, hardly ever', 'No, never' or 'I did not attempt to contact them' to the question. The interpretation of this measure aims to evaluate whether respondents were able to get help if needed for any health problems they may have, and so excludes those who said they did not need to access services.

Key to interpreting the results in this chapter is an understanding of the context in which the EVENS data were collected. At the beginning of the data collection in February 2021, the UK was almost one year into the pandemic. England was one month into its third national lockdown, with the stay-at-home order remaining in place until 31 March 2021. It was not until 19 July 2021 that the majority of limitations on social contact were lifted. The initial effects of the pandemic on the mental health of UK residents were sudden and profound (Pierce et al, 2020), and although levels of anxiety and depression have stabilised, at the time of writing they have not yet returned to pre-pandemic levels (OHID, 2022). The effects on physical health are less clear; however, the potential effect of the COVID-19 pandemic should be considered when interpreting these results, especially where comparisons are made with pre-pandemic findings.

6

Housing, place and community

Joseph Harrison, Nissa Finney, Hannah Haycox and Emma Hill

Key findings

Ethnic minority groups in Britain are subject to material deprivation in residential experience, yet succeed in developing strong local attachment, and enriching this during times of crisis.

- Spatial pressure in households is more prevalent among all ethnic minority groups compared to White British people. It is a notable concern for three-generation households and particularly for Pakistani and Roma groups.
- Rates of living in detached housing are highest for White British, Arab, White Irish and Indian groups, at three times the rate of Black African, Black Caribbean and Bangladeshi groups, who tend to live in typically smaller types of accommodation, such as flats/apartments and terraced housing.
- The prevalence of caravan/mobile home accommodation for Gypsy/Traveller and Roma, which is largely invisible in other datasets, is evident in the Evidence for Equality National Survey (EVENS) results.
- Ethnic minorities are disadvantaged compared to the White British group in terms of access to outdoor space at home. The White British group have the highest rates of access to outdoor space at their property. Arab, Chinese and Other Black groups are four times more likely than the White British group to be without outdoor space at home.
- Residential mobility during the pandemic, which could indicate housing precarity, was considerably higher for Roma, Jewish, Other White, Indian, Mixed White and Asian, and Other Asian groups compared to the White British group, even when considering the different age structures of the ethnic groups.
- All ethnic groups, apart from Roma, feel a strong sense of belonging to their local area. Pakistani, Bangladeshi and Indian people are significantly more likely to report positive local belonging than White British people. For all ethnic groups apart from Roma, the majority of those who reported a change in belonging during the pandemic experienced increased attachment to the local area.

Introduction

This chapter is concerned with the differing residential experiences of ethnic groups in Britain. Using the unique aspects of EVENS, we examine material and affective aspects of 'home', considering household composition and the physical attributes of housing, as well as experiences of neighbourhood and the local environment. The analyses show that ethnic minorities in Britain continue to be subjected to material deprivation in residential experience, yet succeed in developing strong local attachments to people and places.

To understand housing from a holistic perspective – as 'home' – factors beyond the physical structure must be considered (Massey, 1992). Housing is a site that influences a person's access to key infrastructures, as well as their experiences of security, belonging and the complex social relationships developed between individuals and groups (Boccagni and Kusenbach, 2020). Having sufficient space in the home is thus considered an important aspect of homemaking, both materially and affectively. Access to home gardens or public green space has been found to have benefits for mental health (Thompson et al, 2012), particularly for children and young people (Tremblay et al, 2015; Jackson et al, 2021). The notion of home thus captures both the material conditions that constrain or facilitate access to opportunities and the interlinked affective impacts that result.

Experiences of, and access to, housing provisions are shaped by the power relations within wider society, including racial, gender, class and generational dynamics (Ahmed, 1999; Brun and Fábos, 2015). Despite the persistent ethnic inequalities in experience in Britain (Finney and Harries, 2015; Shankley and Finney, 2020; Haycox, 2022), considerations of relationships between ethnicity and housing are often limited in broader debates (Bloch et al, 2013). Minority groups were evidenced by Finney and Harries (2015) to be at greater risk of overcrowding compared to White British people, with overcrowding defined as a situation where there are too few bedrooms to meet household needs. Precarious housing is also more prevalent among ethnic minorities (Shankley and Finney, 2020).

The COVID-19 pandemic has further prompted questions about ethnic inequalities in housing experiences. For example, overcrowding became more prominent in the context of working-from-home initiatives. Moreover, the inability to avoid contact with individuals if someone were to test positive for COVID-19 resulted in the spread of the virus being more likely in overcrowded households (Mikolai et al, 2020). Whilst there has yet to be a full-scale investigation of the long-term outcome of the COVID-19 pandemic on wellbeing, it has been found that access to gardens and the outdoors helps individuals maintain their activity levels

(Corley et al, 2021) and is generally associated with positive wellbeing (de Bell et al, 2020).

Experiences of belonging and cohesion are also paramount to consider in relation to the COVID-19 pandemic, as resilience to crises has been linked with higher levels of neighbourhood trust (Aldrich and Meyer, 2015). Prior research has also shown how the formation of local communities among ethnic minorities acts as a method of support in a context of institutional racism (Alexander, 2018). The idea of belonging is often linked to the level of (ethnic) diversity in a local area, with some arguing that highly homogeneous areas are better for levels of generalised trust (Putnam, 2007), and others suggesting that diverse neighbourhoods foster more trust and cohesion (Bécares et al, 2011; Sturgis et al, 2014). The importance of localised amenities and social support increased during the COVID-19 pandemic, particularly during periods of lockdown in which people were confined to their accommodation and neighbourhoods.

The marked ethnic inequalities in housing are also shaped by broader migration histories and localities of settlement, as well as generational, gender and class dynamics (Alexander et al, 2015). In Britain, ethnic groups have their own historical context relating to their migration history and settlement patterns (Solomos, 2003; Hussain and Miller, 2006; Simpson et al 2008). Initial patterns of settlement in Britain were broadly influenced by ethnic minorities' experience of institutional racism and economic inequality, leading to residential clustering in specific regions as a protective measure (Rex and Moore, 1967; Peach, 1998; Finney and Simpson, 2009; Rhodes and Brown, 2019, Catney et al 2021) and distinct patterns of residential mobility (Simpson and Finney, 2009; Finney 2011). Both migration histories and structural inequalities have therefore shaped the geographical location of ethnic minorities, with different local housing and neighbourhood contexts affecting subsequent residential and housing experiences.

The rich data generated from EVENS enable us to depict the residential experiences of ethnic groups during the COVID-19 pandemic in relation to material and emotional aspects of home. First, we analyse type of housing, outlining the living conditions of ethnic groups across Britain. Second, overcrowding is considered, investigating the suitability of the property for the number of people living there. Third, we investigate ethnic differences in outdoor space, including both public space and private outdoor space at the property itself. Fourth, we consider the residential mobility of individuals during the pandemic and the potential precarity that this represents. Finally, using the unique strengths of EVENS, we develop understanding beyond household composition and housing dynamics of people's connection to the local area and neighbourhood in which they live.

Do ethnic groups live in different types of housing?

Using EVENS, we can establish the differences in the types of accommodation in which ethnic groups live across Britain. Figure 6.1 shows the proportion of each ethnic group in different accommodation types, distinguishing between detached, semi-detached, terraced, flats and apartments[1] and mobile homes or caravans. We acknowledge that there is not necessarily a hierarchy of housing types and that internal space, characteristics, location, value and satisfaction are not straightforwardly correlated with housing type. However, in general, detached and semi-detached housing remain the most desired and sought-after properties (McKee et al, 2015).

A clear outlier in the results is the finding that most Gypsy/Traveller respondents lived in mobile homes or caravans; Roma is the only other group which had a significant proportion in this type of accommodation. White British, White Irish and Arab groups were the most likely to live in detached homes (approximately 25% of these groups); Indian, Jewish, Mixed White and Black African, and Mixed White and Asian groups also featured relatively high levels of detached living. Only 9% of Bangladeshi and Gypsy/Traveller and less than 5% of Roma participants were in detached houses.

We find high proportions living in terraced housing among Bangladeshi people – almost 40%, compared to 22% of White British people. Approximately 20% of people lived in terraced housing, which is consistent across nearly all groups under study, the only other exceptions being the higher rates among Black Caribbean and Mixed White and Black African groups and the very low rates for the Gypsy/Traveller group. A low proportion of White British, Pakistani and Roma people were living in flats/apartments (approximately one in six). In comparison, more than 40% of the White Eastern European, other White, Black African and Any other ethnic groups lived in flats/apartments.

Housing types are not evenly spread across the country, and neither are ethnic groups; some of the ethnic differences may relate to the housing stock in the areas where different groups tend to reside. For example, detached housing is not the norm in central urban areas, particularly London, which is where high proportions of ethnic minorities reside. Furthermore, it has been recognised that there are distinctive features of the housing market in London compared to elsewhere in Britain, including higher housing costs reflecting demand pressures (Holley et al, 2011; Hamnett and Reades 2019). Figure 6.2 shows selected groups' housing type distribution for London and non-London separately. The results highlight the differences in housing patterns between London and the remainder of Britain. As expected, flats and apartments are more common in London compared to outside London and the reverse is true for detached housing. Overall, we observe that ethnic differences in housing type take a different form in London compared to elsewhere in Britain.

FIGURE 6.1: ACCOMMODATION TYPE, BY ETHNIC GROUP

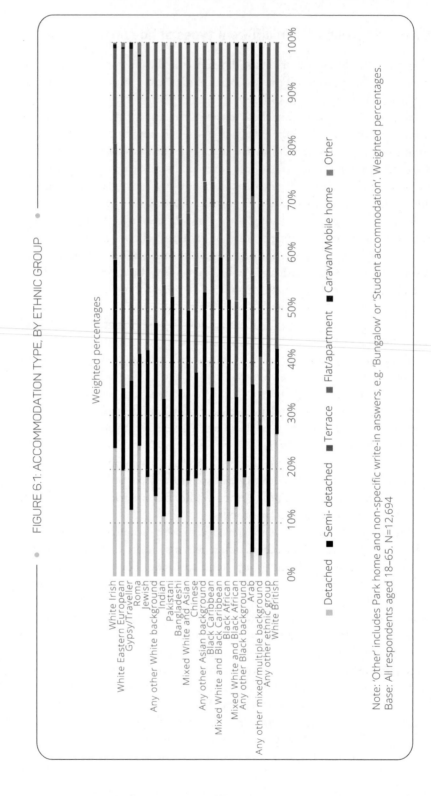

Weighted percentages

White Irish
White Eastern European
Gypsy/Traveller
Roma
Jewish
Any other White background
Indian
Pakistani
Bangladeshi
Mixed White and Asian
Chinese
Any other Asian background
Mixed White and Black Caribbean
Black Caribbean
Black African
Mixed White and Black African
Any other Black background
Arab
Any other mixed/multiple background
Any other ethnic group
White British

0% 10% 20% 30% 40% 50% 60% 70% 80% 90% 100%

■ Detached ■ Semi-detached ■ Terrace ■ Flat/apartment ■ Caravan/Mobile home ■ Other

Note: 'Other' includes Park home and non-specific write-in answers, e.g. 'Bungalow' or 'Student accommodation'. Weighted percentages.
Base: All respondents aged 18–65. N=12,694

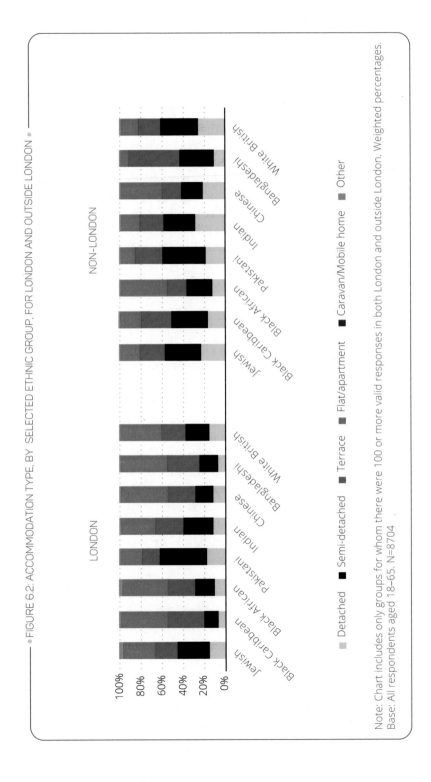

● FIGURE 6.2: ACCOMMODATION TYPE, BY SELECTED ETHNIC GROUP, FOR LONDON AND OUTSIDE LONDON ●

NON-LONDON

LONDON

White British
Bangladeshi
Chinese
Indian
Pakistani
Black African
Black Caribbean
Jewish

100%
80%
60%
40%
20%
0%

■ Detached   ■ Semi-detached   ■ Terrace   ■ Flat/apartment   ■ Caravan/Mobile home   ■ Other

Note: Chart includes only groups for whom there were 100 or more valid responses in both London and outside London. Weighted percentages.
Base: All respondents aged 18–65. N=8704 .

In London, higher proportions of Pakistani and Jewish people (around 60% and 50% respectively) resided in detached and semi-detached houses compared to other ethnic groups, including the White British group. In comparison, high proportions of Black Caribbean, Black African, Bangladeshi and Chinese people live in terraced housing or apartments. Outside London, White British alongside Jewish and Indian households were in the most advantaged position in terms of housing type, with close to 60% living in detached or semi-detached housing. Pakistani respondents outside London also show an advantaged position, but the proportion is skewed towards semi-detached over detached housing. Black African, Bangladeshi and Chinese households experience disadvantage outside of London as they do in London. It should be noted that the Black Caribbean ethnic group experience housing disadvantage in London to a far greater extent compared to their experience outside the capital: in London, 80% live in terrace houses or apartments, whereas outside the capital the majority of Black Caribbean people live in detached or semi-detached housing.

Do ethnic minorities experience more overcrowding?

During the COVID-19 pandemic, restrictions stipulating 'Stay Home, Save Lives, Protect the NHS' were in force in the UK. This placed pressure on household space as the home additionally became the location for work, study and schooling. Figure 6.3 shows the percentage of respondents who were living in overcrowded accommodation based on our derived overcrowding measure (see Box 6.1). The results indicate that there was a higher prevalence of overcrowding among all ethnic minority groups compared to White British households. Almost 60% of Roma were in overcrowded living arrangements, a rate 15 times higher than White British. Additionally, around a quarter of Pakistani and Arab people experienced overcrowding during the COVID-19 pandemic. Along with the White British group, White Irish, Jewish, Black Caribbean, and Mixed White and Black Caribbean groups experienced the lowest levels of overcrowding (around 5%).

Figure 6.4 shows the percentage of households that experienced overcrowding for the 'typical' household configuration of one or two generations, compared to households with three or more generations. It should be noted that three-generation households are more common for some ethnic groups: of EVENS respondents, 2% of White British households reported having three generations, with a similarly low proportion for Gypsy/ Traveller, Any other White, Black Caribbean, Arab and other mixed/multiple background, whereas over a third of Roma respondents, one in seven Bangladeshis and almost one in ten Pakistanis have three or more generations in the household. Figure 6.4 clearly demonstrates that the presence of a third

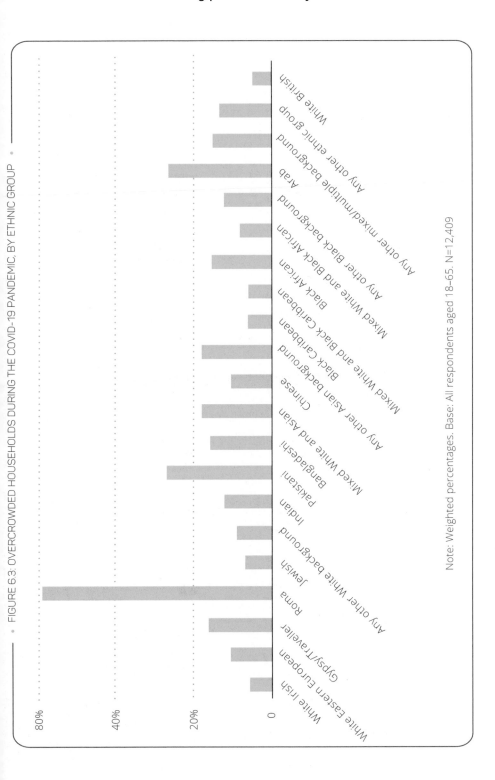

• FIGURE 6.3: OVERCROWDED HOUSEHOLDS DURING THE COVID-19 PANDEMIC, BY ETHNIC GROUP •

Note: Weighted percentages. Base: All respondents aged 18–65. N=12,409

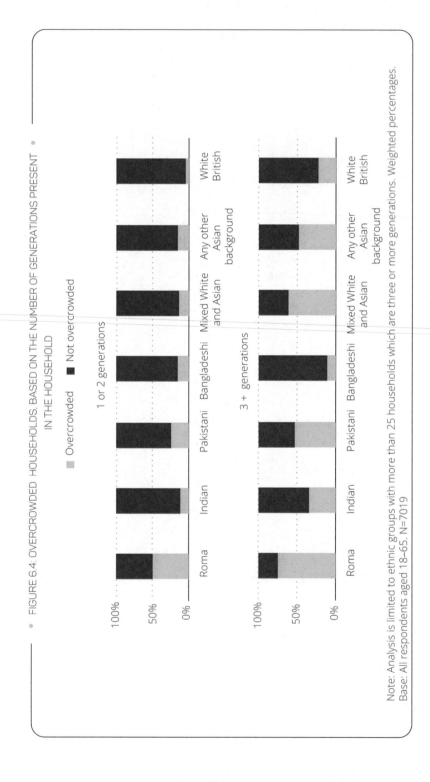

FIGURE 6.4: OVERCROWDED HOUSEHOLDS, BASED ON THE NUMBER OF GENERATIONS PRESENT IN THE HOUSEHOLD

Note: Analysis is limited to ethnic groups with more than 25 households which are three or more generations. Weighted percentages. Base: All respondents aged 18–65. N=7019

generation can be associated with overcrowding. Roma households were particularly affected by overcrowding, as Figure 6.3 showed, but within three-generation households, over 75% are overcrowded compared to only 50% in a more typical household structure. We see particularly high levels of overcrowding for three-generation households – and higher than one and two-generation households – for all Asian groups (including mixed), but it is least pronounced for the Bangladeshi minority group, who to some extent accommodate three-generation living without resulting in high rates of overcrowding.

Are there different experiences in access to the outdoors for ethnic minorities?

With advice against using public transport and travelling outside of the local vicinity during the COVID-19 pandemic, the ability to access outdoor space and nature close to home became a determinant of differential experience. Parks and natural areas remained accessible for those living nearby to enjoy, and the ability to access these spaces was captured in the EVENS. The results are shown in Figure 6.5.

The results indicate that for most ethnic groups, nine in ten people had overall access to outdoor space. Gypsy/Traveller and Roma people had the lowest levels of access to outdoor space (68% and 54% respectively). The figure was also relatively low for Chinese, Any other Asian background, and Mixed White and Asian groups. Analysis into potential differences between London and the remainder of Britain (not shown in the figure) found that higher proportions of those who were resident in London had access to outdoor space locally.

Differences between ethnic groups in access to outdoor spaces at their home are shown in Figure 6.6. Access to private outdoor space was particularly important during the 'stay at home' guidance issued by the UK government as part of the national lockdowns. A total of 94% of White British people reported having outdoor space at home, the highest across all ethnic groups. Pakistani, Jewish, White Irish and Roma were the only ethnic minority groups with similar levels to White British people. For Other White, White Eastern European, Bangladeshi, Chinese, Other Black Arab and Any Other ethnic groups, around one in five respondents reported having no access to outdoor space at their home.

Did ethnic minorities experience more residential mobility during the COVID-19 pandemic?

Using EVENS, we identified the respondents who moved house after the pandemic started in February 2020; these movements were a combination

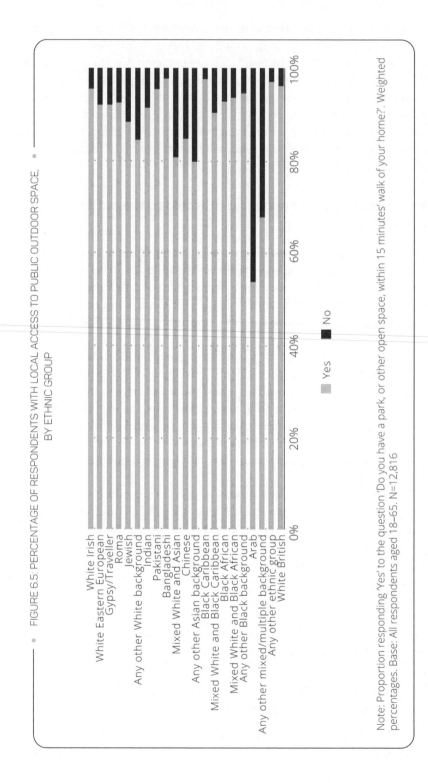

FIGURE 6.5: PERCENTAGE OF RESPONDENTS WITH LOCAL ACCESS TO PUBLIC OUTDOOR SPACE, BY ETHNIC GROUP

Note: Proportion responding 'Yes' to the question 'Do you have a park, or other open space, within 15 minutes' walk of your home?'. Weighted percentages. Base: All respondents aged 18–65. N=12,816

● FIGURE 6.6: PERCENTAGE OF RESPONDENTS WITH PRIVATE OUTDOOR SPACE, BY ETHNIC GROUP ●

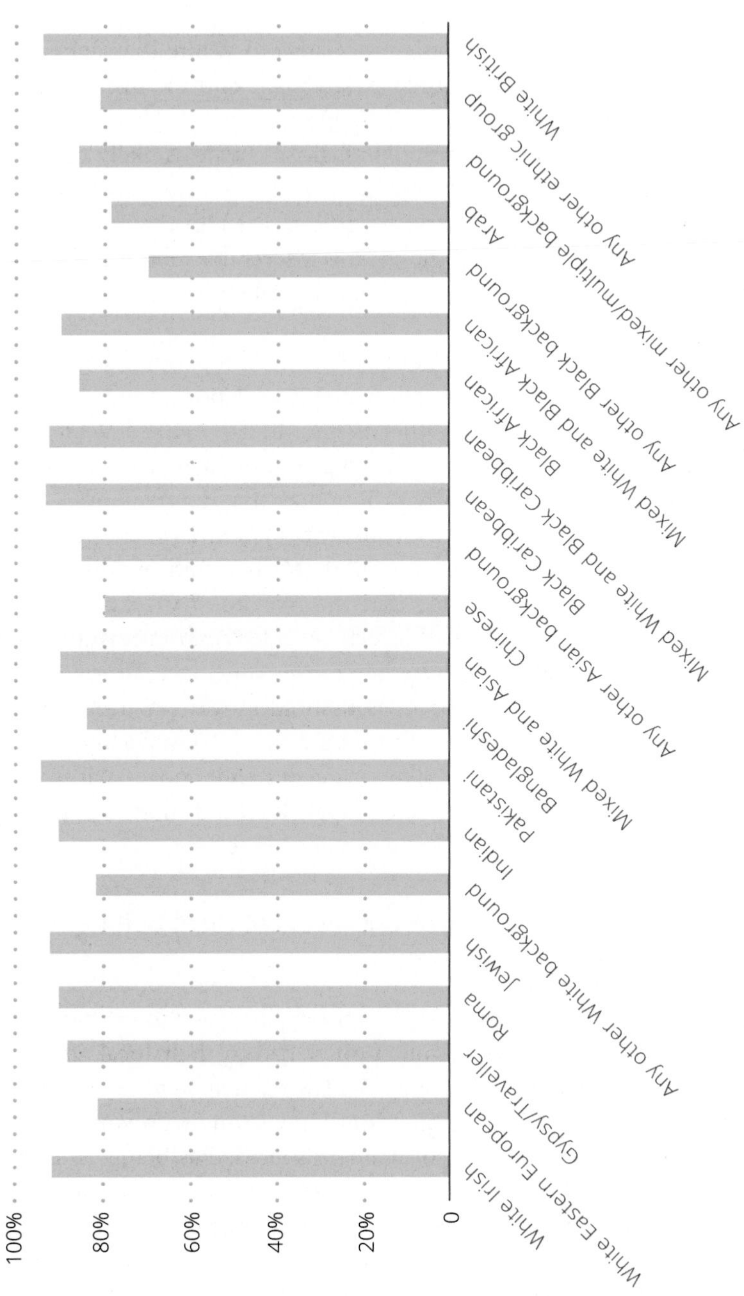

Notes: Proportion responding 'Yes' to the question: 'Does the property you are currently living in have any of the following? A garden, a roof terrace or large balcony, other private outdoor space, other shared outdoor space'. Weighted percentages. Base: All respondents aged 18–65. N=12,499

of individuals leaving an existing household to join or start another, or the movement of an entire household. The results are shown in Figure 6.7, which presents the likelihood (Odds Ratio [OR]) of experiencing a change in location since the start of the pandemic relative to White British people. Since age is such a determinant of life course stage and the events which are inter-related with mobility (Finney, 2011), we control this model for age.[2] An OR of two means that an individual was twice as likely to move house during the pandemic compared to a White British person of the same age. The tails attached to the point indicate the region where we are 95% confident the unknown ratio lies; if this bisects the solid vertical line, the result cannot be deemed to be significantly different from that of the White British reference group.

The results indicate that, compared to White British people, there was a significantly increased likelihood of experiencing residential mobility during the pandemic for Roma, Jewish, Other White, Indian, Mixed White and Asian, Other Asian, Any other mixed background and Any other ethnic group. This likelihood is particularly pronounced for Roma people, who were found to be almost four times more likely than White British people to have experienced a move since February 2020. Whilst significant differences are not observed, there is evidence that the likelihood of experiencing residential mobility during the pandemic was lower for Arab and Bangladeshi people compared to White British people of the same age. Although not shown in the results here, the type of household moves experienced did vary between groups: Roma, Eastern European, Gypsy/Traveller and Mixed White and Asian people are more likely to experience moves within the same household group, whereas Chinese, Bangladeshi and Arab respondents more often reported mobility involving moving alone.

Did ethnic minorities show different levels of local belonging during the COVID-19 pandemic?

The novelty of EVENS' design and questioning allows for the exploration of the connection that different ethnic groups had to their local area at a time when neighbourhoods became particularly salient. Figure 6.8 shows the response in the EVENS to the question 'How strongly do you feel you belong to your local area?' where local area is specified as being 'within a 15-minute walk from home'. Strong local attachment was found for all South Asian, Black African and Black Caribbean ethnic groups: more than 80% of respondents in these groups reported fair or strong local belonging, compared to 77% of White British people. The lowest feeling of local belonging is found in the Roma group, where over two thirds reported no strong belonging to their local area, and less than one in 20 suggested a very strong level of belonging. White Other and Eastern European groups

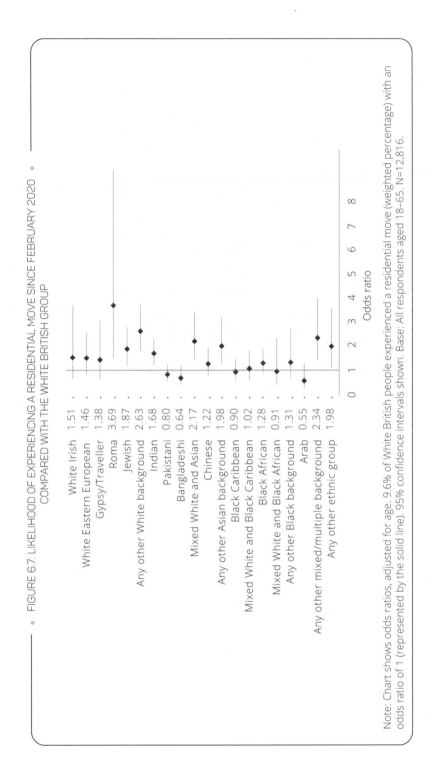

FIGURE 6.7: LIKELIHOOD OF EXPERIENCING A RESIDENTIAL MOVE SINCE FEBRUARY 2020 COMPARED WITH THE WHITE BRITISH GROUP

White Irish	1.51
White Eastern European	1.46
Gypsy/Traveller	1.38
Roma	3.69
Jewish	1.87
Any other White background	2.63
Indian	1.68
Pakistani	0.80
Bangladeshi	0.64
Mixed White and Asian	2.17
Chinese	1.22
Any other Asian background	1.98
Black Caribbean	0.90
Mixed White and Black Caribbean	1.02
Black African	1.28
Mixed White and Black African	0.91
Any other Black background	1.31
Arab	0.55
Any other mixed/multiple background	2.34
Any other ethnic group	1.98

Odds ratio

Note: Chart shows odds ratios, adjusted for age. 9.6% of White British people experienced a residential move (weighted percentage) with an odds ratio of 1 (represented by the solid line). 95% confidence intervals shown. Base: All respondents aged 18–65. N=12,816.

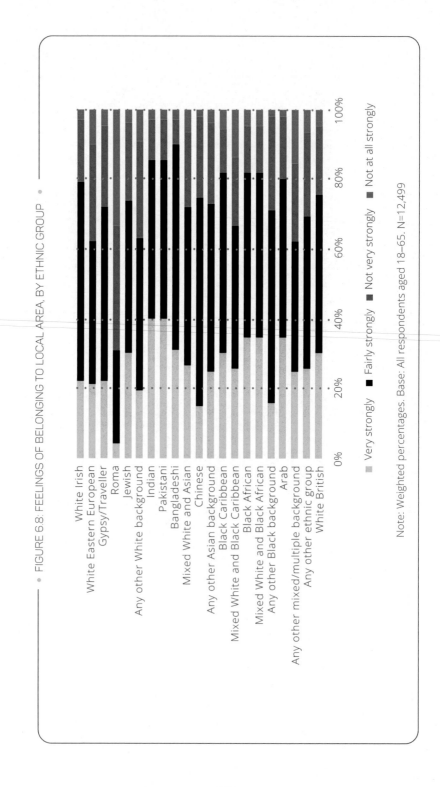

● FIGURE 6.8: FEELINGS OF BELONGING TO LOCAL AREA, BY ETHNIC GROUP ●

■ Very strongly ■ Fairly strongly ■ Not very strongly ■ Not at all strongly

Note: Weighted percentages. Base: All respondents aged 18–65. N=12,499

also stated low levels of belonging compared to White British people. Additionally, many mixed groups reported lower levels of local belonging.

The results in Figure 6.8 do not account for potential biases based on the age and geographical location of respondents. Therefore, we controlled for age and region of residence to estimate the likelihood of an individual responding positively (combining Very strongly and Fairly strongly) when asked about their belonging to the local area. The results are presented in Figure 6.9 and can be interpreted in the same way as those in Figure 6.7.

Indian and Pakistani people were almost twice as likely to express strong local belonging compared to White British people, and Bangladeshi respondents were almost three times as likely to do so. Most other ethnic groups showed positive belonging levels similar to White British people. Some groups clearly showed lower likelihoods of strong local belonging compared to White British people: Eastern European, Other White and Any other mixed background are approximately half as likely to have reported positive local belonging compared to the White British group. Roma people had a substantially smaller likelihood of feeling a strong sense of belonging, which was far lower than all other minority ethnic groups too. The results from Figure 6.9 suggest that the observed differences in Figure 6.8 are only partially explained by different age structures and the different concentration of ethnic minority groups in certain regions of Britain.

EVENS offers an insight into how local belonging changed during the COVID-19 pandemic. Figure 6.10 shows the change in belonging since February 2020 for each ethnic group. An unchanged level of belonging to their local community was reported by the majority in most ethnic groups. Apart from Gypsy/Traveller and Roma, all ethnic groups had more reported increases in belonging rather than decreases. Over half of White Irish people report increased local belonging. Approximately 40% of Jewish, Indian, Pakistani, Mixed White and Asian, Chinese and Black African people experienced increases in local belonging during the pandemic. Amongst White British people, this was around 30%. Almost one in three Gypsy/ Traveller people reported decreases in local belonging, with one in four of those identifying as Any other Black or Any other ethnic group also reporting declines in belonging. This compares to 10% of White British people who reported a decrease. White Irish, Bangladeshi and Mixed White and Black Caribbean people had the lowest proportions reporting a decrease in local belonging.

Discussion

The material and affective ramifications of housing (or 'home') on ethnic minorities throughout the COVID-19 pandemic is the central concern of this chapter. The unique insights generated from EVENS offer the

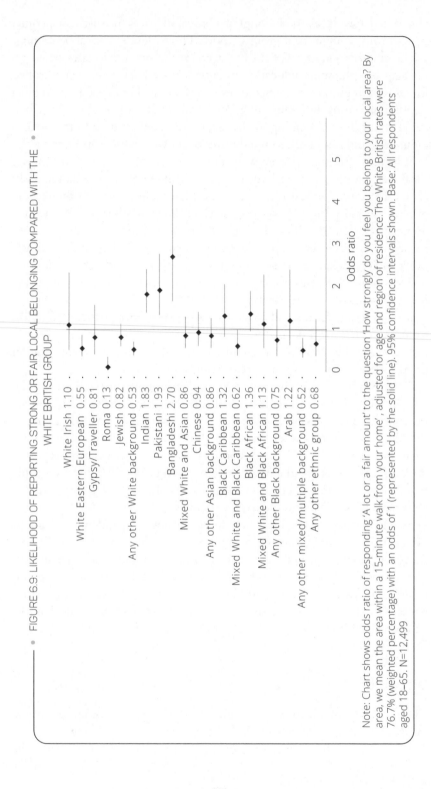

FIGURE 6.9: LIKELIHOOD OF REPORTING STRONG OR FAIR LOCAL BELONGING COMPARED WITH THE WHITE BRITISH GROUP

White Irish 1.10
White Eastern European 0.55
Gypsy/Traveller 0.81
Roma 0.13
Jewish 0.82
Any other White background 0.53
Indian 1.83
Pakistani 1.93
Bangladeshi 2.70
Mixed White and Asian 0.86
Chinese 0.94
Any other Asian background 0.86
Black Caribbean 1.32
Mixed White and Black Caribbean 0.62
Black African 1.36
Mixed White and Black African 1.13
Any other Black background 0.75
Arab 1.22
Any other mixed/multiple background 0.52
Any other ethnic group 0.68

Odds ratio

Note: Chart shows odds ratio of responding 'A lot or a fair amount' to the question 'How strongly do you feel you belong to your local area? By area, we mean the area within a 15-minute walk from your home', adjusted for age and region of residence. The White British rates were 76.7% (weighted percentage) with an odds of 1 (represented by the solid line). 95% confidence intervals shown. Base: All respondents aged 18–65. N=12,499

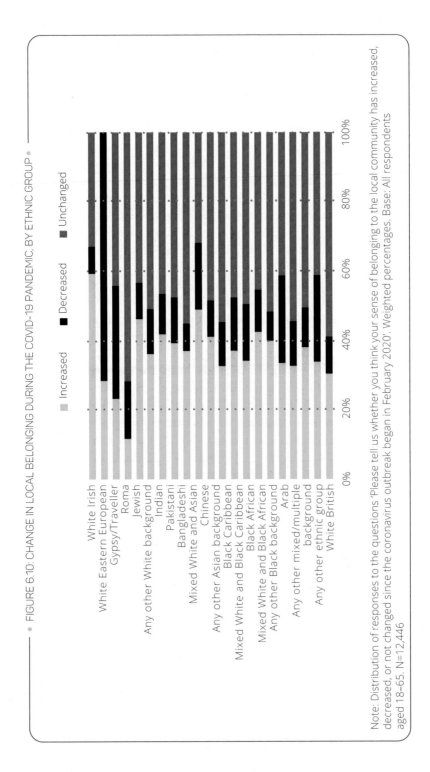

● FIGURE 6.10: CHANGE IN LOCAL BELONGING DURING THE COVID-19 PANDEMIC, BY ETHNIC GROUP ●

■ Increased   ■ Decreased   ■ Unchanged

White Irish
White Eastern European
Gypsy/Traveller
Roma
Jewish
Any other White background
Indian
Pakistani
Bangladeshi
Mixed White and Asian
Chinese
Any other Asian background
Black Caribbean
Mixed White and Black Caribbean
Black African
Mixed White and Black African
Any other Black background
Arab
Any other mixed/multiple background
Any other ethnic group
White British

0%   20%   40%   60%   80%   100%

Note: Distribution of responses to the questions 'Please tell us whether you think your sense of belonging to the local community has increased, decreased, or not changed since the coronavirus outbreak began in February 2020'. Weighted percentages. Base: All respondents aged 18–65. N=12,446

opportunity to heighten our understanding of the systemic exclusions to which different ethnic groups are subjected in housing. This chapter has evidenced inequalities in four inter-related dimensions of housing: household types; overcrowding and space; residential mobility; and levels of belonging.

The desirability of, and access to, different household types and spaces among ethnic minorities is an area that is underexplored in UK scholarship, with a few notable exceptions (Lukes et al, 2019; Shankley and Finney, 2020). The comparatively limited engagement with ethnic minorities' experiences of housing in the broader literature is perhaps surprising, given that studies have identified minorities' disproportionate experiences of overcrowded housing and precarity (Finney and Harries, 2015). EVENS has empirically demonstrated the prominent persistence of smaller housing types among Bangladeshi, Black Caribbean and Black African people. Significant proportions of Gypsy/Traveller and Roma live in caravans and mobile homes, reflecting specific cultures of residence. Interpreting the ethnic differences in housing type – and whether they represent racialisation and stigmatisation (Phillips and Harrison, 2010; Yuval-Davis et al, 2017, Alexander and Byrne 2020) – is difficult without further research to better understand the desirability of different household types, and housing decision making, across ethnic groups.

What is clear from EVENS is disadvantage for many ethnic minority groups in terms of house space not meeting the needs of the household, particularly for multigenerational households. A relatively high prevalence of three-generation households were found among Asian respondents, with Roma also identified as the group with the highest proportion of three-generation households and extremely high levels of overcrowding. In comparison, White British respondents seem more able to acquire housing that matches their needs. As Burgess and Muir (2020) demonstrate, motivations of multigenerational living are diverse and tend to be shaped by both subjective experiences and intersecting structures, such as housing affordability, postponed household formation among younger, adult children and an ageing population requiring care. Whilst multigenerational housing may be indicative of caring responsibilities within the family (Victor et al, 2012), such arrangements can also be contextualised as a defensive mechanism against structural pressures, including institutional racism and stigmatisation (Frost et al, 2022), alongside financial constraints and instability (van Hout and Staniewicz, 2011; Battaglini et al, 2018; Burgess and Muir, 2020; see also Chapters 7 and 8). Findings developed from EVENS thus imply that the availability of housing stock to match the spatial needs of different ethnic groups is lacking, due in part to limited access to the larger accommodation required for multigenerational living. This relates to the exclusion of ethnic minorities from housing planning and provision (Phillips and Harrison, 2010; Shankley and Finney, 2020) and the positioning of the White, nuclear family as normative in institutional imaginaries (Alexander and Byrne, 2020; Fortier, 2021).

In the context of the COVID-19 pandemic, risks of overcrowding and inadequate household space can be highly problematic in relation to following the directives introduced to prevent the spread of COVID-19, to the detriment of both the physical and mental health of those who experience overcrowding (see Chapter 5). Housing access constitutes a key area that shapes risk of exposure to COVID-19 (Nazroo and Bécares, 2021). The future ramifications of such overcrowded living conditions can be long-term socioeconomic and health disparities between the ethnic groups that experience this disadvantage and those that do not.

In addition to inequalities in the interior space available, EVENS unveils differences in access to outdoor spaces. The repercussions of the lack of access to open space can materialise in lower levels of overall health and wellbeing (Thompson et al, 2012; de Bell et al, 2020). Some groups experience a material disadvantage in this aspect of open space in the local area compared to White British people; more than one in ten Pakistani, Mixed White and Asian, Chinese, Other Asian, Mixed White and Black African, and Other Black person experience this disadvantage, compared to only one in 20 White British persons. The lack of access to open green space in the community can be mitigated by access to outdoor space at home, which can be considered even more important for overall wellbeing than access in the local area (Marques et al, 2021) and as a key factor in resilience to COVID-19 restrictions. Whilst most respondents had access to outdoor space at home, we find that all ethnic minority groups had lower proportions of people with outdoor space at home compared to White British people. These continued disadvantages in lack of access to open space are especially problematic when combined with the disparities of interior space and overcrowding that affect many ethnic minority groups disproportionately.

EVENS offers further unique insights into the residential experiences of ethnic minorities by considering aspects of residential mobility among ethnic groups during the pandemic. EVENS data highlighted similarities in the risk of moving during the pandemic for many groups compared to White British, possibly in part due to legal changes which prevented evictions or the additional uncertainty in the economy inhibiting or delaying house buying and moving. However, some groups – Roma, Jewish, Other White, Indian, Mixed White and Asian, Other Asian, Any other mixed background and Any other ethnic group – had a higher likelihood of residential mobility during the pandemic even after controlling for age. To elaborate further, the control for age should limit the effect of residential mobility linked to the life course such as marriage and moving for studies and employment (Billari and Liefbroer, 2010). Therefore, the higher risk of residential mobility among ethnic minority groups could signal precarity, a suggestion that warrants further attention in future studies. Also of interest is the finding that Gypsy/Traveller people did not have a significantly increased risk of moving, despite being a culture traditionally linked with mobility. These findings contribute to discussion of how such groups are homogenised and racialised as nomadic in UK public discourse, despite their varying experiences and levels of residential mobility (Yuval-Davis et al, 2017).

Relatively high levels of local belonging among Indian, Pakistani and Bangladeshi people were found compared to White British people, in line with previous research (Finney and Jivraj, 2013). These differences persist even after controlling for region of residence and age. We posit that high levels of local belonging are linked to strong cultural institutions which have fostered a sense of community that is tied to identity (Bécares et al, 2011) as well as the local geographical area and can operate as a form of community solidarity in response to structural exclusions (Frost et al, 2022). As demonstrated in Chapter 3, high levels of attachment to ethnicity and religion were present among Indian, Pakistani and Bangladeshi respondents, emphasising the importance of local community infrastructure and mechanisms of community. In comparison, low levels of local belonging were experienced by Roma, a group that has been known to experience social exclusion and marginalisation that policy has not remedied (Clark, 2014; Lane and Smith, 2021). The social ostracisation and structural racism they experience sees limited interaction with the wider community, with the overall group size perhaps not large enough for their own ethno-community to reach a critical social mass to combat this 'othering'. Eastern European, Other White and Any other mixed people are also statistically less likely to have high levels of strong local belonging compared to White British people. These groups have particularly high proportions of recent first-generation immigrants, which may mean they have not had sufficient time to build attachment to the local area (Kasarda and Janowitz, 1974; Giuliani, 2003).

EVENS further identifies how local belonging is mobilised during times of crisis in the context of the COVID-19 pandemic. Whilst there is minimal prior research on this topic, links between neighbourhoods, community identity and the pandemic have been shown to be important for resilience and the unlocking of social support (Stevenson et al, 2021). Thus, it is likely that community spirit and belonging increase through the shared bonding experience of multiple lockdowns (Mao et al, 2021), and our findings highlight such developments across most ethnic groups.

Conclusion

Through EVENS, we identify inequalities and illustrate deprivation in the everyday, material lived residential experience of ethnic minorities in Britain. This novel survey has enabled the exploration of the residential experience of ethnic groups in more depth and breadth than previous surveys or administrative data have allowed for, including for Roma and Gypsy/Traveller groups who have previously been understudied. Experiences of housing (or home) have been shown to have material and affective ramifications in relation to precarity, levels of overcrowding, residential mobility and experiences of belonging. We observe distinct levels of material deprivation across almost all ethnic groups compared to White British people, the exceptions being White Irish, Jewish and to a lesser extent Indian people. Smaller housing, higher levels of overcrowding and residential mobility, and increasing pressures on the ability to access the outdoors (locally and at the property) exist for most minority groups. The material inequalities evidenced have implications for other life domains, including health, employment and socioeconomic circumstances (see Chapters 5, 7 and 8).

However, the resilience of ethnic groups in times of crisis has also been implied by the EVENS findings given in this chapter, which have pointed to community mechanisms and networks of solidarity being mobilised during the COVID-19 pandemic. Despite the material disadvantage apparent in housing type and overcrowding, levels of local belonging are high among most ethnic minority groups. These findings can indicate community solidarity, which challenges the stigmatisation of ethnically dense and poor neighbourhoods.

Box 6.1: Housing, place and community: measures and methods

General: All percentages presented in this chapter are weighted percentages calculated using the propensity weights available in the EVENS dataset. The results come from EVENS respondents aged between 18 and 65. Individuals who responded 'Don't know' or 'Prefer not to say' were excluded on a question-by-question basis; hence, each figure presented has a different underlying sample size.

Overcrowding: We create an indicator for overcrowding based on the bedroom standard defined in the UK Parliament in the Housing (Overcrowding) Bill 2003. We take the number of individuals aged over 16 (N) as requiring N-1 bedrooms, under the assumption that two are in some form of intimate relationship. For children we assume that all can share with one other, thus requiring X/2 bedrooms. The total bedrooms required is equal to (N-1) + (X/2), rounding up if necessary. We anticipate that both these assumptions will result in an underestimation of the number of respondents who face overcrowding as we cannot consider the age and gender of children. In some instances, respondents did not report any adult household members. As only those aged 18 or over were eligible for the survey, in these instances we added a single adult to the household on the assumption that the responding adult did not include themselves in the total reported.

Moving house: For Figure 6.7 we apply a logistic regression with the outcome being experiencing a house move since February 2020. This movement covered both moving as an individual and moving with an entire household. We control for continuous age in years. The White British ethnic group is the reference category.

Local belonging: As noted earlier, logistic regression is applied to create Figure 6.9. The outcome is reported 'strong' or 'fair' sense of local belonging. This model was controlled for continuous age and region of residence. The White British ethnic group is the reference category.

Notes

[1]   The survey distinguished between purpose-built flats and house conversions versus flats within commercial properties (for example, above a shop). Overwhelmingly it was the former option; the category in the analysis is a combination.

[2]   Controlling for sex was tested, but was not significant.

7

Work and employment

Nico Ochmann, Ken Clark, Michaela Šťastná and James Nazroo

Key findings

Existing ethnic inequalities in labour market outcomes before the COVID-19 pandemic persisted during the consequent disruption of the labour market, but were not exacerbated for most ethnic minority groups during the pandemic.

- In relation to labour force participation, employment, and unemployment, outcomes during the COVID-19 pandemic varied across ethnic minority groups compared to the White British majority group. Importantly, Bangladeshi men experienced similar outcomes in terms of these three indicators as White British men.
- White Irish and Jewish women had a lower unemployment rate than White British women, whereas women in the Gypsy/Traveller, Any other White background, Indian, Pakistani, Any other Asian background, Black African, Any other Black background and Arab groups had a higher unemployment rate during the pandemic than their White British counterparts.
- White Eastern European and Any other Black background men had a lower unemployment rate during the pandemic than White British men, while Pakistani men had a higher unemployment rate.
- Jewish and Chinese women were more likely to be in precarious employment during the pandemic than White British women. Amongst men, it was Gypsy/Traveller, Roma, Bangladeshi, Any other Asian background and Any other Black background groups that were more likely to experience job precarity than White British men.
- There were similarities across ethnic minority groups relative to the White British group in a range of outcomes related to lockdown, including change in occupation, furlough, increased working hours and reduced pay.
- In addition, Chinese women were more likely to be worried about job security than White British women. The same held true for Indian, Pakistani, Bangladeshi, Chinese, Any other Asian background, Any other Black background, Arab and any other mixed/ multiple background men compared with White British men.

Introduction

Wealth creation plays an integral role in providing productive employment opportunities for members of society. The rise in living standards, fair economic and social institutions, and fair play in the economic process contribute to a good and just society. Since ethnic minority people make up a quarter of British society (Eurostat, 2014; Rienzo and Fernandez-Reino, 2021), their overall contribution to the British economy makes it key that they enjoy equal opportunities and fair treatment in the labour market, over and above a broader requirement for justice. This chapter focuses on the detailed and unique coverage provided by the Evidence for Equality National Survey (EVENS) of standard labour market outcomes, such as labour force participation, employment and unemployment, and on pandemic-related economic indicators, such as change in occupation, furlough, increased working hours, reduced pay and job security.

Evidence on ethnic inequalities in labour market outcomes before the pandemic showed that employment, unemployment and wage gaps existed between most non-White ethnic groups and the White British majority for both men and women (Clark and Shankley, 2020). In particular, Black African and Black Caribbean men showed large gaps for all three labour market outcomes compared to White British men, whereas Pakistani and Bangladeshi women had significantly lower employment rates, much higher unemployment rates and far lower weekly earnings than White British women. In addition, Clark and Ochmann (2022) observe that Pakistani, Bangladeshi and Black African men were more likely to be in bad (precarious) jobs than White British men.

Most of the labour market literature on the COVID-19 pandemic looks at standard economic outcomes, such as employment, unemployment and wages before and during the disruption. For instance, Francis-Devine (2022) compares unemployment rates combining women and men from the first quarter of 2020 to the last quarter of 2021 based on data from the Office for National Statistics (ONS), and finds that Pakistani people had an unemployment rate of 5.9% before the COVID-19 pandemic and a rate of 10.2% after the outbreak. Chinese people also saw an increase in unemployment from 4.7% to 7.6%. In addition, Cribb et al (2021) report an increase in joblessness for a combined group of Pakistani and Bangladeshi people during the pandemic.

This chapter examines economic outcomes during the COVID-19 pandemic across a large number of ethnic groups and a wide range of labour market indicators. It covers 21 different ethnic groups, a number that is unparalleled in other UK datasets that are used to study ethnic differences, such as the UK Labour Force Survey or the UK Household Longitudinal Study. Since the White British group is the majority group in the UK, it is intuitive to compare the outcomes of the ethnic minority groups to the majority group. The overall evidence provided by EVENS suggests that the labour market outcomes during the COVID-19 pandemic were complex with variations across the economic outcomes of interest, though some ethnic minority groups did particularly badly.

Findings

Economic activity

Figure 7.1 reports five major economic outcomes, with a sixth outcome that combines all remaining economic categories (see Box 7.1). Looking at women first, a relatively high percentage of those in the White Eastern European, Black Caribbean and Any other Black background groups were employed full-time. In contrast, Gypsy/Traveller, Roma, Pakistani, Bangladeshi, Mixed White and Asian, and Arab women had relatively low proportions in full-time employment. The relatively low employment and high unemployment rates for Pakistani and Bangladeshi women are consistent with previous literature for the UK (Georgiadis and Manning, 2011; Manning and Rose, 2021). Interestingly, the share of Bangladeshi and Arab women in part-time employment was relatively high, whereas Gypsy/Traveller and Pakistani women had low rates of part-time employment. However, women from both Gypsy/Traveller and Pakistani groups took care of family members (or people in a private home) in relatively large numbers. White Eastern European, Pakistani and Bangladeshi women also had high percentages of full-time students, whereas relatively few Gypsy/Traveller and no women in the Any other Black background group attended universities full-time.

Turning now to men, White Irish, White Eastern European, Bangladeshi, Black Caribbean and White British men displayed high rates of full-time employment. White Irish, White Eastern European, Bangladeshi, Mixed White and Asian, Arab and White British men showed low rates of part-time employment, whereas Gypsy/Traveller, Mixed White and Black Caribbean, Mixed White and Black African, and Any other Black background men had high rates of part-time employment. Gypsy/Traveller, Mixed White and Asian, and Arab men were among the few ethnic groups that had a substantial proportion of men taking care of family members. All other groups had zero or very small proportions of men assuming family care responsibilities. When it comes to being full-time students, Chinese and Any other mixed/multiple background men had relatively proportions attending universities. Gypsy/Traveller, Indian, Pakistani, and Arab men, among others, were also well represented at universities. Gypsy/Traveller, Pakistani and Arab men experienced high rates of unemployment.

• FIGURE 7.1: SELECTED ECONOMIC ACTIVITIES

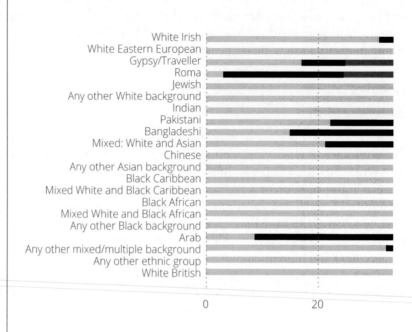

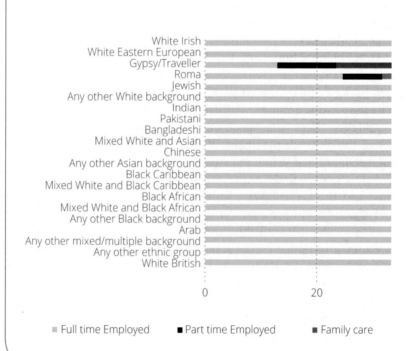

■ Full time Employed   ■ Part time Employed   ■ Family care

FOR WOMEN AND MEN, BY ETHNIC GROUP ●

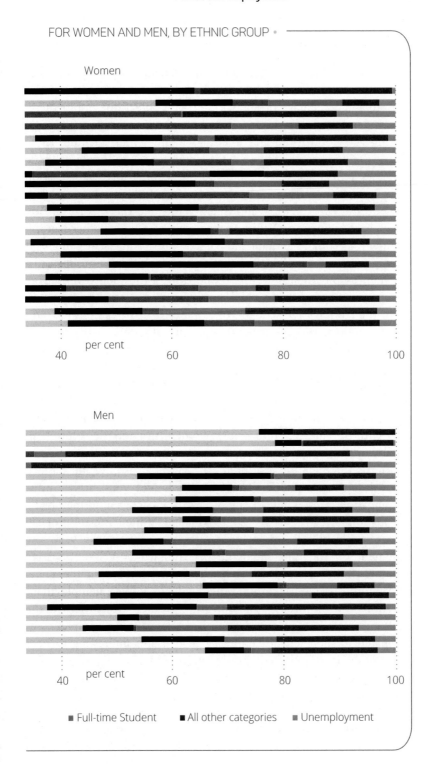

Women

per cent

40   60   80   100

Men

per cent

40   60   80   100

■ Full-time Student   ■ All other categories   ■ Unemployment

Labour market indicators

Table 7.1 looks at three standard labour market indicators: labour force participation, which includes those in the labour force (employed and unemployed) as a percentage of the working age population; employment, which includes those self-employed and employed as a percentage of the working age population; and unemployment, which includes those unemployed as a percentage of those in the labour force (see Box 7.1). These indicators vary a great deal across ethnic groups. Labour force participation was relatively high for White Eastern European, Jewish, Black Caribbean, Mixed White and Black Caribbean, Mixed White and Black African, Any other Black background and White British women. On the other hand, it was very low for Roma, Pakistani and Mixed White and Asian women. It is interesting to observe in Table 7.1 that some female ethnic groups had a relatively high employment rate (the proportion of the total working age population in employment), but a high unemployment rate (the proportion of those in the labour force who are unemployed) at the same time. This held true for Indian, Black Caribbean and Any other Black background women, and underlines the usefulness of defining both the employment and unemployment rate. A small number of ethnic groups had extremely high unemployment rates. For instance, about one in five of Pakistani, Bangladeshi, Any other Asian background and Any other Black background women, and about one in three of the Arab women were unemployed, compared with one in 25 White British women. In contrast, White Irish and Jewish women shared very low unemployment rates.

The patterns for men are also interesting. White Irish, White Eastern European, Jewish and Black Caribbean men had very high labour force participation rates, whereas Any other Black background men had a low participation rate. In addition, White Irish and White Eastern European men reported almost full employment rates accompanied by very low unemployment. On the other end of the spectrum, Mixed White and Asian and Any other Black background men had a relatively low employment rate, and the Any other Black background men had a very low unemployment rate. To show the importance of separating women from men in the analysis, Roma, Pakistani and Arab men had relatively high employment rates compared to their female counterparts. It is also interesting to note that Bangladeshi men reported similar labour force participation rates, employment rates and unemployment rates to White British men, although they were in more precarious employment situations (Figure 7.4).

Figure 7.2 reports the difference between ethnic minority groups and the White British majority for all three standard labour market indicators once differences in the age structures across the groups have been taken into account. No female ethnic minority group had a higher labour force

TABLE 7.1: LABOUR FORCE PARTICIPATION, EMPLOYMENT AND
UNEMPLOYMENT RATES DURING THE COVID-19 PANDEMIC,
BY ETHNIC GROUP

	Weighted percentage					
	Women			Men		
	Partici-pation	Employ-ment	Unemploy-ment	Partici-pation	Employ-ment	Unemploy-ment
White Irish	74.8	74.1	0.8	96.2	96.2	0.0
White Eastern European	77.4	74.5	3.8	99.6	99.0	0.6
Gypsy/Traveller	58.4	48.2	17.5	80.5	72.2	10.2
Roma	41.9	34.2	18.5	79.6	74.7	6.1
Jewish	79.0	77.6	1.8	90.7	87.1	3.9
Any other White background	72.1	62.7	13.0	83.7	81.4	2.7
Indian	74.4	65.7	11.7	84.4	80.4	4.7
Pakistani	50.2	40.2	19.9	84.9	77.4	8.9
Bangladeshi	64.6	52.8	18.2	88.7	84.8	4.5
Mixed White and Asian	43.0	39.8	7.5	65.6	60.8	7.2
Chinese	75.3	71.7	4.8	71.4	65.6	8.1
Any other Asian background	63.9	50.7	20.7	81.8	76.6	6.3
Black Caribbean	78.5	72.2	8.1	90.4	82.6	8.6
Mixed White and Black Caribbean	79.9	75.3	5.8	82.7	73.4	11.3
Black African	73.2	64.8	11.4	87.1	83.1	4.6
Mixed White and Black African	80.2	75.3	6.1	78.1	76.6	1.8
Any other Black background	86.6	67.4	22.2	54.0	53.2	1.5
Arab	63.1	40.9	35.2	75.7	66.5	12.3
Any other mixed/multiple background	57.4	54.5	5.1	72.4	66.4	8.4
Any other ethnic group	56.6	53.4	5.7	84.1	80.3	4.5
White British	77.4	74.4	3.8	87.8	84.4	3.9

participation rate than White British women. Gypsy/Traveller, Roma, Pakistani, Mixed White and Asian, and Any other Asian background women, among others, had a significantly lower participation rate than White British women. As for the female employment rates, no ethnic minority group had a statistically significantly higher employment rate than White British women, whereas Gypsy/Traveller, Roma, Any other White background, Indian, Pakistani, Bangladeshi, Mixed White and Asian, Any other Asian background, Black African and Arab women, among others, had a lower rate than their White British counterparts. While some ethnic minority women

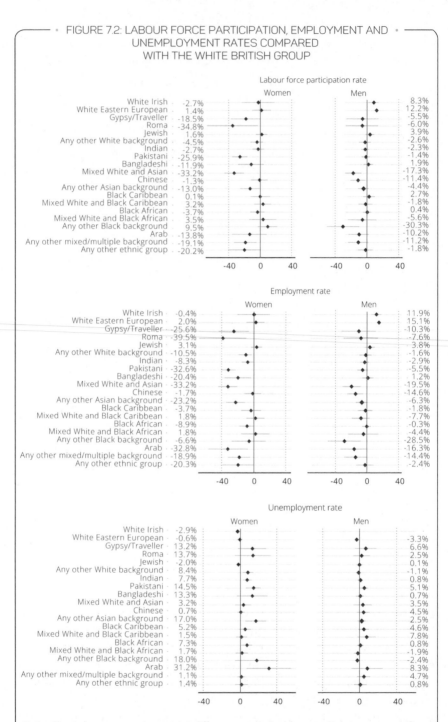

FIGURE 7.2: LABOUR FORCE PARTICIPATION, EMPLOYMENT AND UNEMPLOYMENT RATES COMPARED WITH THE WHITE BRITISH GROUP

Note: Chart shows percentage point difference, adjusted for age. Outcomes are defined as in Table 7.1. White Irish men do not report any unemployment in the sample, hence there is no estimate for this group.

had a significantly higher unemployment rate than White British women, notably Indian, Pakistani, Any other Asian background and Arab women, some, such as White Irish and Jewish women, also had a statistically significantly lower unemployment rate.

Looking at the labour force participation rate for men, White Irish and White Eastern European men showed a significantly higher participation rate than White British men, whereas only Mixed White and Asian, Chinese and Any other Black background men reported a lower labour force participation rate than White British men. And only White Irish and White Eastern European men had a higher employment rate than White British men, whereas men in some ethnic minority groups had a lower employment rate: Mixed White and Asian, Chinese, Any other Black background, Arab and Any other mixed/multiple background. In terms of unemployment, White Eastern European and Any other Black background men experienced lower unemployment rates than White British men, which is in contrast to Pakistani men, who had a higher unemployment rate than White British men.

Precarious employment

For those who are employed, Figure 7.3 looks at standard versus precarious employment. Temporary, solo self-employed and zero-hours contracts make up the precarious employment category. Solo self-employed workers are people without employees. Zero-hours contract workers are people without a guaranteed minimum number of working hours provided by the employer. Precarious employment tends to be defined by lower pay and less job security (Clark and Ochmann, 2022), and in general workers tend to have a preference for job security (Datta, 2019). Some foreign-born ethnic minority people in the UK come from countries with relatively poorer working conditions and fewer work place safety standards than the UK, and these reasons, coupled with workplace discrimination, mean that some of them then take on jobs that White British people are able to avoid. It is also important to note that some of those educated abroad have qualifications and work experience that are imperfectly transferable to the domestic labour market (Fortin et al, 2016). As a result, they might start out in more precarious employment.

Looking at Figure 7.3 for women, about 45% of Gypsy/Traveller and Roma women were in precarious employment. Looking at their precarious employment in more detail, none of the Roma women had temporary employment; instead, they were either solo self-employed or had zero-hours contracts. In the case of Gypsy/Traveller women, they were mostly solo self-employed with a small number in temporary employment. In contrast, Arab women had a relatively high percentage in standard employment (roughly 85%).

Gypsy/Traveller and Roma men also had a high percentage in precarious employment (approximately 85 and 65%, respectively). A small percentage

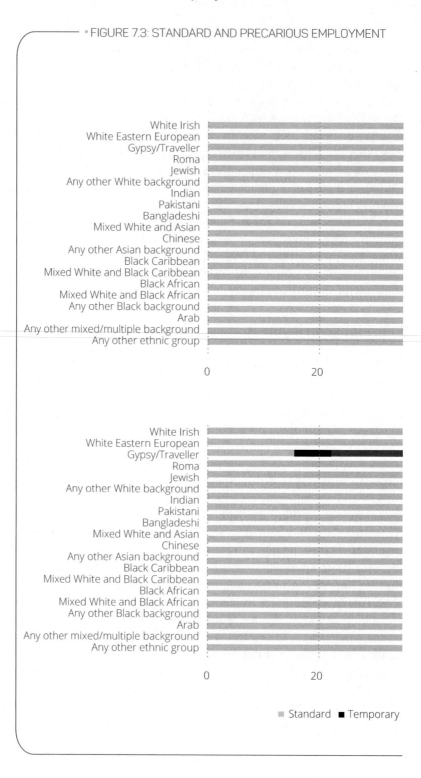

• FIGURE 7.3: STANDARD AND PRECARIOUS EMPLOYMENT

DURING THE COVID-19 PANDEMIC, BY ETHNIC GROUP •

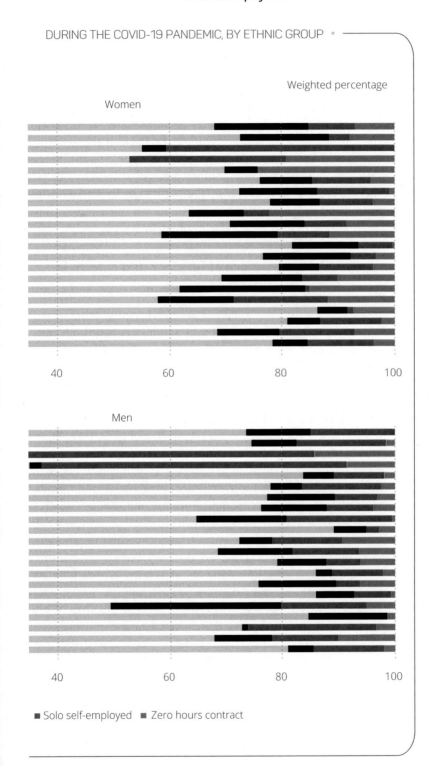

Weighted percentage

Women

Men

■ Solo self-employed ■ Zero hours contract

of Gypsy/Traveller and Roma men were in temporary employment, while both Gypsy/Traveller and Roma men were mostly solo self-employed. In contrast, about 90% of Mixed White and Asian men were in standard employment.

Figure 7.4 shows differences in level of precarious employment, among those who are employed, for ethnic minority groups relative to the White British group. The findings are adjusted for age. Looking at these relative outcomes, for two of the ethnic minority groups – Jewish and Chinese women – women had a higher percentage of job precarity than White British women, while for men, Gypsy/Traveller, Roma, Bangladeshi, Any other Asian background and Any other Black background men were significantly more likely than White British men to be in precarious jobs.

Change in occupation, experience of furlough and change in working hours, during the COVID-19 pandemic

The question associated with Table 7.2 is unique with regard to other surveys on the COVID-19 pandemic, because it asks about occupation changes. It would be expected that those who are the margins of the labour market would be more affected by economic downturns. For that reason, they might be more likely to change occupations during a recession in order to stay employed. Numerous ethnic groups have a high percentage of women who changed occupations after the beginning of the COVID-19 pandemic. 25% or more of White Eastern European, Gypsy/Traveller, Roma, Mixed White and Asian, Chinese and Any other mixed/multiple background women changed occupations during the COVID-19 pandemic. For men, Mixed White and Black African and Any other Black background groups had over 30% of men changing occupations since the outbreak of COVID-19. Interestingly, about 20% more Roma women switched occupations than Roma men. The same held true for Gypsy/Traveller women versus men.

The fifth and sixth columns of Table 7.2 compare the ethnic minority groups to the White British group. Looking first at women, Roma, Chinese, Any other Black background, and Any other mixed/multiple background women were significantly more likely to change occupations than White British women. It is interesting to note that at least Chinese and any other Black background women had a relatively high employment rate (see Table 7.1). As for men, Jewish, Indian, Chinese and Black African groups were more likely to change occupations and, except for men in the Chinese group, also had high employment rates (see Table 7.1). However, there were also groups that were less likely than White British people to change their occupations during the COVID-19 pandemic. For women, they were Pakistani, Bangladeshi, and Mixed White and Black Caribbean women, where Pakistani and Bangladeshi women had relatively high unemployment

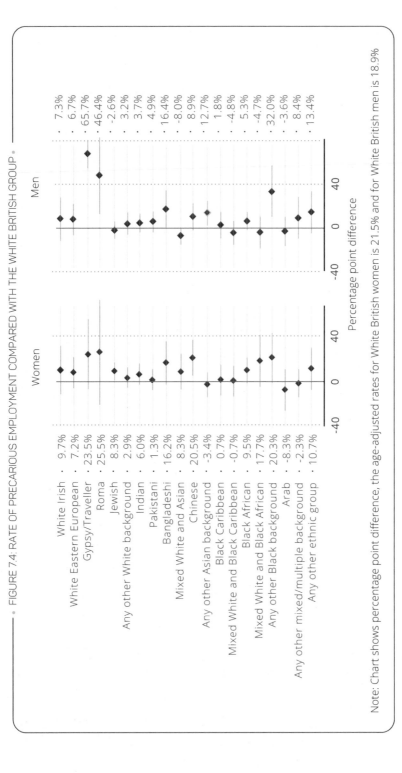

FIGURE 7.4: RATE OF PRECARIOUS EMPLOYMENT COMPARED WITH THE WHITE BRITISH GROUP

Women

Men

	Women	Men
White Irish	9.7%	7.3%
White Eastern European	7.2%	6.7%
Gypsy/Traveller	23.5%	65.7%
Roma	25.5%	46.4%
Jewish	8.3%	-2.6%
Any other White background	2.9%	3.2%
Indian	6.0%	3.7%
Pakistani	1.3%	4.9%
Bangladeshi	16.2%	16.4%
Mixed White and Asian	8.3%	-8.0%
Chinese	20.5%	8.9%
Any other Asian background	-3.4%	12.7%
Black Caribbean	0.7%	1.8%
Mixed White and Black Caribbean	-0.7%	-4.8%
Black African	9.5%	5.3%
Mixed White and Black African	17.7%	-4.7%
Any other Black background	20.3%	32.0%
Arab	-8.3%	-3.6%
Any other mixed/multiple background	-2.3%	8.4%
Any other ethnic group	10.7%	13.4%

Percentage point difference

Note: Chart shows percentage point difference, the age-adjusted rates for White British women is 21.5% and for White British men is 18.9%

TABLE 7.2: CHANGE IN OCCUPATION DURING THE COVID-19 PANDEMIC AND AGE-ADJUSTED DIFFERENCE BETWEEN ETHNIC MINORITY PEOPLE AND WHITE BRITISH PEOPLE

	Had a change in occupation				Change in occupation (difference compared with White British)	
	Women	n	Men	n	Women	Men
White Irish	16.6	38	17.3	41	-1.3	0.0
White Eastern European	26.0	206	9.3	100	10.6	-5.6
Gypsy/Traveller	38.4	40	15.7	83	19.6	-4.5
Roma	35.0	25	13.9	17	18.9*	-5.9
Jewish	17.8	210	27.1	142	0.6	8.1*
Any other White background	22.2	295	17.6	184	2.0	2.0
Indian	16.5	449	24.1	439	-1.8	8.3**
Pakistani	16.7	262	22.1	277	-5.6*	7.2
Bangladeshi	15.8	138	9.7	136	-7.0*	-6.0*
Mixed White and Asian	35.5	187	16.5	137	9.0	-0.6
Chinese	27.6	285	29.7	193	15.2**	10.0**
Any other Asian background	22.0	222	24.3	197	4.0	8.5
Black Caribbean	9.9	277	14.8	152	-3.7	0.8
Mixed White and Black Caribbean	13.3	161	26.0	103	-7.5*	5.4
Black African	21.4	416	22.4	350	1.6	5.9*
Mixed White and Black African	23.3	71	38.9	39	6.0	10.6
Any other Black background	36.5	82	30.9	46	20.0*	13.2
Arab	15.6	42	27.0	39	5.3	11.6
Any other mixed/multiple background	37.8	157	20.5	84	17.9**	4.4
Any other ethnic group	31.3	104	28.8	70	9.0	11.2
White British	17.9	1275	14.6	1195		

$* p < 0.1, ** p < 0.05$

Note: Only includes those who reported being employed as defined in the question

rates (see Table 7.1). Bangladeshi men were less likely than their White British counterparts to change occupations, perhaps because they had high rates of solo self-employment (see Figure 7.3).

Figures 7.5 and 7.6 describe other work-related implications of the coronavirus outbreak by ethnic group, with Figure 7.5 showing the rate

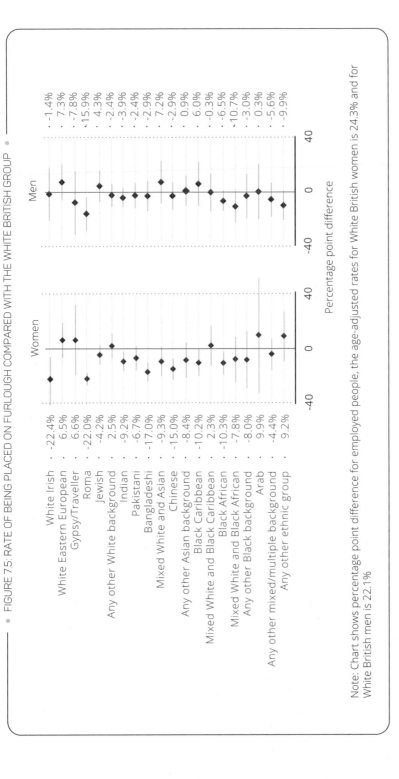

FIGURE 7.5: RATE OF BEING PLACED ON FURLOUGH COMPARED WITH THE WHITE BRITISH GROUP

	Women	Men
White Irish	-22.4%	-1.4%
White Eastern European	6.5%	7.3%
Gypsy/Traveller	6.6%	-7.8%
Roma	-22.0%	-15.9%
Jewish	-4.2%	4.3%
Any other White background	2.5%	-2.4%
Indian	-9.2%	-3.9%
Pakistani	-6.7%	-2.4%
Bangladeshi	-17.0%	-2.9%
Mixed White and Asian	-9.3%	7.2%
Chinese	-15.0%	-2.9%
Any other Asian background	-8.4%	0.9%
Black Caribbean	-10.2%	6.0%
Mixed White and Black Caribbean	2.3%	-0.3%
Black African	-10.3%	-6.5%
Mixed White and Black African	-7.8%	-10.7%
Any other Black background	-8.0%	-3.0%
Arab	9.9%	0.3%
Any other mixed/multiple background	-4.4%	-5.6%
Any other ethnic group	9.2%	-9.9%

Percentage point difference

Note: Chart shows percentage point difference for employed people, the age-adjusted rates for White British women is 24.3% and for White British men is 22.1%

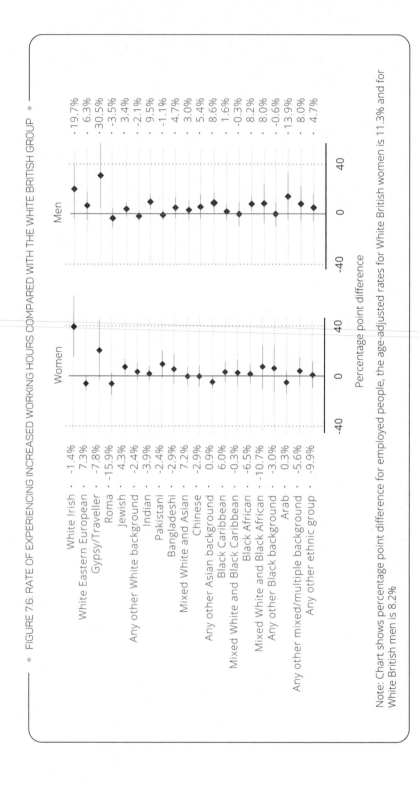

• FIGURE 7.6: RATE OF EXPERIENCING INCREASED WORKING HOURS COMPARED WITH THE WHITE BRITISH GROUP •

		Women	Men
White Irish	-1.4%		19.7%
White Eastern European	7.3%		6.3%
Gypsy/Traveller	-7.8%		30.5%
Roma	-15.9%		-3.5%
Jewish	4.3%		3.4%
Any other White background	-2.4%		-2.1%
Indian	-3.9%		9.5%
Pakistani	-2.4%		-1.1%
Bangladeshi	-2.9%		4.7%
Mixed White and Asian	7.2%		3.0%
Chinese	-2.9%		5.4%
Any other Asian background	0.9%		8.6%
Black Caribbean	6.0%		1.6%
Mixed White and Black Caribbean	-0.3%		-0.3%
Black African	-6.5%		8.2%
Mixed White and Black African	-10.7%		8.0%
Any other Black background	-3.0%		-0.6%
Arab	0.3%		13.9%
Any other mixed/multiple background	-5.6%		8.0%
Any other ethnic group	-9.9%		4.7%

Percentage point difference

Note: Chart shows percentage point difference for employed people, the age-adjusted rates for White British women is 11.3% and for White British men is 8.2%

of being placed on furlough and Figure 7.6 showing the rate of having extended working hours due to the COVID-19 outbreak, and both figures comparing ethnic minority groups with the White British group. Being placed on furlough means that a person temporarily stops working while receiving reduced pay and not being made redundant. White Irish, Roma, Indian, Bangladeshi, Chinese, Black Caribbean and Black African women were less likely to be furloughed than White British women, while no female ethnic minority group was more likely to be placed on furlough than White British women. For men, Roma men were less likely to be furloughed than White British men, and no ethnic minority group was more likely than White British men to be placed on furlough.

White Eastern European and Any other Asian background women experienced a lower likelihood than White British women to have had an increase in their working hours, and White Irish and Jewish women were more likely to have had an increase in their hours than their White British counterparts. For men, no ethnic minority group had a lower probability of increasing their working hours, whereas Gypsy/Traveller, Indian, Any other Asian background and Black African men had a higher probability of increasing their working hours. Women and men in all other ethnic minority groups showed the same likelihood of having an increase in their working hours as their White British counterparts.

Pay and concerns about job loss during the COVID-19 pandemic

Economic downturns generate a great deal of uncertainty for employers and workers. Businesses find it hard to predict future income streams, meaning workers therefore face uncertainties with regard to income, working hours and job security. In this context, labour market policies, such as furlough, to control the pandemic become crucial. Figure 7.7 shows the probability of reduced pay for ethnic minority people compared with their White British counterparts. People in most ethnic minority groups in the UK were not more likely than the White British group to receive a pay cut. However, White Irish, Mixed White and Asian, and Any other Black background men were more likely to experience a pay cut than White British men. Of these groups White Irish and Any other Black background men had a very low unemployment rate (see Table 7.1). It is possible that these ethnic minority groups might have traded a pay cut for further employment. Interestingly, Roma women were less likely than White British women to receive a pay cut.

When it comes to job security, Figure 7.8 shows that Chinese women were more worried about losing their jobs than White British women. Among men, this was the case for several of the ethnic minority groups, White Irish, Indian, Pakistani, Bangladeshi, Chinese, Any other Asian background, Any other Black background, Arab and Any other mixed/multiple background

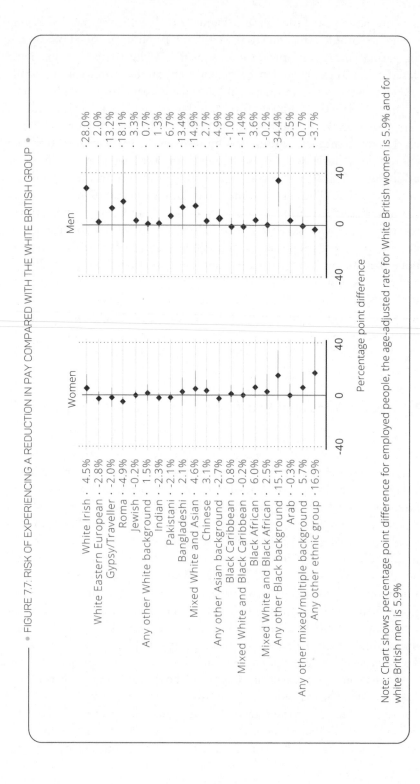

• FIGURE 7.7: RISK OF EXPERIENCING A REDUCTION IN PAY COMPARED WITH THE WHITE BRITISH GROUP •

Note: Chart shows percentage point difference for employed people, the age-adjusted rate for White British women is 5.9% and for white British men is 5.9%

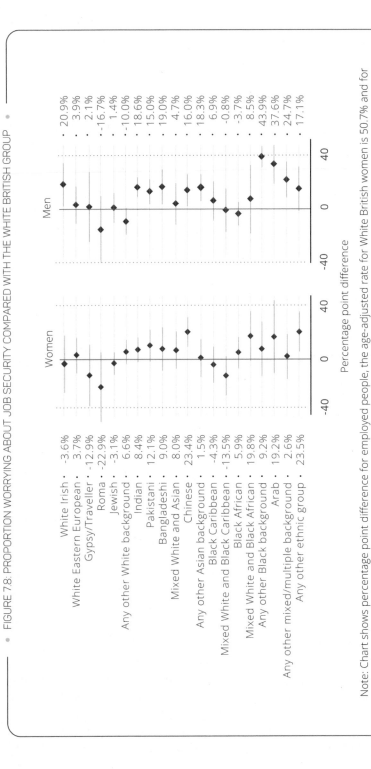

FIGURE 7.8: PROPORTION WORRYING ABOUT JOB SECURITY COMPARED WITH THE WHITE BRITISH GROUP

	Women	Men
White Irish	-3.6%	20.9%
White Eastern European	3.7%	3.9%
Gypsy/Traveller	-12.9%	2.1%
Roma	-22.9%	-16.7%
Jewish	-3.1%	1.4%
Any other White background	6.6%	-10.0%
Indian	8.4%	18.6%
Pakistani	12.1%	15.0%
Bangladeshi	9.0%	19.0%
Mixed White and Asian	8.0%	4.7%
Chinese	23.4%	16.0%
Any other Asian background	1.5%	18.3%
Black Caribbean	-4.3%	6.9%
Mixed White and Black Caribbean	-13.5%	-0.8%
Black African	5.9%	-3.7%
Mixed White and Black African	19.8%	8.5%
Any other Black background	9.2%	43.9%
Arab	19.2%	37.6%
Any other mixed/multiple background	2.6%	24.7%
Any other ethnic group	23.5%	17.1%

Percentage point difference

Note: Chart shows percentage point difference for employed people, the age-adjusted rate for White British women is 50.7% and for White British men is 50.9%

men were more likely to worry about job security than White British men. No ethnic minority group for both men and women was less worried about job security than its White British counterparts.

Discussion and conclusion

Prior to the pandemic, evidence suggested that there has been substantial variation in unemployment, employment and wage outcomes across ethnic groups (Manning and Rose, 2021). In general, ethnic minority groups experienced an unemployment penalty compared to the White British group, with only Indian women and Pakistani men showing a consistent downward trend in unemployment over the years before the pandemic. Similarly, there existed an employment penalty for both ethnic minority men and women compared with their White British counterparts, although the penalty has been declining for most ethnic minority men. In addition, a persistent pay penalty for all ethnic minority groups has been in existence for both women and men (Manning and Rose, 2021). It seems to be the case that labour market discrimination, at least in the hiring and possibly at the promotion and pay stage, is one part of the story of differential labour market outcomes of ethnic minority people in the UK (Clark and Shankley, 2020; Manning and Rose, 2021). Other powerful factors are the imperfect transferability of foreign human capital in the form of qualification and work experience to the country of destination (Fortin et al, 2016; Zwysen and Demireva, 2018), family influence on child outcome (Heckman and Landersø, 2021), and the quality and associated pay scale of firms people work for (Phan et al, 2022).

Compared to the White British group, the COVID-19 pandemic did not affect ethnic minority groups more adversely, or at least not when it comes to labour market outcomes, such as change in occupations, increased working hours and pay reduction. However, it is important to note that for some ethnic minority groups, disadvantages in the labour market persisted during the COVID-19 pandemic. For instance, Pakistani women and men reported high unemployment rates relative to White British people. Cribb et al (2021) come to a similar conclusion from their analysis of a combined Pakistani/Bangladeshi group. Importantly, for the EVENS data, Bangladeshi men showed high labour force participation, high employment and low unemployment rates, although they were more likely to be in precarious employment than White British men. Moreover, other ethnic minority men, such as Gypsy/Traveller and Roma, among others, were also more likely to be in precarious employment during the COVID-19 pandemic, which remains a troublesome element of the UK labour market (Clark and Ochmann, 2022).

In sum, there is a need for careful description in terms of labour market patterns as no ethnic minority group faced disadvantages across all outcomes during the COVID-19 pandemic. The wide range of ethnic minority groups included in EVENS and the separate treatment of women and men in the analysis allow for a more comprehensive accounting of ethnic differences in economic outcomes. The government's job retention scheme enacted during the pandemic to place people on furlough was probably effective in preventing high unemployment rates (Cribb et al, 2021). This pandemic policy possibly mitigated further inequalities across ethnic groups. Of course, this may have been a consequence of the unintended outcomes of policies that impacted differentially across the employment sectors in which ethnic minority people are and are not concentrated. For example, many ethnic minority people work in sectors that continued to operate through the pandemic, so were, if anything, less likely to experience furlough.

Box 7.1: Work and employment: measures and methods

The target population in this chapter is restricted to those aged 18–65 and includes students, but excludes retirees of all ages. Furthermore, this chapter only estimates population percentages, and all model estimates are made relative to White British people, while including an age variable in the regression. Age differences are taken into consideration if noted in the tables and figures because ethnic minority people tend to be younger than White British people, which might significantly impact labour market outcomes. Only statistically significant results at the 5% level are discussed in most instances. Confidence intervals at the 95% level are reported by gender. Weights are used for all estimates.

Twelve employment categories are used: self-employed; in full-time paid employment (including furlough); in part-time paid employment (under 35 hours a week and, again, including furlough); unemployed; on maternity leave; looking after family or home; full-time student; long-term sick or disabled; on a government training scheme; unpaid worker in family business; working in an apprenticeship; or doing something else. Figure 7.1 then categorises selected employment responses into six outcomes: full-time employed; part-time employed; family care; full-time student; all other categories; and unemployment. It is important to note that in this context, the unemployment rate is the percentage of the working age population that is unemployed and not the percentage of the labour force (employed and unemployed) that is unemployed.

In Table 7.1, labour force participants (self-employed; in full-time paid employment (including furlough); in part-time paid employment (under 35 hours a week and, again, including furlough); unemployed) were coded as one, the employed (self-employed; in full-time paid employment (including furlough); in part-time paid employment (under 35 hours a week and, again, including furlough)) were coded as one, and the unemployed were coded as one. The labour force participation rate is the percentage of the reference population of working-age people. The employment rate is the percentage of the reference population of working-age people that is employed. The employed include self-employed and part-time and full-time workers. The unemployment rate is the percentage of the labour force that is unemployed. The employment rate includes the economically inactive in the reference population, whereas the unemployment rate does not, suggesting that it entertains a smaller reference population.

The definitions of the variables included in Figure 7.3 are based on four separate questions. First: 'Which best describes your employment situation after the outbreak of the pandemic?' (self-employed; in full-time paid employment (including furlough); in part-time paid employment (under 35 hours a week and, again, including furlough)). Second: 'Is your employment contract permanent or temporary?' Third: 'Do you currently employ anybody else?' Fourth: 'Does your contract have a guaranteed number of minimum employment hours, or do you have a "zero hours" contract?' Standard employed workers are all employed workers minus the sum of temporary, solo self-employed and zero-hour contract workers. This definition produces four outcomes: standard employment and the three other categories.

Figure 7.4 combines the temporary, solo self-employed and zero-hours contract categories from Figure 7.3 into a non-standard category and uses this combined category with the standard category from Figure 7.3 to form a binary outcome.

Table 7.2 is based on the following question: 'Has your occupation changed since the coronavirus outbreak began in February 2020?', with a response of yes or no. Please note that the number of employed in each ethnic category slightly exceeds the number of employed which can be derived from the information in Table 7.1. The reason for this deviation is that Table 7.2 does not restrict the sample to employed individuals according to the definition in Table 7.1.

Figures 7.5, 7.6 and 7.7 are based on binary variables categorised to one if the answer is yes and to zero if the answer is no. For Figure 7.8, the answer to the question on worry allows for four responses: not worried at all; somewhat worried; very worried; and extremely worried. The constructed binary variable is categorised to one if the answer is somewhat worried, very worried or extremely worried, and to zero if the answer is not worried at all.

8

Socioeconomic circumstances

*Michaela Šťastná, Dharmi Kapadia, Ken Clark, James Nazroo
and Nico Ochmann*

Key findings

Persisting ethnic inequalities in socioeconomic circumstances have been exacerbated
by the COVID-19 pandemic.

- Despite increasing educational and occupational levels, ethnic minority people
  continue to face financial difficulties and disadvantages with regards to housing.
- Financial difficulties have been exacerbated by the impact of the COVID-19 pandemic,
  with many ethnic minority groups reporting almost double the rates of financial
  difficulties in the midst of the pandemic compared to the pre-pandemic period,
  especially for people from Chinese, Any other Black, Mixed White and Black Caribbean
  and Any other White backgrounds.
- Further, the detrimental financial impact of the pandemic has been greater for ethnic
  minority people than for the White British group.
- Compared to White British people, particularly high rates of worries about financial
  circumstances are seen for people from Arab, Bangladeshi, Pakistani, Any other Asian
  and Any other ethnic groups.
- People from Roma and Gypsy/Traveller ethnic groups experience the highest levels of
  socioeconomic deprivation; they are more likely to have no educational qualifications,
  less likely to be in the highest occupational positions, and have high rates of financial
  difficulties and benefit receipt.
- People from Arab and Any other ethnic groups show exceptionally high rates of
  disadvantage in terms of housing, financial difficulties (both pre-pandemic and in the
  midst of the COVID-19 pandemic), receipt of benefits and worries about finances.

Introduction

This chapter focuses on ethnic inequalities in socioeconomic outcomes
for people in the UK. We illustrate longstanding inequalities, especially in
relation to education, occupation and tenure, and compare these with the

socioeconomic impact of the COVID-19 pandemic. The Evidence for Equality National Survey (EVENS) data map all of these domains in great detail; this is reflected in the inclusion of questions on socioeconomic status as well as financial situation, both before and during the COVID-19 pandemic, income change, receipt of benefits and worries about finances. Investigating the potential unequal socioeconomic impact before and during the pandemic is crucial as ethnic minority groups in the UK have been shown to experience disadvantages in many of these spheres (Kapadia, Nazroo and Clark, 2015; Byrne et al, 2020). Moreover, these disadvantages seem to have been further exacerbated by the COVID-19 crisis (Benzeval et al, 2020; Hu, 2020; Allen et al, 2021). The EVENS data provide the opportunity to undertake a detailed investigation into the experiences of ethnic minority people's socioeconomic circumstances and how the COVID-19 pandemic has affected them.

Ethnic inequalities in socioeconomic status have been shown to be widespread in domains such as education, housing, job opportunities and income, with many ethnic minority groups faring worse than the White British population (Kapadia, Nazroo and Clark, 2015; Byrne et al, 2020; Allen et al, 2021; Zwysen, Di Stasio and Heath, 2021). Focusing on people who attained either degree-level qualifications or who have no qualifications, Lymperopoulou and Parameshwaran (2015) used three UK censuses (1991, 2001 and 2011) to explore whether there is an educational gap between ethnic minority people and the White British group. The results show that in the past 20–30 years, educational attainment has been increasing for ethnic minority groups, with Indian, Pakistani and Bangladeshi groups showing the highest increases in the proportion of degree-educated people (Lymperopoulou and Parameshwaran, 2015). But stark inequalities remain for some groups – for example, the highest rates of having no qualifications were seen for Gypsy/Traveller people (60% compared to 24% of the White British group in 2011) (Lymperopoulou and Parameshwaran, 2015). Despite high levels of degree education for some ethnic minority groups, there is evidence for a lower chance of admission to elite Russell Group universities for ethnic minority people (Boliver, 2016).

Even though many ethnic minority people have high levels of degree-level education compared to the White British population in the UK, they are much more likely to be in occupations that pay lower than the living wage (for example, sales, hospitality, personal care and retail) or to be overqualified for their jobs (Brynin and Longhi, 2015). Brynin and Longhi (2015) explore the link between occupation and poverty for ethnic minority groups in the UK using the Labour Force Survey (LFS) and the UK Household Longitudinal Survey (UKHLS). They report that ethnic minority people are more likely to be employed in the education and health sectors, within which they experience unequal wages. For example, in the nursing and midwifery professions, 23.1% come from an ethnic minority group, and these ethnic minority nurses and midwives earn £1.20 less per hour compared to their White British counterparts (Brynin and Longhi, 2015). There is also evidence to show that Pakistani and Bangladeshi people in particular are concentrated in low-paying occupations, where they also experience lower wages compared to White employees (Brynin and Longhi, 2015).

Further, there are also marked inequalities for ethnic minority groups in the housing market. Data from the English Housing Survey (2015/16 and 2016/17) and the Census (2001 and 2011) show that ethnic minority people, and especially people from Any other White, Chinese and Any other ethnic groups were most likely to privately rent, which indicates a higher level of housing precarity (Shankley and Finney, 2020). Social renting (from local authorities) was highest for Black African, Mixed White and Black Caribbean, and Black African people.

Due to economic adversity and inequality experienced across ethnic groups during the COVID-19 pandemic, persistent disadvantages may have been exacerbated for some ethnic minority groups (Gardiner and Slaughter, 2020; Witteveen, 2020). For example, Benzeval et al (2020) report that overall 45% of people have experienced an income loss of at least 10% and that the extent of the income loss is accentuated for people belonging to an ethnic minority group. Similarly, a report by the Financial Conduct Authority (2021) stated that due to the COVID-19 pandemic, almost 40% of adults have experienced income loss, especially self-employed individuals, low-income households and people belonging to ethnic minority groups. The report of their COVID-19 survey, conducted in October 2020 (Financial Conduct Authority, 2021), also shows that people from Any other ethnic backgrounds (22%), Mixed background (19%) and Black or Black British (17%) people had high rates of reporting their financial situation 'to be a lot worse than prior the pandemic' (compared to 14% of White people). Job losses, particularly in hospitality, tourism and retail, have led to income reduction and financial hardship (see also Chapter 7). Using data from the UKHLS COVID-19 survey, Hu (2020) reports that ethnic minority people born outside of the UK were at a higher risk of losing their job, and ethnic minority people born in the UK experienced lower furloughing rates compared to White British people. This indicates lower employment protection for both migrant and UK-born ethnic minority groups (Hu, 2020; Allen et al, 2021). Pakistani and Bangladeshi people have been identified as two of the most vulnerable groups when it comes to job security, as they make up to 30% of workers in the sectors most affected by restrictions put in place in response to the COVID-19 outbreak (Platt and Warwick, 2020; Allen et al, 2021).

Previous research, then, points to persistent ethnic inequalities in many socioeconomic domains. The aim of this chapter is to explore how pre-existing ethnic inequalities relate to the differential experiences of the COVID-19 pandemic of ethnic minority people compared to White British people. We describe ethnic inequalities in a range of socioeconomic measures: education, occupation, tenure and financial situation before the COVID-19 outbreak. We then focus on how people's financial situation has changed during the COVID-19 pandemic, whether they have experienced income change and have been receiving income-related benefits, and to what extent they worry about their financial situation. Using EVENS data, we map the socioeconomic circumstances for 21 distinct ethnic groups in the UK. Thus, we are able to thoroughly investigate ethnic inequalities in socioeconomics in Britain and illustrate how these were amplified under the influence of the COVID-19 pandemic.

Results

Education

Compared to the White British group (32.4%), higher proportions of degree-educated people are seen in most ethnic minority groups, with the exception of people from Roma (5.9%), Gypsy/Traveller (18.8%) and Any other Black (26.8%) ethnic groups (Table 8.1). We observe the highest proportions of attaining degree-education for people from White Irish (65.3%), Indian (62.9%), Any other White (60.9%), Black African (60.8%) and Jewish (60.3%) ethnic groups – these are especially high compared to the 32.4% of degree-educated among the White British group. The rates of having no qualifications are most pronounced for Roma (54.6%) and Gypsy/Traveller (51.2%) people, but are also substantial for Arab (9.1%) people in comparison to the White British group (2.4%).

In Table 8.1, we present rates for people aged 18–65. Figure 8.1 shows the percentage point difference relative to the White British group once age and sex differences are accounted for (see Box 8.1). We find that, compared to the White British group, many ethnic minority groups are more likely to be degree-educated. This is especially the case for White Irish people (whose rate of degree-educated is 33 percentage points higher), Indian people (30 percentage points higher), Black African people (28 percentage points higher), people from Any other White backgrounds (28 percentage points higher) and Jewish people (28 percentage points higher), but is also present for people from Any other Asian, Chinese, Any other ethnic group, White Eastern European, Pakistani and Mixed White and Asian ethnic groups. Thus, we continue to see an educational advantage once differences in age and sex are taken into account for most ethnic minority groups. Significantly lower rates of being degree-educated compared to the White British group are only seen for Roma (27 percentage points lower), Gypsy/Traveller (14 percentage points lower) and Mixed White and Black Caribbean (12 percentage points lower) ethnic groups.

Occupation

Here, we present self-reported occupation before the outbreak of COVID-19 in February 2020. Looking at Table 8.2, we see the proportion of people in

TABLE 8.1: HIGHEST EDUCATIONAL QUALIFICATION, BY ETHNIC GROUP

Weighted percentage
Highest educational qualification

	Degree-educated	Diploma/apprenticeship	A-level or equivalent	GCSE or equivalent	Other/don't know	No qualifications	N
White Irish	65.3	12.8	12.9	1.7	4.7	2.6	97
White Eastern European	48.8	13.7	21.5	6.8	3.8	5.4	360
Gypsy/Traveller	18.8	4.6	12.2	10.2	3.0	51.2	227
Roma	5.9	16.7	16.0	2.6	4.1	54.6	73
Jewish	60.3	11.7	11.7	9.9	0.4	5.9	476
Any other White background	60.9	10.2	13.9	4.2	4.7	6.2	650
Indian	62.9	13.1	12.5	9.4	1.5	0.6	1255
Pakistani	47.1	13.6	15.4	11.9	6.3	5.7	849
Bangladeshi	44.2	12.6	21.8	9.2	6.4	5.8	406
Mixed White and Asian	45.3	18.6	18.6	5.2	8.6	3.8	520
Chinese	52.6	20.4	16.8	7.3	2.4	0.4	663
Any other Asian background	56.2	16.6	15.2	6.2	3.7	2.0	663
Black Caribbean	42.9	23.8	16.7	12.1	3.8	0.8	558
Mixed White and Black Caribbean	21.4	38.3	17.6	16.9	4.0	1.8	354
Black African	60.8	16.2	12.2	7.7	1.2	1.9	1042
Mixed White and Black African	52.1	24.3	20.5	3.0	0.1	0.0	155
Any other Black background	26.8	29.5	8.1	10.1	18.8	6.7	176
Arab	50.2	10.6	3.6	15.1	11.5	9.1	152
Any other mixed/multiple background	42.2	22.3	16.3	6.5	8.8	3.9	363
Any other ethnic group	54.7	13.6	15.9	3.0	12.7	0.0	252
White British	32.4	21.1	21.9	21.3	1.0	2.4	3523
N	7270	1931	1840	1173	229	371	12814

higher managerial, administrative and professional occupations (the highest class) is greater for people from Jewish (62.9%), Any other White (60.4%), White Irish (55.9%), Mixed White and Asian (55.4%) and Indian (53.7%) ethnic groups. These rates are considerably higher than that of the White British group

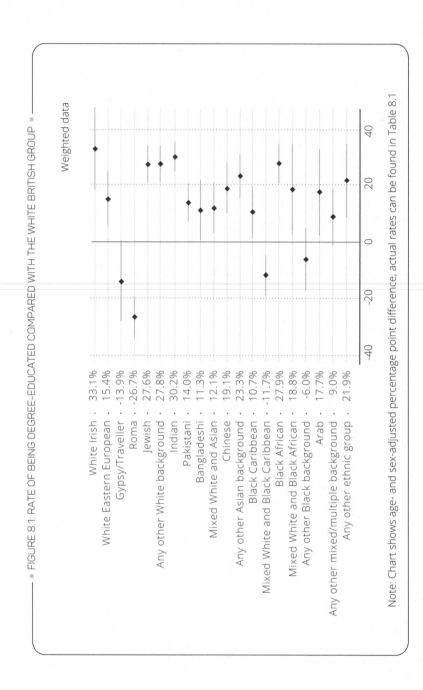

• FIGURE 8.1: RATE OF BEING DEGREE-EDUCATED COMPARED WITH THE WHITE BRITISH GROUP •

Weighted data

White Irish	33.1%
White Eastern European	15.4%
Gypsy/Traveller	-13.9%
Roma	-26.7%
Jewish	27.6%
Any other White background	27.8%
Indian	30.2%
Pakistani	14.0%
Bangladeshi	11.3%
Mixed White and Asian	12.1%
Chinese	19.1%
Any other Asian background	23.3%
Black Caribbean	10.7%
Mixed White and Black Caribbean	-11.7%
Black African	27.9%
Mixed White and Black African	18.8%
Any other Black background	-6.0%
Arab	17.7%
Any other mixed/multiple background	9.0%
Any other ethnic group	21.9%

Note: Chart shows age- and sex-adjusted percentage point difference, actual rates can be found in Table 8.1

Box 8.1: Socioeconomic circumstances: measures and methods

We undertake descriptive analyses for eight outcomes and show tables for each by ethnic group: highest educational qualification, occupational class, type of tenure, financial difficulties three months prior to the COVID-19 outbreak and in the midst of the pandemic, income change, receipt of benefits, and worries about financial situation.

Logistic regression models are used to plot percentage point difference figures for degree-level education, highest occupational class, homeownership, financial difficulties, income decrease as well as no change in income, receipt of benefits and financial worries. We code each outcome of interest as 1 (for example, having a degree-level education, being in the highest occupational class, being a homeowner, having financial difficulties). We adjust these models for age and sex, and compare the adjusted percentage point differences for ethnic minority people to those of White British people. The estimates are shown with 95% confidence intervals. Age is used as a continuous variable (18–65 years). Stata 16.1 (StataCorp, 2019) statistical software was used to conduct the analyses.

Education: We combine university higher degree and first-level degree qualifications into a 'degree-educated' category. From hereon in, we use the term 'degree-educated' to address those who are educated to at least undergraduate degree level, so this category also includes people who have postgraduate qualifications.

Occupational class: We use the five category version of the National Statistics Socioeconomic Classification (NS-SEC; ONS, 2022) from the occupation types coded according to the Standard Occupational Classification 2020 (SOC2020; ONS, 2021a). We present analyses using occupation type reported prior to the COVID-19 pandemic.

Tenure: Homeownership is defined as both without and with a mortgage. Renting includes people who are private or social renting.

Financial difficulties: In EVENS, the question on the financial situation before the COVID-19 outbreak specifically asks: 'In the 3 months before the coronavirus outbreak, how well were you managing financially?' The question mapping the financial situation during the pandemic asks: 'And now, how are you managing financially?' and thus provides information on people's financial circumstances between February and October 2021 – the months affected by COVID-19 lockdowns and subsequent policy changes. The possible answers to these two questions were: living very comfortably, living somewhat comfortably, finding it somewhat difficult, finding it very difficult or prefer not to say. We show the proportions of people having financial difficulties who answer that managing financially is either somewhat or very difficult.

Income change: The EVENS question about income change asks: 'Is your current household income higher than, about the same as or lower than before the coronavirus outbreak in February 2020?' We show the rates of income change categorised as income increase (combining 'much higher' or 'a little higher' answers), no change in income ('about the same') and income decrease (combining 'a little lower' or 'much lower').

Benefits receipt: We define a person as receiving income-related benefit(s) if they indicate receiving any of the following benefit payments: universal credit, job seeker's allowance, employment and support allowance, pension credit, housing benefit, council tax support, statutory sick pay, attendance allowance, personal independence payments, asylum/home office/section 95 support, carer's allowance, child tax credits, income support, industrial injuries disablement benefit, tax credits or a working tax credit.

Worries about financial situation: In the figure showing percentage point difference in reporting financial worries, we combine the answers 'very worried' and 'extremely worried'.

(43.7%). The lowest proportions in the highest occupational class are observed for Gypsy/Traveller and Roma people (12.4% and 17.1%, respectively). People from Any other Black backgrounds also show lower proportions of having an occupation in the highest class (25.7%) – many of them have intermediate occupations (29.3%) or semi-routine and routine occupations (31.9%). A large proportion of people in the Any other ethnic (35.5%), Arab (31.9%) and Pakistani (31.5%) groups are also in intermediate occupations. When it comes to semi-routine and routine occupations, high rates are seen for Roma (51.5%), White Gypsy/Traveller (42.6%), White Eastern European (37.4%) and Mixed White and Black Caribbean (33.8%) ethnic groups.

Figure 8.2 shows the percentage point difference relative to the White British group of the proportion who are in a higher managerial, administrative or professional occupation once differences in age and sex are accounted for. Compared to the White British group, people from Jewish, Any other White and Indian ethnic groups show significantly higher rates of being in these occupations (see Figure 8.2). This is especially true for people from the Jewish and Any other White ethnic groups, who have rates of being in the highest occupational class that are 19 percentage points and 17 percentage points higher than those for White British people. People from Gypsy/ Traveller, Mixed White and Black Caribbean, Any other Black and White Eastern European ethnic groups show lower rates of being in a higher managerial, administrative or professional occupation compared to the White British group. Even though the White British group exhibits a lower proportion of people in the highest occupational class, many differences between White British people and ethnic minorities are not statistically significant. Thus, even though at first sight, we might see an occupational advantage for some ethnic minority groups, this does not seem to be the case for many once age and sex differences are accounted for.

TABLE 8.2: OCCUPATIONAL CLASS (NS-SEC CLASSIFICATION), BY ETHNIC GROUP

| | Weighted percentage | | | | | |
| | Occupational class | | | | | |
	Higher managerial, administrative and professional occupations	Intermediate occupations	Small employers and own account workers	Lower supervisory and technical occupations	Semi-routine and routine occupations	N
White Irish	55.9	22.5	0.1	4.9	16.6	72
White Eastern European	28.4	15.0	5.1	14.0	37.4	259
Gypsy/Traveller	12.4	6.6	16.2	22.2	42.6	117
Roma	17.1	2.8	28.5	0.0	51.5	31
Jewish	62.9	16.5	9.8	3.4	7.5	322
Any other White background	60.4	14.1	4.6	4.5	16.3	429
Indian	53.7	22.5	4.5	2.7	16.6	801
Pakistani	35.4	31.5	8.5	0.6	24.1	487
Bangladeshi	33.5	21.5	7.5	5.7	31.9	242
Mixed White and Asian	55.4	18.1	4.6	5.2	16.7	296
Chinese	48.1	14.0	10.8	9.3	17.9	430
Any other Asian background	41.1	17.6	4.8	7.2	29.2	370
Black Caribbean	35.9	27.8	6.8	7.9	21.6	388
Mixed White and Black Caribbean	26.5	26.5	10.1	3.1	33.8	246
Black African	43.8	22.4	2.7	7.5	23.6	698
Mixed White and Black African	46.9	18.8	1.8	4.3	28.2	100
Any other Black background	25.7	29.3	5.3	7.8	31.9	111
Arab	41.5	31.9	3.2	6.5	17.0	70
Any other mixed/multiple background	36.4	19.6	4.8	6.8	32.5	224
Any other ethnic group	35.5	35.5	16.0	5.7	7.3	152
White British	43.7	19.9	7.3	6.6	22.5	2329
N	4266	1780	485	296	1347	8174

Tenure

The highest proportions of home ownership without a mortgage are seen for Gypsy/Traveller (44%), Roma (38.6%), White British (31.4%), Jewish

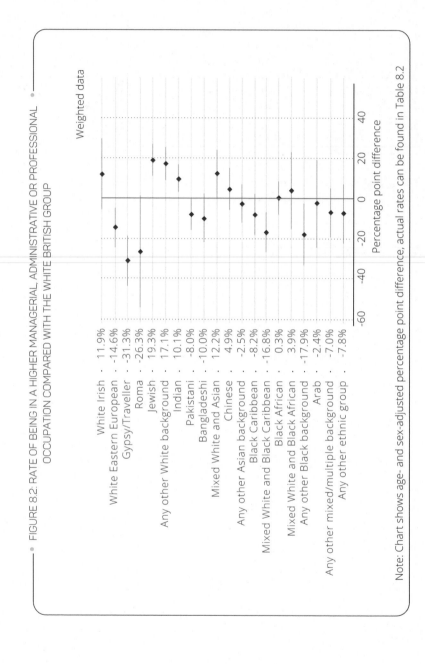

FIGURE 8.2: RATE OF BEING IN A HIGHER MANAGERIAL, ADMINISTRATIVE OR PROFESSIONAL OCCUPATION COMPARED WITH THE WHITE BRITISH GROUP

Weighted data

White Irish	11.9%
White Eastern European	-14.6%
Gypsy/Traveller	-31.3%
Roma	-26.3%
Jewish	19.3%
Any other White background	17.1%
Indian	10.1%
Pakistani	-8.0%
Bangladeshi	-10.0%
Mixed White and Asian	12.2%
Chinese	4.9%
Any other Asian background	-2.5%
Black Caribbean	-8.2%
Mixed White and Black Caribbean	-16.8%
Black African	0.3%
Mixed White and Black African	3.9%
Any other Black background	-17.9%
Arab	-2.4%
Any other mixed/multiple background	-7.0%
Any other ethnic group	-7.8%

Percentage point difference

-60 -40 -20 0 20 40

Note: Chart shows age- and sex-adjusted percentage point difference, actual rates can be found in Table 8.2

• TABLE 8.3: TENURE, BY ETHNIC GROUP •

Weighted percentage

Tenure

	Own outright	Own with mortgage	Rent	Rent-free/ with parents	Other	N
White Irish	20.0	44.1	32.0	3.9	-	97
White Eastern European	6.9	25.0	67.2	0.4	0.5	360
Gypsy/Traveller	44.0	13.5	37.6	3.1	1.9	227
Roma	38.6	1.4	57.5	2.6	-	73
Jewish	30.6	37.8	27.9	2.1	1.7	476
Any other White background	11.8	28.7	53.8	2.4	3.3	650
Indian	27.5	38.2	29.3	3.2	1.8	1255
Pakistani	22.0	38.1	29.5	4.9	5.5	849
Bangladeshi	21.6	34.2	38.0	1.6	4.7	406
Mixed White and Asian	19.1	28.5	39.7	9.7	3.0	520
Chinese	24.2	28.1	44.3	1.9	1.5	663
Any other Asian background	16.9	30.8	44.3	4.1	3.9	663
Black Caribbean	19.4	35.9	40.0	3.1	1.5	558
Mixed White and Black Caribbean	12.2	23.3	56.7	2.6	5.2	354
Black African	10.1	20.0	64.0	3.7	2.1	1043
Mixed White and Black African	13.3	35.2	50.4	1.1	0.0	155
Any other Black background	19.8	20.6	42.1	8.3	9.2	176
Arab	13.0	15.8	61.9	3.5	5.8	152
Any other mixed/multiple background	10.5	21.9	57.4	2.9	7.2	364
Any other ethnic group	13.1	29.2	48.2	3.7	5.8	252
White British	31.4	36.7	28.3	2.2	1.4	3523
N	2881	4278	4908	415	334	12816

(30.6%) and Indian (27.5%) people (Table 8.3). It is important to note that for Gypsy/Traveller and Roma people, their dwelling type might be different from conventional home ownership (see Chapter 6). The survey indicates that a high proportion of Gypsy/Traveller people live on a traveller site (59%)

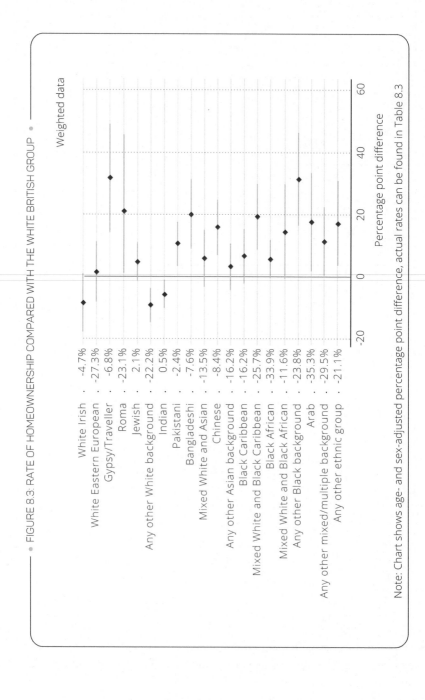

● FIGURE 8.3: RATE OF HOMEOWNERSHIP COMPARED WITH THE WHITE BRITISH GROUP ●

Weighted data

White Irish	-4.7%
White Eastern European	-27.3%
Gypsy/Traveller	-6.8%
Roma	-23.1%
Jewish	2.1%
Any other White background	-22.2%
Indian	0.5%
Pakistani	-2.4%
Bangladeshi	-7.6%
Mixed White and Asian	-13.5%
Chinese	-8.4%
Any other Asian background	-16.2%
Black Caribbean	-16.2%
Mixed White and Black Caribbean	-25.7%
Black African	-33.9%
Mixed White and Black African	-11.6%
Any other Black background	-23.8%
Arab	-35.3%
Any other mixed/multiple background	-29.5%
Any other ethnic group	-21.1%

Percentage point difference

Note: Chart shows age- and sex-adjusted percentage point difference, actual rates can be found in Table 8.3

and do not own the land they live on (58%). The lowest rates of owning a home without a mortgage are seen for people from the White Eastern European (6.9%), Black African (10.1%), Any other mixed background (10.5%) and Any other White background (11.8%) groups. For these groups, we simultaneously see high rates of renting.

Figure 8.3 shows the percentage point difference relative to the White British group of the proportion of homeownership (either outright or with a mortgage) once age and sex differences are accounted for. It illustrates that, compared to the White British group, no other ethnic group has significantly higher rates of being a homeowner. Similar rates of home ownership to those for White British people are observed for Jewish, White Irish, Indian and Pakistani people. We see disadvantage particularly for Arab and Black African people compared to White British people when it comes to homeownership; rates are lower by 35 percentage points for Arab people and by 34 percentage points for Black African people. Such a pattern indicates clear White British advantage in terms of homeownership across ethnic groups, with people from Arab, Black African, White Eastern European and Any other White backgrounds at a particular disadvantage.

Financial difficulties before and during the COVID-19 pandemic

In Table 8.4, we show proportions of people reporting financial difficulties before the COVID-19 outbreak and during the COVID-19 pandemic, together with a calculation of the relative rate of the change in financial difficulties. We see high proportions of reporting financial difficulties before the pandemic for people from Arab (40.6%), Any other (39.8%), Mixed White and Black African (37.8%), Any other mixed (34.2%) and Any other Black (31.2%) ethnic groups.

Table 8.4 also shows that for all ethnic groups, except Mixed White and Black African people, there were increases in financial difficulties during the pandemic. The 'Relative rate' column in Table 8.4 shows that, relative to the rates before the COVID-19 pandemic, the highest increases are seen for people from Chinese (1.9 times higher), Any Other Black (1.7 times higher), Mixed White and Black Caribbean, Gypsy/Traveller, Roma (all 1.6 times higher) and Any Other White (1.5 times higher) ethnic groups. We only see a decrease in reporting financial difficulties for Mixed White and Black African people; however, they initially report extraordinarily high rates of financial difficulties (36.9%), and the rates of difficulties reported during the pandemic are still high and comparable to rates reported by other ethnic minority groups (for example, people from Indian or Any other White ethnic groups).

We present two figures illustrating the percentage point difference in reporting financial difficulties before the pandemic (Figure 8.4) and during the pandemic (Figure 8.5) compared to the White British group, adjusted for differences in age and sex. Before the COVID-19 outbreak, we observe that people from

TABLE 8.4: FINANCIAL DIFFICULTIES IN THE THREE MONTHS BEFORE THE COVID-19 OUTBREAK AND DURING THE PANDEMIC, BY ETHNIC GROUP

	Weighted percentage			
	Financial difficulties			
	Before the pandemic	During the pandemic	Relative rate	N
White Irish	30.7	34.5	1.1	96
White Eastern European	19.4	23.9	1.2	353
Gypsy/Traveller	25.5	39.9	1.6	218
Roma	27.8	45.3	1.6	73
Jewish	20.1	26.8	1.3	451
Any other White background	19.2	29.8	1.5	621
Indian	18.7	27.7	1.5	1205
Pakistani	27.4	38.4	1.4	789
Bangladeshi	31.3	39.3	1.3	383
Mixed White and Asian	26.0	38.2	1.5	497
Chinese	18.3	34.3	1.9	644
Any other Asian background	28.1	40.1	1.4	636
Black Caribbean	28.0	38.8	1.4	536
Mixed White and Black Caribbean	28.4	44.5	1.6	344
Black African	26.8	33.7	1.3	1000
Mixed White and Black African	37.8	28.1	0.7	153
Any other Black background	31.2	53.2	1.7	162
Arab	40.6	53.8	1.3	141
Any other mixed/multiple background	34.2	45.9	1.3	350
Any other ethnic group	39.8	49.8	1.3	240
White British	23.4	29.8	1.3	3438
N	3,117	4303		12,330

the Arab and Any other ethnic groups show higher rates of reporting financial difficulties compared to the White British group, by 17 percentage points and 10 percentage points respectively. By contrast, Indian people were less likely to report having financial difficulties than White British people, by 5 percentage

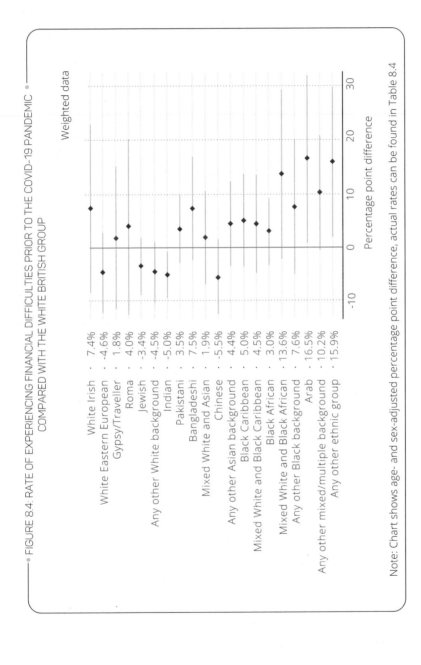

FIGURE 8.4: RATE OF EXPERIENCING FINANCIAL DIFFICULTIES PRIOR TO THE COVID-19 PANDEMIC COMPARED WITH THE WHITE BRITISH GROUP

Weighted data

White Irish	7.4%
White Eastern European	-4.6%
Gypsy/Traveller	1.8%
Roma	4.0%
Jewish	-3.4%
Any other White background	-4.5%
Indian	-5.0%
Pakistani	3.5%
Bangladeshi	7.5%
Mixed White and Asian	1.9%
Chinese	-5.5%
Any other Asian background	4.4%
Black Caribbean	5.0%
Mixed White and Black Caribbean	4.5%
Black African	3.0%
Mixed White and Black African	13.6%
Any other Black background	7.6%
Arab	16.5%
Any other mixed/multiple background	10.2%
Any other ethnic group	15.9%

Percentage point difference

Note: Chart shows age- and sex-adjusted percentage point difference, actual rates can be found in Table 8.4

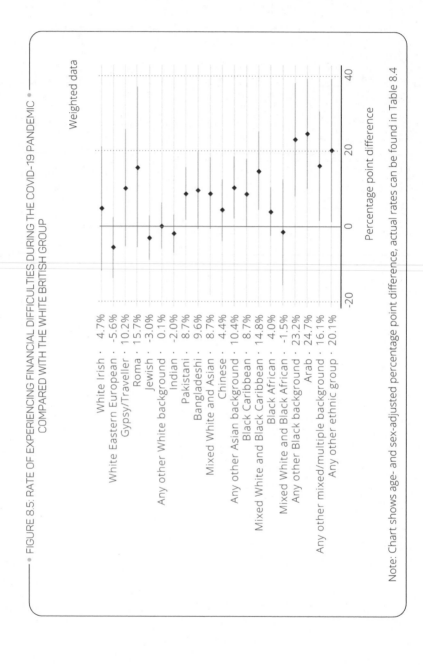

FIGURE 8.5: RATE OF EXPERIENCING FINANCIAL DIFFICULTIES DURING THE COVID-19 PANDEMIC
COMPARED WITH THE WHITE BRITISH GROUP

Weighted data

White Irish	4.7%
White Eastern European	-5.6%
Gypsy/Traveller	10.2%
Roma	15.7%
Jewish	-3.0%
Any other White background	0.1%
Indian	-2.0%
Pakistani	8.7%
Bangladeshi	9.6%
Mixed White and Asian	8.7%
Chinese	4.4%
Any other Asian background	10.4%
Black Caribbean	8.7%
Mixed White and Black Caribbean	14.8%
Black African	4.0%
Mixed White and Black African	-1.5%
Any other Black background	23.2%
Arab	24.7%
Any other mixed/multiple background	16.1%
Any other ethnic group	20.1%

Percentage point difference

-20   0   20   40

Note: Chart shows age- and sex-adjusted percentage point difference, actual rates can be found in Table 8.4

points. However, looking at the differences in financial situations during the pandemic, we see that ethnic minority groups were more likely to report struggling financially compared to the White British group – especially people from Arab (by 25 percentage points), Any other Black (by 23 percentage points), Any other (by 20 percentage points), Any other mixed (by 16 percentage points) and Mixed White and Black Caribbean (by 15 percentage points) ethnic groups. During the pandemic, no ethnic minority group was less likely to have financial difficulties compared to White British people, with ethnic inequalities further increasing compared to the pre-pandemic rates.

Income change

Table 8.5 shows income change rates by ethnic group. The highest rates of income increase during the pandemic are seen for people from Mixed White and Black African (49.9%), White Irish (25.7%), Any other Black (26.1%), Mixed White and Asian (25%) and Black African (24.9%) ethnic groups. Conversely, the highest rates of experiencing income decrease are reported by people from Roma (55.6%), Irish (41.5%), Any other Black (39.5%), Chinese (38.1%) and Gypsy/Traveller (36%) ethnic groups. The highest rates of reporting no change to their income are seen for Black Caribbean (51%), Indian (52.2%), White British (52.6%) and Eastern European (51.5%) people.

Even though, intuitively, income increase should indicate advantage, in the light of the events throughout the COVID-19 pandemic, the association might not be as straightforward. For example, key workers' workload and hours could have initially increased, resulting in higher income, but so could their exposure to the virus in addition to further psychological strain (May et al, 2021). People who had been furloughed might report decreased income, but also more savings due to reduced transport or other costs; however, such a pattern does not necessarily indicate advantage in comparison to people whose income had not changed. We could thus speculate that people whose income has remained stable are at an advantage as their financial stability was not shaken by the COVID-19 crisis.

Figure 8.6 shows the percentage point difference in reporting an income decrease compared to the White British group when controlling for differences in age and sex. We observe significantly higher rates of experiencing an income decrease for Roma (by 30 percentage points), Irish (by 15 percentage points), Any other Black (by 14 percentage points) and Chinese (by 13 percentage points) ethnic groups.

Figure 8.7 shows the percentage point difference in reporting no change in income compared to White British people, adjusted for differences in age and sex. No change in income, rather than an income increase, might hint at higher stability, both in terms of employment and finances. Less income volatility might thus indicate an overall advantage. Figure 8.7 illustrates that

TABLE 8.5: INCOME CHANGE DURING THE COVID-19
PANDEMIC, BY ETHNIC GROUP

Weighted percentage

Income change by ethnicity

	Increased	No change	Decreased	Don't know	N
White Irish	25.7	31.3	41.5	1.5	96
White Eastern European	22.7	51.5	21.0	4.8	356
Gypsy/Traveller	20.9	42.2	36.0	0.9	215
Roma	3.5	38.5	55.6	2.5	73
Jewish	20.6	47.9	29.1	2.4	463
Any other White background	24.0	41.9	28.0	6.1	630
Indian	20.7	52.2	23.5	3.5	1220
Pakistani	17.4	43.9	30.5	8.2	807
Bangladeshi	19.4	41.0	34.4	5.3	392
Mixed White and Asian	25.0	37.0	28.8	9.2	506
Chinese	17.6	38.2	38.1	6.1	648
Any other Asian background	19.2	48.8	28.2	3.9	636
Black Caribbean	19.7	51.0	26.2	3.1	545
Mixed White and Black Caribbean	20.2	40.5	34.0	5.2	344
Black African	24.9	45.5	25.6	3.9	1009
Mixed White and Black African	49.9	33.8	15.9	0.4	153
Any other Black background	26.1	31.1	39.5	3.3	162
Arab	11.5	43.9	41.8	2.8	150
Any other mixed/multiple background	25.0	44.8	22.7	7.6	356
Any other ethnic group	23.8	45.8	25.7	4.6	243
White British	20.1	52.0	26.3	1.7	3459
N	2907	5550	3494	512	12463

compared to the White British majority, no ethnic group had higher rates of experiencing stability in their income. Conversely, significantly lower rates of experiencing no change in income are seen especially for people from White Irish (by 21 percentage points), Any other Black (by 19 percentage points) and Mixed White and Asian (by 12 percentage points) backgrounds.

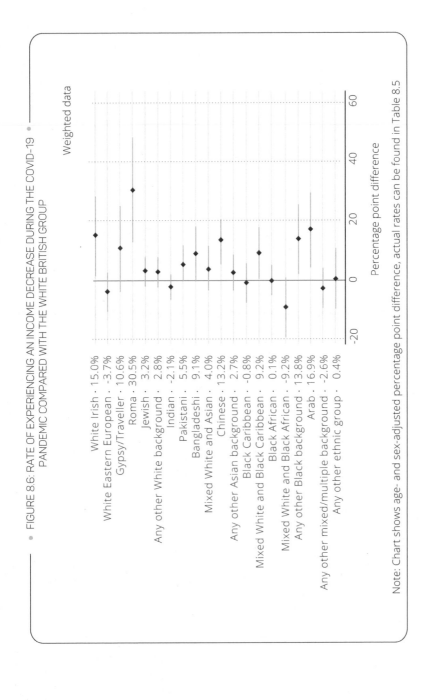

FIGURE 8.6: RATE OF EXPERIENCING AN INCOME DECREASE DURING THE COVID-19 PANDEMIC COMPARED WITH THE WHITE BRITISH GROUP

Weighted data

White Irish · 15.0%
White Eastern European · -3.7%
Gypsy/Traveller · 10.6%
Roma · 30.5%
Jewish · 3.2%
Any other White background · 2.8%
Indian · -2.1%
Pakistani · 5.5%
Bangladeshi · 9.1%
Mixed White and Asian · 4.0%
Chinese · 13.2%
Any other Asian background · 2.7%
Black Caribbean · -0.8%
Mixed White and Black Caribbean · 9.2%
Black African · 0.1%
Mixed White and Black African · -9.2%
Any other Black background · 13.8%
Arab · 16.9%
Any other mixed/multiple background · -2.6%
Any other ethnic group · 0.4%

Percentage point difference

Note: Chart shows age- and sex-adjusted percentage point difference, actual rates can be found in Table 8.5

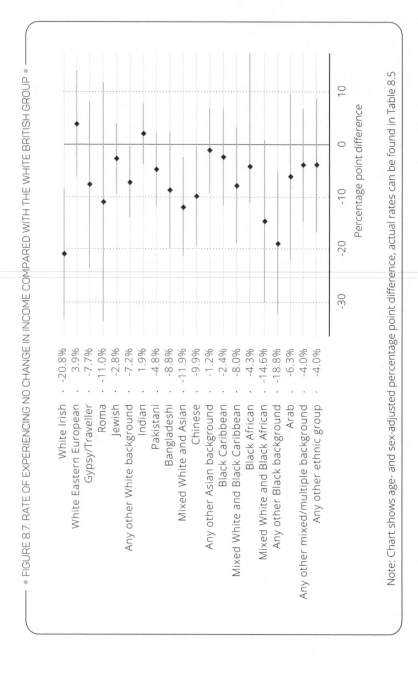

FIGURE 8.7. RATE OF EXPERIENCING NO CHANGE IN INCOME COMPARED WITH THE WHITE BRITISH GROUP

White Irish	-20.8%
White Eastern European	3.9%
Gypsy/Traveller	-7.7%
Roma	-11.0%
Jewish	-2.8%
Any other White background	-7.2%
Indian	1.9%
Pakistani	-4.8%
Bangladeshi	-8.8%
Mixed White and Asian	-11.9%
Chinese	-9.9%
Any other Asian background	-1.2%
Black Caribbean	-2.4%
Mixed White and Black Caribbean	-8.0%
Black African	-4.3%
Mixed White and Black African	-14.6%
Any other Black background	-18.8%
Arab	-6.3%
Any other mixed/multiple background	-4.0%
Any other ethnic group	-4.0%

Percentage point difference

Note: Chart shows age- and sex-adjusted percentage point difference, actual rates can be found in Table 8.5

TABLE 8.6: RECEIVING INCOME-RELATED BENEFITS, BY ETHNIC GROUP AND AGE

Weighted percentage

Yes, receiving income-related benefits by ethnicity

	Yes	18–29	30–49	50–65	N
White Irish	17.9	29.1	15.3	19.2	97
White Eastern European	29.6	32.8	29.7	11.3	350
Gypsy/Traveller	58.9	79.0	66.5	20.9	187
Roma	50.6	57.3	48.2	46.4	73
Jewish	31.7	38.9	31.1	27.9	447
Any other White background	18.0	20.7	14.6	28.1	627
Indian	21.4	30.6	18.5	19.7	1188
Pakistani	38.3	46.1	36.5	29.3	777
Bangladeshi	47.5	52.3	49.4	38.7	354
Mixed White and Asian	33.6	41.2	33.5	13.0	470
Chinese	44.0	46.2	51.6	18.3	631
Any other Asian background	30.3	28.8	36.0	19.8	608
Black Caribbean	32.4	50.1	30.0	28.6	532
Mixed White and Black Caribbean	47.4	56.1	44.1	35.8	340
Black African	33.1	33.0	37.5	23.3	983
Mixed White and Black African	42.6	64.1	28.5	26.4	148
Any other Black background	59.0	78.8	58.5	31.5	159
Arab	44.8	33.0	40.6	61.7	143
Any other mixed/multiple background	39.1	31.2	41.1	48.6	341
Any other ethnic group	44.5	44.3	39.5	61.0	240
White British	26.5	29.0	27.6	24.0	3428
N	3944	1403	1820	721	12123

Current receipt of benefits

Increase in financial difficulties during the pandemic might have led people to seek additional help from the government. We explore the receipt of benefits across ethnic groups to illustrate the levels of financial hardship experienced during the pandemic. The four main types of benefits claimed were universal credit (40.5%), council tax support or reduction (29.3%), housing benefit (24.9%) and personal independence payments (21.2%).

Table 8.6 shows that highest proportions of people receiving benefits are seen for people from Any other Black (59%), Gypsy/Traveller (58.9%), Roma (50.6%), Bangladeshi (47.5%), Mixed White and Black Caribbean (47.4%), Arab (44.8%), Any other ethnic group (44.5%) and Chinese (44%) ethnic groups. We observe different patterns of benefit receipt rates by age – while for some groups, the proportion of people claiming benefits remains quite stable across age groups (for example, Bangladeshi, White British or Indian people), for others, different patterns emerge. We see large differences in receiving benefits by age for people from Gypsy/Traveller (79% of those aged 18-29 compared to 20.9% of those aged 50-65), Any other Black (78.8% of those aged 18-29 compared to 31.5% of those aged 50-65) and Mixed White and Black African (64% of those aged 18-29 compared to 26.4% of those aged 50-65) ethnic groups. In contrast, higher rates of benefit receipt are seen for older people aged 50-65 compared to the 18-29 age group in any other (61% compared to 44.3%) and Arab (61.7% compared to 33%) ethnic groups.

Figure 8.8 shows the percentage point difference in benefits receipt compared to White British people, adjusted for differences in age and sex. Compared to the White British group, people from Gypsy/Traveller, Any other Black, Bangladeshi, Mixed White and Black Caribbean, Any other, Arab, Pakistani and Chinese ethnic groups have higher rates of receiving income-related benefits (Figure 8.8). Especially high percentage point differences are seen for people from Gypsy/Traveller (an increase by 32 percentage points) and Any other Black (31 percentage points) ethnic groups. Conversely, only people from Any other White, White Irish and Indian ethnic groups show lower rates of receiving income-related benefits compared to White British people. Such patterns show that for most ethnic minority groups, additional financial support from the government was essential during the COVID-19 pandemic.

Worries about financial situation

Table 8.7 shows that high rates of reporting being extremely worried about their financial situation are seen for people from Bangladeshi (14.9%), White Irish (13.5%), Any other (12.2%), Black African (9.4%) and Mixed White and Black Caribbean (9%) ethnic groups. Conversely, we see low rates of extreme worry in terms of financial situation for Roma (0.1%), White Eastern European (2.5%) and Chinese (3.5%) people.

Figure 8.9 shows the percentage point difference in being worried about finances compared to White British people, while controlling for differences in age and sex. Compared to the White British group, people from Arab,

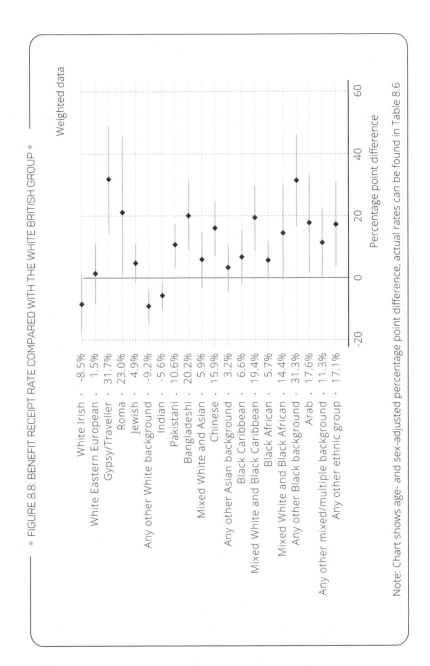

• FIGURE 8.8: BENEFIT RECEIPT RATE COMPARED WITH THE WHITE BRITISH GROUP •

Weighted data

White Irish ·	-8.5%
White Eastern European ·	1.5%
Gypsy/Traveller ·	31.7%
Roma ·	23.0%
Jewish ·	4.9%
Any other White background ·	-9.2%
Indian ·	-5.6%
Pakistani ·	10.6%
Bangladeshi ·	20.2%
Mixed White and Asian ·	5.9%
Chinese ·	15.9%
Any other Asian background ·	3.2%
Black Caribbean ·	6.6%
Mixed White and Black Caribbean ·	19.4%
Black African ·	5.7%
Mixed White and Black African ·	14.4%
Any other Black background ·	31.3%
Arab ·	17.6%
Any other mixed/multiple background ·	11.3%
Any other ethnic group ·	17.1%

Percentage point difference

Note: Chart shows age- and sex-adjusted percentage point difference, actual rates can be found in Table 8.6

TABLE 8.7: WORRIES ABOUT FINANCIAL SITUATION, BY ETHNIC GROUP

Weighted percentage

Worried about financial situation by ethnicity

	Not at all worried	Somewhat worried	Very worried	Extremely worried	N
White Irish	32.3	43.2	10.9	13.5	96
White Eastern European	27.7	52.8	17.1	2.5	356
Gypsy/Traveller	39.2	39.6	14.8	6.4	220
Roma	30.8	45.0	24.1	0.1	73
Jewish	31.0	51.8	11.6	5.6	456
Any other White background	26.6	58.2	9.6	5.6	628
Indian	28.7	50.9	11.9	8.5	1215
Pakistani	17.8	52.6	19.7	9.9	815
Bangladeshi	23.9	45.9	15.4	14.9	393
Mixed White and Asian	24.2	58.8	9.6	7.4	505
Chinese	20.3	58.9	17.4	3.5	652
Any other Asian background	23.4	48.8	19.7	8.1	641
Black Caribbean	27.9	53.2	11.4	7.6	543
Mixed White and Black Caribbean	22.2	53.7	15.1	9.0	349
Black African	27.3	52.0	11.3	9.4	1012
Mixed White and Black African	25.4	58.0	14.3	2.3	154
Any other Black background	25.0	50.2	19.3	5.5	164
Arab	17.9	41.3	32.5	8.3	146
Any other mixed/multiple background	21.4	55.6	16.1	6.9	354
Any other ethnic group	12.5	54.0	25.3	8.1	247
White British	36.4	48.4	8.7	6.5	3453
N	3230	6488	1630	1124	12472

Any other, Pakistani, Bangladeshi and Any other Asian groups show higher rates of being worried about their financial situation (Figure 8.9). The difference is especially high for Arab (by 25 percentage points), Any other (by 18 percentage points), Bangladeshi (by 14 percentage points), Pakistani (by 13 percentage points) and Any other Asian (by 12 percentage points) ethnic groups. No ethnic minority group is less likely to report being worried

Socioeconomic circumstances

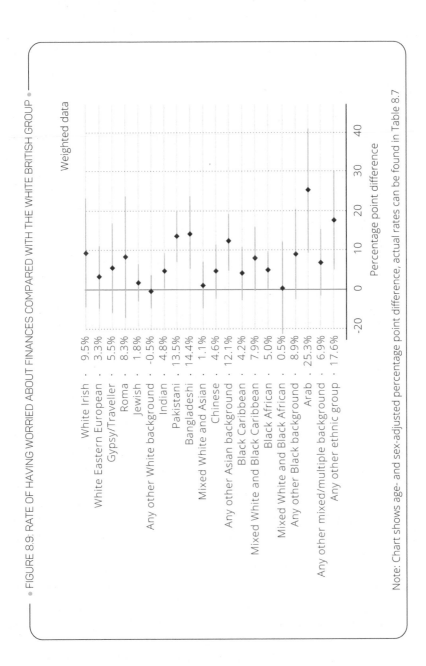

FIGURE 8.9: RATE OF HAVING WORRIED ABOUT FINANCES COMPARED WITH THE WHITE BRITISH GROUP

Weighted data

White Irish	9.5%
White Eastern European	3.3%
Gypsy/Traveller	5.5%
Roma	8.3%
Jewish	1.8%
Any other White background	-0.5%
Indian	4.8%
Pakistani	13.5%
Bangladeshi	14.4%
Mixed White and Asian	1.1%
Chinese	4.6%
Any other Asian background	12.1%
Black Caribbean	4.2%
Mixed White and Black Caribbean	7.9%
Black African	5.0%
Mixed White and Black African	0.5%
Any other Black background	8.9%
Arab	25.3%
Any other mixed/multiple background	6.9%
Any other ethnic group	17.6%

Percentage point difference

Note: Chart shows age- and sex-adjusted percentage point difference, actual rates can be found in Table 8.7

165

about finances than the White British group. For both Arab and Any other ethnic groups, high rates of financial worries correspond with high rates of reporting financial difficulties, both in pre-pandemic times as well as in the midst of the COVID-19 pandemic. Such a pattern highlights that both groups are at a considerable risk financially.

Discussion and conclusion

In this chapter, we explored ethnic inequalities in socioeconomic status (education, occupational class, tenure, receipt of benefits and financial worries), documenting pre-pandemic inequalities as well as inequalities evident during the COVID-19 pandemic. We found that ethnic minority groups show high educational attainment levels. For some ethnic minority groups, high occupational class is also more commonly observed compared to the White British groups. Despite this educational and, for some, occupational advantage, severe ethnic inequalities are apparent across most other socioeconomic domains. This is marked by lower homeownership rates, higher financial difficulties (further exacerbated by the COVID-19 pandemic), high rates of receipt of benefits and worries about finances. We note that these trends are likely due to the structural and institutional racism ethnic minority people have experienced over their life courses and continue to experience to this day (see Chapter 4), which then leads to a disjuncture between educational success and socioeconomic security.

We observe that ethnic minority people, especially those from White Irish, Indian, Black African, Any other White and Jewish ethnic groups, show significantly higher rates of having a degree-level education compared to the White British group. High rates of having no qualifications are seen especially for Roma (54.6%) and Gypsy/Traveller (51.2%) people. Similarly, although some ethnic minority groups are more likely to be in higher occupational positions, we see that ethnic minority people are more likely to be represented in the lowest occupational class of semi-routine and routine occupations compared to White British people. This is particularly pronounced for Roma, Gypsy/Traveller, Mixed White and Black Caribbean and Eastern European people.

In terms of tenure, our results show that no other ethnic minority group is more likely to own their home, both without or with a mortgage, than White British people. Nonetheless, even when owning a home, the quality of housing might differ for ethnic minorities compared to the White British (see Chapter 6). The lowest rates of owning a home are seen among Eastern European, Mixed White and Black Caribbean, Black African and Arab people. Simultaneously, these ethnic groups show very high rates of renting. In this analysis we are unable to distinguish between private and social renting. Nonetheless, either type of renting indicates a level of housing instability and could be especially damaging during the COVID-19 pandemic when paired with job and income uncertainty.

High rates of people reporting financial difficulties before the pandemic are seen for people from Arab, Any other, Mixed White and Black African and Any other Black ethnic groups. However, these rates increased further for all ethnic groups when asked about their financial situation in the midst of the COVID-19 pandemic (February–October 2021), with the exception of the Mixed White and Black African group. The highest rates of financial difficulties during the pandemic are seen for people from Arab, Any other Black, Any other and Roma ethnic groups. Compared to White British people, people from Roma, Irish, Arab, Any other Black and Chinese ethnic groups also more often reported that their income decreased during the pandemic. Nonetheless, the income decrease reported might be qualitatively very different for individuals as well as ethnic groups. It could be argued that while those people who report no change have missed out on potential gains, their financial situation as well as their employment type (see Chapter 7) remained the most stable and thus most resilient during the COVID-19 crisis. Our findings show that compared to White British people, no other ethnic group experienced more income stability, and that people from White Irish, Any other Black and Mixed White and Asian ethnic groups experienced the least stability.

Related to income (in)stability, high rates of benefit receipts were seen for people from Any other Black, Gypsy/Traveller, Roma, Bangladeshi and Chinese ethnic groups, indicating high levels of financial hardship, and also indicating that people had to seek additional governmental help due to the financial effects of the pandemic. Lowest rates of receiving income-related benefits were observed for people from White Irish (17.9%), Any other White (18%) and Indian (21.4%) ethnic groups, but these figures still show a noticeable share of people struggling in relation to their income. Moreover, some ethnic minority groups might have been less aware of the available help, and thus not claimed the benefits they were entitled to (Haque et al, 2020). Highly differentiated patterns of benefit receipt by age are seen for ethnic minority groups, while the rates for the White British group remain stable across age groups. Lastly, we observe high rates of being extremely worried about their financial situation for people from Bangladeshi, White Irish, Pakistani, Black African, Mixed White and Black Caribbean, Arab and Any other ethnic groups.

In this chapter, we illustrate ethnic differences in socioeconomic circumstances using unrivalled EVENS data mapping the lives of 21 ethnic groups in the UK. We show that despite some decrease in ethnic inequalities in educational attainment and, for some groups, occupational level, we still see large inequalities when comparing ethnic minority groups to the White British population on other socioeconomic indicators, especially in tenure, financial difficulties, income fluctuations, receipt of benefits and worries about finances. Gypsy/Traveller people are particularly disadvantaged across most domains, a finding that has not been possible to examine with survey data prior to EVENS due to the undersampling of this group. Also, people belonging to the Arab and Any other ethnic groups appear to be disproportionately struggling financially. Our findings show persistent socioeconomic inequalities for ethnic minority people in the UK, with worse outcomes related to finances having been further exacerbated by the COVID-19 pandemic. The groups considerably affected by the COVID-19 pandemic in terms of financial struggles, worries and income fluctuations are people from Arab, Any other Black, Any other, Any other mixed, Chinese, Gypsy/ Traveller, Roma, White Irish, Bangladeshi, Pakistani and Any other Asian ethnic groups. Thus, we present evidence showing that ethnic minority groups were much less immune to the socioeconomic strain of the COVID-19 outbreak compared to White British people, with some groups being severely affected while already experiencing longstanding inequalities prior to the COVID-19 crisis.

9

Political participation and Black Lives Matter

Magda Borkowska, Neema Begum, Nissa Finney and Joseph Harrison

---

Key findings

Despite experiencing adversities, ethnic minority people report relatively high levels of political trust and continue to have high levels of political engagement indicated by interest in politics and political party affiliation.

- In relation to pandemic management, people across all ethnic backgrounds are more likely to trust the Scottish Parliament, the Welsh Assembly and local mayors than the UK Parliament.
- Among ethnic minority people, the lowest levels of trust in the UK Parliament are reported by those from the Black Caribbean group, and the highest by those from Black African, Arab and Chinese groups.
- Most ethnic minority groups (with the exception of Roma, Gypsy/Traveller and White Eastern European groups) report higher levels of political interest than the White British group.
- People from the Roma group are the least likely to report having a political party preference, while the White Irish group has the highest proportion of people who identify with a political party.
- The distribution of political party preferences varies considerably across groups. Among ethnic minority people, Pakistani, Bangladeshi, Black African and Black Caribbean people report the highest support for Labour. Conservatives gain the highest share of Jewish and the lowest share of Black Caribbean votes. Highest levels of support for the Liberal Democrats are found for White Eastern European, Chinese, White Irish and White other groups.
- The highest support for the Black Lives Matter (BLM) movement is reported by Black Caribbean, Black African, and Arab groups; people from Roma, Gypsy/Traveller and White Eastern European groups are the least likely to support BLM.

Introduction

This chapter examines ethnic differences in the levels of political trust, political party preferences and attitudes towards BLM during the COVID-19 pandemic. We know that ethnic inequalities in health and some labour market outcomes were exacerbated during this time (see Chapters 5, 7 and 8), but there is little evidence on what happened to the levels of political trust and other political attitudes. This is of interest because of the crucial role of political trust for crisis management (Devine et al, 2021; Jennings et al, 2021; Zahariadis et al, 2021; Busemeyer, 2022; Goldstein and Wiedemann, 2022; Weinberg, 2022). The effectiveness of government restrictions and guidelines in relation to health protective behaviours (such as social distancing, self-isolation, vaccination and restrictions on travelling) requires trust in the government and policy makers at the national, regional and local levels. This chapter exploits the high granularity of ethnic minority categories available in the Evidence for Equality National Survey (EVENS) to compare political attitudes (including trust in different levels of government) across different ethnic groups at the time of the COVID-19 crisis. This is not only the first large-scale study on political attitudes of British ethnic minority groups during this period, but also the first large-scale survey evidence since the 2010 Ethnic Minority British Election Study.

Political trust

Political trust during the COVID-19 pandemic is usually assessed based on general population surveys with insufficient numbers of ethnic minority people for interethnic comparisons. This is an important gap in the literature because of potential implications of political trust for public behaviour and the differential impact of the pandemic on ethnic minority groups. For example, we know that some ethnic minority groups experienced particularly adverse health outcomes (see Chapter 5). Health protective behaviours such as vaccination or social distancing are some of the exemplar measures that are crucial for mitigating the higher risks of infection and complications from COVID-19. Political trust is one the key correlates of vaccine acceptance and compliance with other government-imposed measures (Han et al, 2021; Weinberg, 2022). Therefore, from the policy perspective, it is vital to understand whether there are significant interethnic differences in political trust, which could affect people's choices in relation to health protective guidelines. Given the long history of systemic ethnic discrimination (Byrne et al, 2020), which was acutely felt during the pandemic, we might expect that the levels of trust in government among ethnic minority people could be quite low. On the other hand, we know that historically ethnic minority groups expressed relatively high levels of political trust (Maxwell 2010a; Heath et al. 2013).

The general population studies (Davies et al, 2021) show that political trust fluctuated during the pandemic period, with heightened trust observed around the first lockdown, and the subsequent decline of trust to pre-pandemic levels. In relation to interethnic differences, there is little evidence on the levels of trust of ethnic minority groups in Britain during this period. At the time of writing, we found only two studies which addressed political trust question across ethnic groups: the evidence from the YouGov poll (Abraham, 2021) as well as from the five UK cohort studies (Parsons and Wiggins, 2020) suggested that ethnic minorities have lower levels of trust in the UK government than White British people.

Political interest and participation

Survey data on ethnic minority political participation is increasingly outdated. The Ethnic Minority British Election Study (EMBES), the largest representative quantitative survey of ethnic minority political behaviour, was conducted in 2010. The existing work tends to focus on ethnic differences in voter registration, voting turnout and political party choice, with somewhat less attention paid to political interest.

Historical trends show that there tend to be lower levels of registration to vote in elections among some ethnic minority groups, particularly the Black African group, 25% of whom are not on electoral registers compared to 11% of White British people (Sobolewska and Barclay, 2021). However, turnout in elections for ethnic minorities tends to be similar to the White British population (after accounting for under-registration). Ethnic minority people also do not lag behind in terms of levels of political interest or having a political party affiliation (Heath et al, 2013). Traditionally, all ethnic minority groups have expressed consistently high support for the Labour Party. For example, in the 2017 general election, the Labour Party gained 77% of the ethnic minority vote (Martin and Khan, 2019).

While ethnic minorities have generally been found to be more left-leaning and supporting more liberal parties, the Labour Party has also been credited with bringing in different forms of anti-discrimination legislation, including the 1965 Race Relations Acts and its successors. This does not mean that Labour has a blemish-free record in terms of supporting ethnic minority rights. The 1968 Commonwealth Immigrants Act further reduced the rights of Commonwealth citizens to migrate to the UK and recently Labour has been criticised for tolerating the anti-Semitism of some of its prominent members. The controversial invasion of Iraq in 2003 has also resulted in a significant loss of ethnic minority support for Labour.

Arguably, however, out of the main political parties, the Labour Party has been perceived as relatively sympathetic towards ethnic minority rights. On the contrary, the Conservative Party has been deemed more hostile towards ethnic minority and immigrant groups. Notable examples include former cabinet minister Enoch Powell's 1968 'Rivers of Blood' speech criticising Commonwealth migration to the UK and former Prime Minister Margaret Thatcher referring to Britain becoming 'swamped' by immigration. Former Prime Minister David Cameron's modernisation of the party in the 2000s aimed to move the Conservative Party away from its 'nasty party' image with a concerted effort to bring greater diversity among Conservative candidates and to appeal to ethnic minority voters, particularly the Indian group. Indeed, support for the Conservatives has increased slightly in recent years among the Indian group, who were also the most pro-Brexit ethnic minority group in the 2016 EU referendum.

Due to small sample sizes, the existing studies generally examine patterns of political behaviour of five broad ethnic minority groups (Indian, Pakistani, Bangladeshi, Black Caribbean and Black African), with almost no evidence on what these patterns look like among other ethnic groups. In this chapter we present the first evidence on political party preferences across 21 ethnic minority groups. We also take advantage of the wide coverage of EVENS to compare political party preferences for ethnic minority and majority people across England, Scotland and Wales. The time of the COVID-19 pandemic presents a unique opportunity to see how sensitive political attitudes are to the unfolding crisis situation. The 'rally around the flag' hypothesis suggests that in a time of crisis, people tend to support their political leaders more. On the other hand, the government's failure to address the uneven impact of the pandemic on ethnic minority groups could create a sense of grievance and political apathy.

Attitudes towards BLM

The COVID-19 pandemic has coincided with the murder of George Floyd by a police officer in Minneapolis in the US in May 2020. The ensuing BLM protests around the world placed racial inequalities firmly in the spotlight. Thus far, little has been known about the extent to which different ethnic minority groups in Britain support or oppose the BLM movement. As expected, the limited evidence that exists shows higher levels of support for BLM among ethnic minority people compared to White British people. However, given the strong focus of the BLM movement on police discrimination based on skin colour, it is not clear whether the level of support across different ethnic minority groups should be similarly high. The poll by Ipsos MORI conducted in 2020 shows that about 47% of White British respondents support the BLM movement compared to 75% of those who identify as ethnic minorities (Ipsos MORI, 2020). The same poll also reports that the highest support was among those who identified as Black (81%). Similar interethnic differences across broadly defined ethnic groups were found in the US. The 2020 survey conducted by the Pew Research Center (Parker et al, 2020) shows the highest level of BLM support among Black respondents (about 86%), followed by those from Hispanic (77%) and Asian (75%) backgrounds. In the same survey, the level of BLM support among White Americans was around 60%. Younger respondents (irrespective of ethnic background) also reported more positive attitudes towards BLM than older ones.

This chapter brings new evidence into our understanding of political trust and political attitudes during a global health crisis. In the next, empirical section, we first look at the patterns of political trust in different levels of government (national, subnational, mayoral and local) and examine how they compare across ethnic minority groups. We then turn to questions on the levels of political interest and political party support, and in the last section, we examine levels of support and opposition towards the BLM movement. In the final section of the chapter, we discuss our results in the context of past trends and reflect on what they mean in view of the ethnic minority experiences during the COVID-19 pandemic.

Ethnic differences in political trust across levels of the UK government

The EVENS survey asked all respondents to what extent they trusted the UK Parliament in relation to its management of the coronavirus outbreak. Those living in Scotland and Wales were also asked how much they trusted the Scottish Parliament/Welsh Assembly respectively in their management of the coronavirus outbreak. The last question in relation to trust considered those living in local authorities with directly elected mayors and asked how much they trusted their mayor in terms of handling the COVID-19 outbreak. Figure 9.1 shows the likelihood that people would generally trust the UK Parliament in handling the pandemic for each ethnic group in EVENS.

All ethnic minority groups (except for Black Caribbean) expressed more trust in the UK Parliament's ability to handle the pandemic than the White British group. Overall, approximately 35% of White British respondents said they generally trust Parliament in terms of managing the pandemic. This figure dropped to 34% when we adjusted the predicted probability of trust for age and sex composition of the White British group. The highest levels of trust (over 60%) were reported by those from Arab (72%), Black African (72%), Chinese (68%), Other Asian (64%), Any other (62%) and Indian (61%) ethnic groups. Some of the white groups (Jewish, White Irish and Other White) and some of the mixed groups (White and Black African,

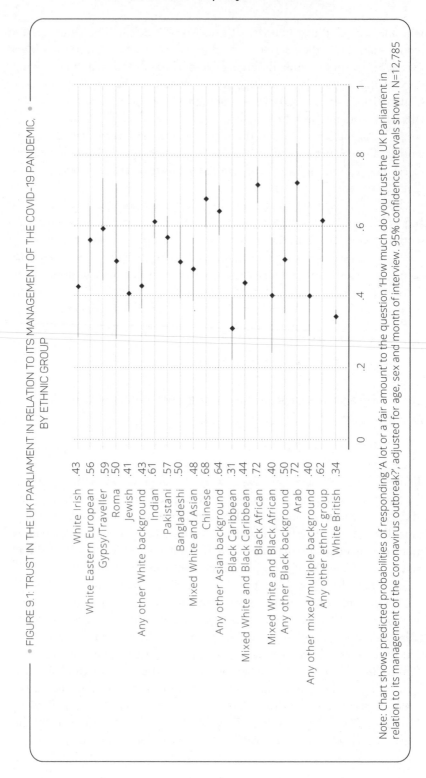

● FIGURE 9.1: TRUST IN THE UK PARLIAMENT IN RELATION TO ITS MANAGEMENT OF THE COVID-19 PANDEMIC, ●
BY ETHNIC GROUP

White Irish	.43
White Eastern European	.56
Gypsy/Traveller	.59
Roma	.50
Jewish	.41
Any other White background	.43
Indian	.61
Pakistani	.57
Bangladeshi	.50
Mixed White and Asian	.48
Chinese	.68
Any other Asian background	.64
Black Caribbean	.31
Mixed White and Black Caribbean	.44
Black African	.72
Mixed White and Black African	.40
Any other Black background	.50
Arab	.72
Any other mixed/multiple background	.40
Any other ethnic group	.62
White British	.34

Note: Chart shows predicted probabilities of responding 'A lot or a fair amount' to the question 'How much do you trust the UK Parliament in relation to its management of the coronavirus outbreak?', adjusted for age, sex and month of interview. 95% confidence intervals shown. N=12,785

White and Black Caribbean, and Other mixed) expressed somewhat lower levels of trust (around 40%) compared to other ethnic minority groups. Interestingly, White Eastern European people had much higher levels of trust (around 56%) compared to the Other White group. The lowest probability of trusting the UK Parliament (31%) was reported by those from a Black Caribbean background, but the difference between Black Caribbean and White British groups was not statically significant (at 95% confidence level).

The large geographical coverage of EVENS allows us to compare broad patterns of trust in the UK Parliament between different constituent countries of Britain. Figure 9.2 shows the percentage of people from non-White British and White British backgrounds living in England, Scotland and Wales who declared they generally trust the UK Parliament. Among White British respondents, the level of trust was significantly higher in England (37%), compared to Scotland (24%) and Wales (27%), whereas among ethnic minority respondents the level of trust was very high in both Wales (61%) and England (52%) and somewhat lower (41%) in Scotland. Although the nominal difference between ethnic minority trust in England and Wales seems substantial (nine percentage points), it was not statistically significant at the 95% confidence level.

With respect to trust in devolved governments, the evidence from EVENS suggests that people from both White British and ethnic minority backgrounds are much more likely to trust the Scottish Parliament and the Welsh Assembly than the UK Parliament. For most ethnic groups, the level of devolved government's trust is over 60%. Figure 9.3 and Figure 9.4 report predicted probabilities of having trust in the Scottish Parliament and the Welsh Assembly, respectively. We report the results for all ethnic groups. However, the smaller number of respondents in Scotland and Wales means we cannot confidently make detailed interethnic comparisons in these two UK countries and, instead, we only comment on broad patterns of trust among ethnic minority and White British groups. Similar to the levels of trust in the UK Parliament, ethnic minority people show higher levels of trust in their devolved governments than the White British group, but the difference between ethnic minority and White British with respect to a regional level of trust is much smaller than that for trust in the UK Parliament.

Our final question on political trust considered trust in local mayors. As shown in Figure 9.5, people from most ethnic groups are somewhat more likely to trust their local mayors than the UK Parliament, but less likely to trust the mayors than the devolved governments. Among White British, around 50% of respondents said they generally trust their mayors, which is about 15 percentage points more than levels of trust in the UK Parliament and about 10 percentage points less than levels of trust in the Scottish Parliament or the Welsh Assembly. Similar to other types of political trust, most ethnic minority groups have more trust in their local mayor than

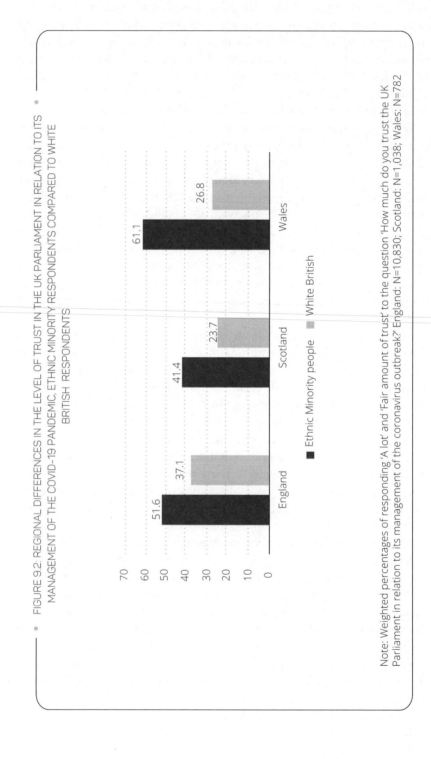

FIGURE 9.2: REGIONAL DIFFERENCES IN THE LEVEL OF TRUST IN THE UK PARLIAMENT IN RELATION TO ITS MANAGEMENT OF THE COVID-19 PANDEMIC, ETHNIC MINORITY RESPONDENTS COMPARED TO WHITE BRITISH RESPONDENTS

Note: Weighted percentages of responding 'A lot' and 'Fair amount of trust' to the question 'How much do you trust the UK Parliament in relation to its management of the coronavirus outbreak?' England: N=10,830; Scotland: N=1,038; Wales: N=782

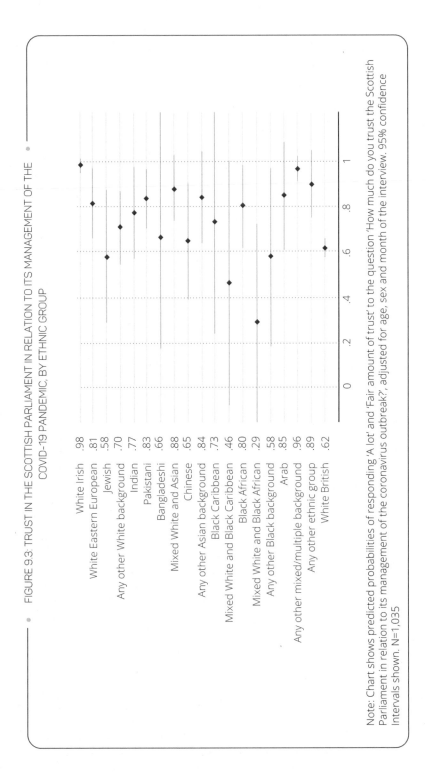

FIGURE 9.3: TRUST IN THE SCOTTISH PARLIAMENT IN RELATION TO ITS MANAGEMENT OF THE COVID-19 PANDEMIC, BY ETHNIC GROUP

Note: Chart shows predicted probabilities of responding 'A lot' and 'Fair amount of trust' to the question 'How much do you trust the Scottish Parliament in relation to its management of the coronavirus outbreak?', adjusted for age, sex and month of the interview. 95% confidence intervals shown. N=1,035

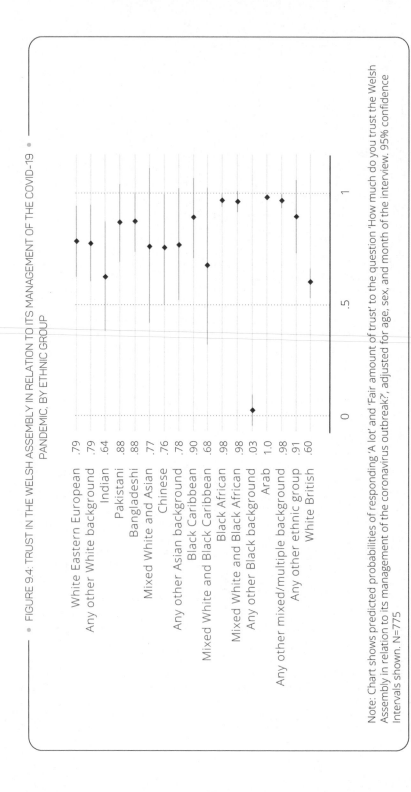

• FIGURE 9.4: TRUST IN THE WELSH ASSEMBLY IN RELATION TO ITS MANAGEMENT OF THE COVID-19 •
PANDEMIC, BY ETHNIC GROUP

White Eastern European	.79
Any other White background	.79
Indian	.64
Pakistani	.88
Bangladeshi	.88
Mixed White and Asian	.77
Chinese	.76
Any other Asian background	.78
Black Caribbean	.90
Mixed White and Black Caribbean	.68
Black African	.98
Mixed White and Black African	.98
Any other Black background	.03
Arab	1.0
Any other mixed/multiple background	.98
Any other ethnic group	.91
White British	.60

Note: Chart shows predicted probabilities of responding 'A lot' and 'Fair amount of trust' to the question 'How much do you trust the Welsh Assembly in relation to its management of the coronavirus outbreak?', adjusted for age, sex, and month of the interview. 95% confidence Intervals shown. N=775

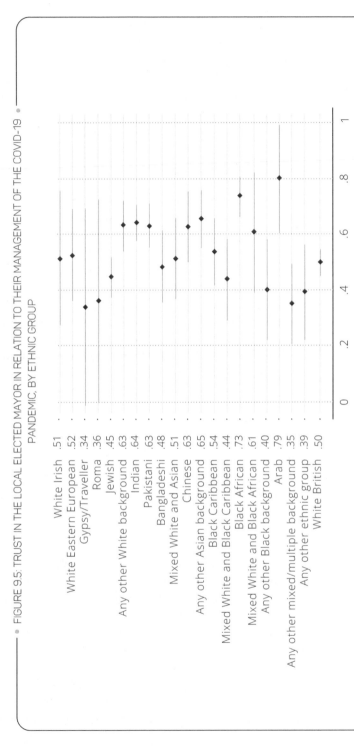

FIGURE 9.5: TRUST IN THE LOCAL ELECTED MAYOR IN RELATION TO THEIR MANAGEMENT OF THE COVID-19 PANDEMIC, BY ETHNIC GROUP

White Irish	.51
White Eastern European	.52
Gypsy/Traveller	.34
Roma	.36
Jewish	.45
Any other White background	.63
Indian	.64
Pakistani	.63
Bangladeshi	.48
Mixed White and Asian	.51
Chinese	.63
Any other Asian background	.65
Black Caribbean	.54
Mixed White and Black Caribbean	.44
Black African	.73
Mixed White and Black African	.61
Any other Black background	.40
Arab	.79
Any other mixed/multiple background	.35
Any other ethnic group	.39
White British	.50

Note: Chart shows predicted probabilities of responding 'A lot' and 'Fair amount of trust' to the question 'How much do you trust your elected [named area and mayor] in relation to their management of the coronavirus outbreak?', adjusted for age, sex and month of the interview. 95% confidence intervals shown. N=5,519

their White British counterparts. Somewhat lower levels of trust in local mayors were reported by the Gypsy/Traveller, Roma, Other mixed, Other Black and Any other groups, but the difference between these groups and the White British group was not statistically significant. However, we need to note here that in our sample, those who answered the question about trust in local mayors had a high proportion of London-based respondents, which means the results might not be generalisable to all local authorities with directly elected mayors.

Ethnic differences in political interest

Interest in politics is a key dimension of democratic engagement. EVENS asked respondents 'How interested would you say you are in politics?', measured on a scale from 1 (Very interested) to 4 (Not at all interested). On average, as shown in Figure 9.6, between 60% and 80% of respondents reported being at least fairly interested in politics (when the age and gender composition of different ethnic groups was accounted for). The level of political interest was the lowest among the Roma group (31%) and the highest among White Irish (83%) and Jewish (81%) groups. Those from Eastern European and Gypsy/Traveller backgrounds had the same levels of political interest as the White British group (around 60%), whereas all other ethnic minority groups (except Roma) were more likely to report being interested in politics.

Ethnic differences in political affiliation

With respect to political party preferences, the EVENS respondents were asked 'If there were a UK general election tomorrow, which party would you vote for?', with an option to choose from seven main UK political parties, specify an 'Other' party, indicate a lack of political party preference, a lack of voting intention or declare an ineligibility to vote. In this analysis, people who self-identified as ineligible to vote were excluded. Figure 9.7 shows the likelihood that people from different ethnic groups expressed a political party preference. On average, between 60% and 80% of respondents indicated having a political party preference, which is similar to the proportion of people who reported having at least a fair amount of political interest. Relative to the White British group (73%), a higher proportion of people from White Irish (84%), Jewish (80%), Pakistani (79%) and Bangladeshi (79%) backgrounds declared having a political party affiliation. In contrast, a relatively low proportion of people from the Roma (33%), Other Black (52%), Any other (60%), White and Asian (62%), and White Eastern European (63%) groups reported a political party preference.

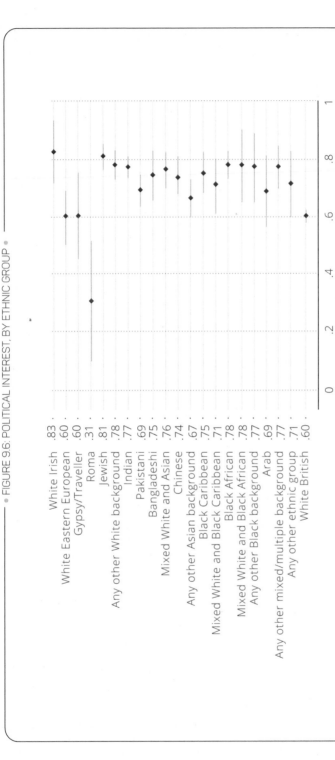

● FIGURE 9.6: POLITICAL INTEREST, BY ETHNIC GROUP ●

White Irish .83
White Eastern European .60
Gypsy/Traveller .60
Roma .31
Jewish .81
Any other White background .78
Indian .77
Pakistani .69
Bangladeshi .75
Mixed White and Asian .76
Chinese .74
Any other Asian background .67
Black Caribbean .75
Mixed White and Black Caribbean .71
Black African .78
Mixed White and Black African .78
Any other Black background .77
Arab .69
Any other mixed/multiple background .77
Any other ethnic group .71
White British .60

Note: Chart shows predicted probabilities of responding 'Very' and 'Fairly interested' to the question 'How interested would you say you are in politics?', adjusted for age and sex. 95% confidence intervals shown. N=12,411

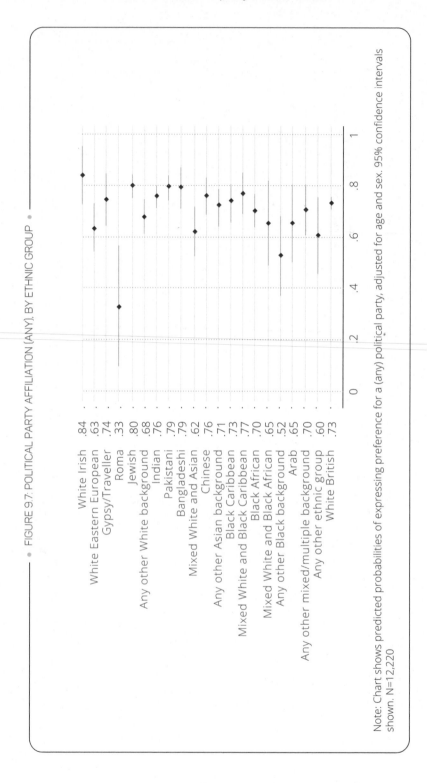

● FIGURE 9.7: POLITICAL PARTY AFFILIATION (ANY), BY ETHNIC GROUP ●

Note: Chart shows predicted probabilities of expressing preference for a (any) political party, adjusted for age and sex. 95% confidence intervals shown. N=12,220

Figure 9.8 considers how patterns of political party preferences differ across ethnic groups. It shows that Labour still garners the majority of the ethnic minority vote, although there is a significant variation across groups. The highest support for Labour (over 60%) is found among Pakistani, Bangladeshi, Black African and Black Caribbean groups, whereas the lowest (30% or lower) is found among those from Chinese, Other Black, White Eastern European and Jewish groups. In our sample, the White British vote is split evenly between Labour and the Conservatives, with 35% of respondents supporting Labour and 35% supporting the Conservatives. Support for the Conservatives is the highest among those from a Jewish background (50%), followed by Indian (37%), Chinese (37%) and Other Black (36%). Liberal Democrats can count on a significant proportion of the White Eastern European (30%), Chinese (26%), Other White (20%) and White Irish (18%) vote, whereas the Greens do best among those from Roma (21%), Other White (17%), White and Black Caribbean (17%), White Eastern European (16%), Black Caribbean (14%) and Gypsy/Traveller (13%) backgrounds. The ability to observe clear, distinctive patterns of political party preferences among those from Roma, Gypsy/Traveller, Jewish, White Eastern European and Chinese groups is unique to EVENS. Previously we had very little evidence on political party preferences of these ethnic groups.

Ethnic differences in political affiliation across the constituent countries of Britain

There are stark differences in political affiliation between the White British majority and ethnic minority voters in the constituent countries of Britain, as shown in Figure 9.9. In England, ethnic minority people have much higher support for Labour compared to the White British majority (49% versus 36%), whereas in Scotland and Wales, both ethnic minority and White British people report similar levels of Labour affiliation. Support for the Scottish National Party (SNP) among ethnic minority voters is also on a par with the White British majority in Scotland (around 52%). As expected, there is a generally lower level of Conservative support in Scotland (14–15%) and Wales (19–25%) compared to England (26–39%) among both White British and ethnic minority people. Liberal Democrats in Wales turn out to be a more popular choice among ethnic minority groups compared to White British voters (16% vs 3%), whereas in England and Scotland, this is on a par with the White British majority. In contrast, support for Plaid Cymru in Wales is much lower among ethnic minority (11%) compared to White British (20%) voters. The Green Party fares better with minority voters (8%) in Scotland compared to the White British (4%) majority.

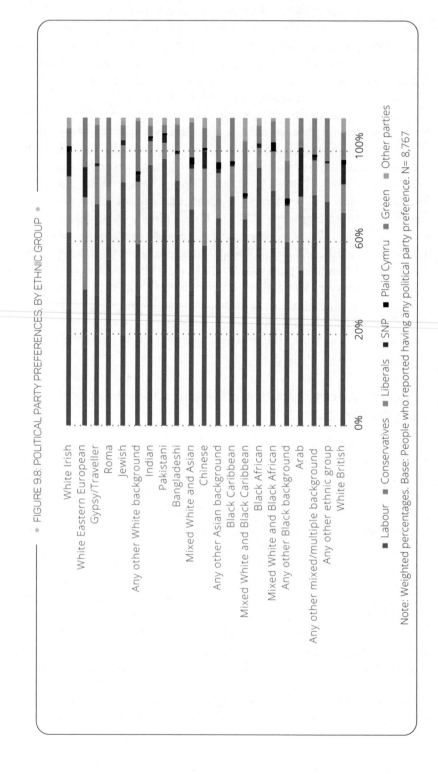

● FIGURE 9.8: POLITICAL PARTY PREFERENCES, BY ETHNIC GROUP ●

Note: Weighted percentages. Base: People who reported having any political party preference. N= 8,767

■ Labour ■ Conservatives ■ Liberals ■ SNP ■ Plaid Cymru ■ Green ■ Other parties

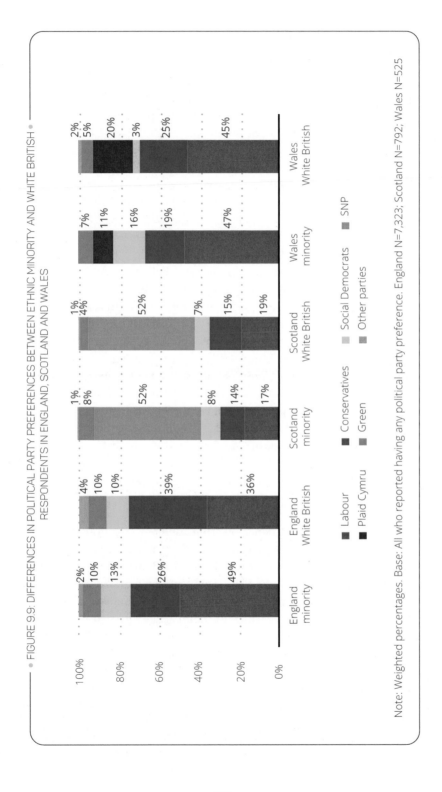

● FIGURE 9.9: DIFFERENCES IN POLITICAL PARTY PREFERENCES BETWEEN ETHNIC MINORITY AND WHITE BRITISH ● RESPONDENTS IN ENGLAND, SCOTLAND AND WALES

Note: Weighted percentages. Base: All who reported having any political party preference. England N=7,323; Scotland N=792; Wales N=525

Ethnic differences in support for BLM

To shed light on the BLM support across different ethnic groups in Britain, EVENS asked 'To what extent do you support or oppose the Black Lives Matter movement?', measured on a five-point scale from 1 (strongly support) to 5 (strongly oppose). Figure 9.10 reports the predicted probabilities of supporting the BLM movement for people from different ethnic groups. On average, a little over half of the White British respondents (55%) declare support for the BLM movement. With a few exceptions, the level of BLM support among ethnic minority groups is considerably higher. Particularly strong support is reported by those from Black Caribbean (78%), Black African (78%), Arab (78%) and White Irish (78%) groups, followed by those from Pakistani (77%), Indian (76%) and Bangladeshi (73%) backgrounds. People who identify as Jewish, Chinese, those with different mixed backgrounds and those who belong to Any other Black groups report somewhat lower levels of support (between 57% % and 70% declare they support BLM). People from Roma, Gypsy/Traveller and White Eastern European backgrounds are the least likely to support BLM, with estimates ranging from 28% to 41% for people from these groups, which is significantly less than the estimated level of support among the White British group. Importantly, however, most people who do not support BLM report neutral attitudes. The opposition towards BLM is generally low, especially among ethnic minority respondents (Figure 9.10). The highest proportion of people who oppose the BLM movement is found among those from Roma, Jewish, White Eastern European, Any other and White British backgrounds (between 20% and 35%).

Discussion

EVENS provides unique evidence on ethnic differences in political attitudes during the turbulent time of the COVID-19 pandemic. This chapter has shown that, despite continuous experience of disadvantage, most ethnic minority people report higher levels of trust in national, regional and local governments compared to White British respondents. We do not find evidence of political alienation of ethnic minority people in relation to other indicators of political engagement such as interest in politics and having a political party affiliation. Similar to the measures of trust, most ethnic minority respondents score higher on our political engagement measures than their White British counterparts. This, however, does not mean that people from ethnic minority backgrounds are indifferent to ethnic discrimination. The support for the BLM movement is very high across most ethnic minority groups, which can be interpreted as a strong voice against experienced injustice.

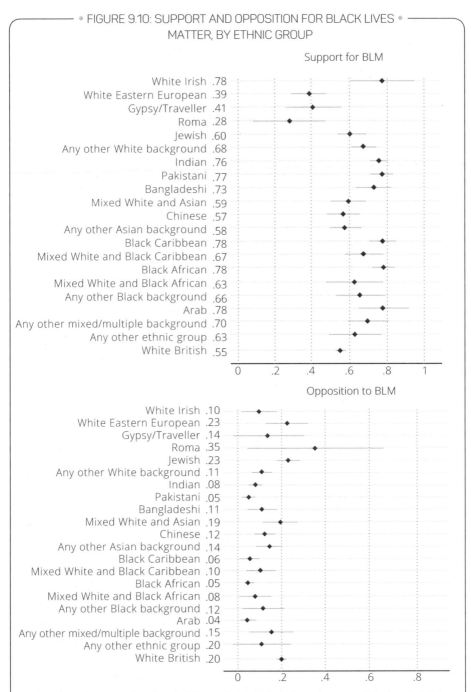

FIGURE 9.10: SUPPORT AND OPPOSITION FOR BLACK LIVES
MATTER, BY ETHNIC GROUP

Support for BLM

White Irish .78
White Eastern European .39
Gypsy/Traveller .41
Roma .28
Jewish .60
Any other White background .68
Indian .76
Pakistani .77
Bangladeshi .73
Mixed White and Asian .59
Chinese .57
Any other Asian background .58
Black Caribbean .78
Mixed White and Black Caribbean .67
Black African .78
Mixed White and Black African .63
Any other Black background .66
Arab .78
Any other mixed/multiple background .70
Any other ethnic group .63
White British .55

Opposition to BLM

White Irish .10
White Eastern European .23
Gypsy/Traveller .14
Roma .35
Jewish .23
Any other White background .11
Indian .08
Pakistani .05
Bangladeshi .11
Mixed White and Asian .19
Chinese .12
Any other Asian background .14
Black Caribbean .06
Mixed White and Black Caribbean .10
Black African .05
Mixed White and Black African .08
Any other Black background .12
Arab .04
Any other mixed/multiple background .15
Any other ethnic group .20
White British .20

Note: Chart shows predicted probabilities of responding chart shows predicted probabilities of reporting 'Strongly support/oppose' and 'Tend to support/oppose' to the question 'To what extent do you support or oppose the Black Lives Matter movement?', adjusted for age and sex. 95% confidence intervals shown. N=12,200

Political trust

Consistent with pre-pandemic periods, we find that, during the COVID-19 crisis, ethnic minority people tended to trust the UK Parliament more than White British people did. The patterns of political trust for six broad ethnic groups (Indian, Pakistani, Bangladeshi, Black Caribbean, Black African and Mixed Black/White) sampled in the EMBES 2010 survey (the last nationally representative UK survey of ethnic minorities' political attitudes) are similar to those found in EVENS. In both surveys (conducted 11 years apart), Black Caribbean and Mixed Black/White groups were less likely to trust the UK Parliament than Indian, Pakistani, Bangladeshi and Black African groups. In 2010, however, the level of trust among the Black Caribbean and Mixed Black/White groups was lower than the level of trust among the White British group, whereas during the COVID-19 pandemic, it was on par with the White British group. It might be that, during times of crisis, even the sceptics tend to have more faith that political leaders will act responsibly in order to manage a global health threat. The notable differences in the levels of trust between different ethnic minority groups might to some extent reflect the differences in experiences of racism and discrimination (see Chapter 4). Unsurprisingly, perceptions of institutional discrimination and trust in democratic institutions often go hand in hand (Maxwell, 2010b).

Existing research points to two factors that can be used to interpret the relatively high levels of political trust among Arab, Chinese, Other Asian, Jewish and White Eastern European groups. First, a significant proportion of people from these ethnic groups are foreign-born and the literature suggests that immigrants tend to express more favourable opinions about the quality of democracy and its institutions in their new country (Maxwell, 2010a, 2010b). Second, a sizeable proportion of people from these groups are likely to be born in countries with less well-functioning democracies than the UK (at least according to commonly used measures of quality of democracy such as polity2 [Teorell et al, 2020]). We can speculate that their positive opinion of the UK Parliament might be a relative one, as comparison is made between government performance in their origin countries and the performance of the UK government. The rationale for the relatively high level of trust reported by those from Gypsy/Traveller and Roma backgrounds is less clear, given that both groups have been traditionally politically marginalised and, for these reasons, we would expect them to have relatively low levels of trust. To date, however, we have had no quantitative evidence on political attitudes of these groups and further work in this area is undoubtedly required.

The generally higher level of trust in devolved governments reported by EVENS respondents is in line with the existing evidence from the polls (ONS, 2022; Scottish Government, 2022; YouGov, 2022). However, what is interesting here is that the higher levels of trust in the Scottish Parliament/ Welsh Assembly are equally, or even more so, felt by ethnic minority respondents as the White British respondents. None of the quantitative surveys to date was explicitly able to compare the levels of trust in central and devolved governments for White British and ethnic minority groups. The EVENS finding of elevated political trust for some ethnic minority groups warrants further investigation.

Political interest

This chapter has shown that ethnic minority people were slightly more likely than White British people to be interested in politics. This is generally in line with the past evidence from the 2010 EMBES (Heath et al, 2013), as well as more recent evidence from the 2021 Joseph Rowntree Reform Trust bespoke poll (Sobolewska and Barkley 2021). However, we note some differences compared to previously reported patterns. The 2010 EMBES showed that people from Pakistani and Bangladeshi backgrounds were somewhat less likely to be interested in politics than White British people, whereas EVENS suggests that all ethnic minority groups (that were included in both surveys) reported similar or slightly higher levels of political interest than White British people.

A few explanations can be posited for these differences. First, the higher levels of political interest among ethnic minority people found in EVENS might be due to the age and generational composition of the EVENS sample compared to the EMBES 2010. Over the past 11 years, immigration patterns and demographic momentum have meant that the proportion of ethnic minority people born in the UK has increased, which could have affected the relative patterns of political engagement across ethnic groups.

Second, the EVENS ethnic minority sample is slightly younger than the EMBES sample; due to the online nature of questionnaire completion, it is likely that some of the least politically engaged young respondents were not covered in the EVENS sample, as it is generally expected that political interest and the likelihood of completing online social surveys are positively correlated. Finally, it is also important to keep in mind that the 2010 EMBES asked respondents two separate questions about interest in 'British politics' and interest in 'home country' politics, whereas EVENS asked about interest in 'politics' more generally. It is unlikely that this would have a major impact on the patterns of responses, as Heath et al (2013) have shown that interest in 'home country' and 'British politics' go hand in hand, suggesting that people who are politically engaged tend to follow political debates in multiple country contexts.

With respect to the political interest of groups that are not usually the focus of political research largely due to the previous lack of quantitative data, those from Jewish and White Irish backgrounds are the most likely to report at least a fair amount of interest in politics. On the contrary, those from Roma, Gypsy/Traveller and White Eastern European backgrounds tend to be the least interested in politics. Despite the lack of a direct source of comparative survey data for these groups, plausible interpretations can be made for the observed patterns. For example, some of the common correlates of political interest include high levels of education, a high sense of belonging to the country and having citizenship or voting rights. These reasons could help us understand why people from Jewish background are likely to report relatively high levels of political interest (as shown in Chapters 3 and 8, Jewish people have some of the highest levels of education and a sense of belonging to British society across ethnic groups). A relatively high education level (see Chapter 8) and the privileged access to voting in the UK elections (Johnston, 2021) among the White Irish group might also partially explain why White Irish people are more likely to report positive political interest. On the contrary, the socioeconomic marginalisation of Roma and Gypsy/Traveller groups can be linked to higher levels of political alienation.

The Eastern European case of relatively low levels of political interest is a novel and interesting finding from EVENS. On the one hand, the traditionally low naturalisation rates of migrants from the post-2004 EU accession countries (Fernandez-Reino and Sumption, 2022) as well as generally low levels of political trust and political participation in Eastern European countries (Hooghe and Quintelier, 2014; OECD 2021) provide plausible reasons for why we could expect low levels of political interest among this group. On the other hand, in the post-Brexit reality, one could expect that the increased political salience of immigration, especially from the Eastern European EU countries, together with the recent increase in citizenship applications made by Eastern Europeans (Fernandez-Reino and Sumption, 2022), could have led to heightened political interest among this group. The results from EVENS suggest that the actual political interest of this group is somewhere in the middle – Eastern Europeans are equally as likely to be politically interested as White British people, but less likely to be interested than other ethnic minority groups (except Gypsy/Traveller and Roma groups).

Political affiliation

High support for the Labour Party among ethnic minority people has traditionally been attributed to the idea of 'linked fate', which can be broadly understood as a belief that the fate of one's ethnic group affects individual life chances. In other words, when people feel they are not getting their fair share of resources because of their ethnicity, they are more likely to vote in order to further their interests as a group rather than just as individuals. For example, Dawson (1994) found that in the US, African Americans vote for the Democrats because it is the party they associate with promoting the interests of Black people as a group. As members of a discriminated ethnic minority group, their fates are 'linked' to one another, which results in a shared political agenda. Similarly, the idea of 'relative ethnic deprivation' (Vanneman and Pettigrew, 1972) is linked to ethnic minority voter support for left-wing parties that have traditionally promoted policies to provide welfare and equalise society socioeconomically. Higher support for the Conservatives among the Indian group, for example, has been attributed to them having a weaker sense of relative ethnic deprivation (Heath et al, 2011).

The EVENS analysis in this chapter has demonstrated the continuing trend of historically low support for the Conservatives among Black Caribbean people. The policing of Black communities under the Conservative governments (2010–22) as well as the Windrush Scandal (Byrne et al, 2020) are factors that might have contributed to the continuation of this trend. The relatively high levels of support for the Liberal Democrats among the Chinese, White Irish, White Eastern European and White Other groups may be related to their pro-EU membership stance and relatively pro-immigration position (Liberal Democrats, 2019).

The analyses presented in this chapter reveals new patterns of political affiliation across ethnic minority groups. In the absence of other recent evidence or polling the interpretations are rather speculative and further research on ethnic differences in voting motivations is needed to complement the EVENS analysis.

BLM

The findings on the high levels of support for BLM across ethnic minority groups (with the exception of the Roma and Gypsy/Traveller groups) can be interpreted as an expression of past and contemporary experiences of racism and discrimination (see Chapter 4) and the levels of perceived ethnic inequalities in the UK. Historically, levels of police discrimination have been arguably highest among the Black Caribbean group, which also tends to report the highest perceived levels of ethnic discrimination (Maxwell, 2012; Heath et al, 2013; see also Chapter 4). On the other hand, White Eastern Europeans usually report some of the lowest levels of ethnic discrimination, with Chinese and Jewish people situated somewhere in the middle. Those from a White Irish background, despite being less exposed to ethnic discrimination (see Chapter 4), tend to express relatively a low level of political trust, which together with their longstanding ambiguous position as both ethnic insiders and outsiders (Walter, 2001) might help to explain why they might be particularly sensitive to racial injustice matters.

The influence of country of origin is also likely to play a role in support for BLM, especially among immigrants. Given that all Eastern European respondents in EVENS are first-generation immigrants, their low level of support for BLM might reflect the relative absence of racial equality discourse in most Eastern European countries and a relatively high prevalence of xenophobic attitudes in these countries (Eurobarometer, 2019). However, the relatively low levels of support for BLM among the Roma and Gypsy/Traveller groups are somewhat more difficult to interpret. On the one hand, these groups have been highly marginalised and exposed to ethnic discrimination, including discrimination by the police, so one might expect that the BLM movement should particularly resonate with their experiences. On the other hand, they might have a sense of being forgotten, given that the incidents of police violence against people from Gypsy/Traveller and Roma backgrounds are rarely picked up by the national media and, even if they are, public outrage in response to such reports seems to be much quieter. Furthermore, the relatively low level of political interest among these groups suggests that they are generally more disconnected from political debates, which might affect their level of engagement with the BLM movement.

Conclusion

This chapter demonstrates that in the time of COVID-19 crisis, most ethnic minority groups in Britain expressed relatively high levels of political trust in central and devolved governments in relation to pandemic management. This might be somewhat surprising given the hardships experienced by ethnic minority people during the COVID-19 pandemic. Most ethnic minority groups also express equally high or higher levels of political interest compared to the White British group and do not lag behind this group in terms of having political party affiliation. However, the level of support for different political parties differs significantly across ethnic groups. Some of these patterns, such as generally high levels of support for the Labour Party among ethnic minority people, are in line with the long-term trends; other findings, such as a relatively high level of support for the Conservatives and/or the Liberal Democrats among Chinese, Jewish, Any Other Black, Eastern Europeans, White Irish and White other groups, represent the first quantitative, nationally representative evidence on political party preferences for these groups. For the first time, we are also able to show comparative statistics of political engagement and political trust for the Gypsy/Traveller and Roma groups. We find that Gypsy/Traveller patterns of political engagement and trust are generally similar to those of other ethnic minority groups, but that people from a Roma background feel particularly politically alienated. We also find that not all ethnic minority people are equally likely to support the BLM movement – those from Roma, Gypsy/Traveller and

White European backgrounds tend to feel less positively about the BLM. Although the descriptive findings in relation to the political engagement differences of the groups about which we knew very little are illuminating in their own right, further work is needed to uncover the key drivers and mechanisms behind these apparent differences.

Box 9.1: Political participation and Black Lives Matter: measures and methods

All the analyses in this chapter use propensity score weights, which have been implemented using the svy package in Stata 16.

Figures 9.1, 9.3, 9.4, 9.5, 9.6, 9.7 and 9.10 report predicted probabilities based on logistic regression models adjusted for age and sex (all models) and month of the interview (models of political trust). This is to account for the fact that these demographic characteristics are strongly associated with political attitudes and behaviours. However, in most cases, the models adjusted for the respondent's age and sex do not alter the differences between ethnic groups observed when no demographic characteristics are controlled for. Given that levels of political trust fluctuated considerably during the pandemic (Davies et al, 2021), accounting for the month of survey completion is particularly important in the models of trust compared to other political outcomes that are less time sensitive. The predicted probabilities can be interpreted as the predicted proportion of people who reported outcome y (that is, trusted the UK Parliament), after respondents' age and sex were taken into account.

Figures 9.2, 9.8 and 9.9 report weighted percentages for ethnic groups without any additional adjustments.

Variable coding:

Trust in the UK Parliament/Scottish Parliament/Welsh Assembly/local mayor is based on the following question(s): 'How much do you trust the UK Parliament (GOV01)/ Scottish Parliament (GOV02)/Welsh Assembly(GOV03)/local mayor (GOV04) in relation to its management of the coronavirus outbreak? 1. A lot; 2. A fair amount; 3. Not very much; 4. Not at all.' Responses 1 and 2 are coded as (1) 'generally trusting' and responses 3 and 4 are coded as (2) 'generally not trusting'.

Political interest is based on the following question: 'How interested would you say you are in politics? (GOV05) 1. Very interested; 2. Fairly interested; 3. Not very interested; 4. Not at all interested.' Responses 1 and 2 are coded as (1) 'generally interested in politics' and responses 3 and 4 are coded as (2) 'generally not interested in politics'.

Political party affiliation is measured by the following question: 'If there were a UK general election tomorrow, which party would you vote for? (GOV06) 1. Labour; 2. Conservatives; 3. Liberal Democrats; 4. Scottish National Party (SNP); 5. Plaid Cymru; 6. Green Party; 7. Reform UK (previously known as the Brexit Party); 8. Other (please specify); 9. I would not vote; 10. I am not eligible to vote; 11. Don't know; 12. Prefer not to say.' Respondents who self-identified as non-eligible are excluded from the analysis. Those who replied 'don't know' or 'would not vote' are coded as (0) 'no political party preference'. Respondents who chose any political party are coded as 1 'Has political party preference'.

Support for Black Lives Matter is based on the following question: 'To what extent do you support or oppose the Black Lives Matter movement? (BLM01) 1. Strongly support; 2. Tend to support; 3. Neither support nor oppose; 4. Tend to oppose; 5. Strongly oppose.' Responses 1 and 2 are coded as (1) 'generally supports BLM' and responses 4 and 5 are coded as (2) 'generally opposes BLM'.

10

Conclusion: ethnic inequality, racism and the potential for racial justice

*James Nazroo, Nissa Finney, Laia Bécares, Dharmi Kapadia
and Natalie Shlomo*

Introduction

The Evidence for Equality National Survey (EVENS) was commissioned, and designed, at the height of the COVID-19 pandemic as part of a broader programme of work that the ESRC Centre on the Dynamics of Ethnicity (CoDE) was undertaking. By this time, a clear pattern of ethnic inequalities in COVID-related risk of mortality had been documented, inequalities in relation to other social and economic outcomes as a result of the pandemic were beginning to be identified, and social and political protests both led, and inspired by, the Black Lives Matter (BLM) movement were at their peak in the UK. Consequently, as described in the Introduction to this volume, the research agenda established by CoDE was as follows:

1. To document new and changing forms of racial and ethnic inequality in the wake of the COVID-19 pandemic and responses to it.
2. To explore emergent forms of social, political and cultural mobilisation around racism and racial inequality during and following the resurgence of the BLM movement.
3. To examine responses within particular social arenas and from institutions (education, health, housing, welfare, culture, employment and businesses, and policing) to the COVID-19 pandemic and BLM.
4. To work with community, policy and third sector partners to understand how racial and ethnic inequality was being addressed during the pandemic, and to formulate future plans for addressing racial injustice.

EVENS encapsulated each of these objectives, working in partnership with key race equality and voluntary sector organisations to produce evidence on the extent of, and responses to, ethnic inequalities with the intention of informing action.

Nevertheless, the sociopolitical environment at the time when the pandemic started (only three years prior to the publication of this volume) meant that state and, to a lesser extent, public sector and private institutions were unwilling to recognise the importance of racism in shaping ethnic inequalities within British society. Reflecting the active downplaying of inequalities, initial reporting of the COVID-19 pandemic and the consequent setting of the policy framework to respond to it were inattentive to the variation of risk across segments of the population, even according to age. Public health surveillance systems were not capable of documenting ethnic inequalities in COVID-related mortality, so these ethnic inequalities were only, and eventually, pushed onto the agenda by a growing public and media recognition that a large proportion of the NHS and care staff who were dying were from an ethnic minority background. Research evidence was slow to emerge and required innovative use of various forms of administrative data (ICNARC, 2020; Nazroo and Bécares, 2020; Platt and Warwick, 2020). The Office for National Statistics (ONS) moved quickly to fill this gap, ambitiously linking mortality records (which do not contain data on ethnicity) with census and NHS records (which do contain data on ethnicity) to estimate ethnic differences in risk of COVID-related mortality (ONS, 2020). These analyses showed large inequalities for all ethnic and religious minority groups (with the sole exception of Chinese women).

Despite this evidence, public health responses to the pandemic have, in general, failed to address the question of inequalities in outcomes. They also did not take seriously the possibility that the policies put in place to manage the pandemic would have unequal negative impacts in relation to economic, social, psychological and health outcomes, even though they recognised this possibility. In relation to ethnicity, this, in part at least, reflected an ongoing denial of the significance of racism to ethnic inequalities in outcomes (Commission on Race and Ethnic Disparities, 2021; Race Disparity Unit, 2022). Rather ethnic 'disparities' in the risk of COVID-related mortality were (and are) seen as a consequence of particular geographical and economic locations of ethnic minority people, differences in living arrangements (presented largely as a result of culturally informed preferences) and varying levels of risk generated by differences in the patterning of chronic illness, biology and underlying genetics. There is, of course, evidence for each of these explanations (ONS, 2020; ONS 2021c) – with the exception of genetics, where the evidence was drawn from laboratory settings (Downes et al, 2021) and did not translate into social settings (Singh et al, 2021), and living arrangements, where the contribution to ethnic differences was negligible (ONS, 2020). However, there is no evidence for the reductionist interpretations of these explanations – that differences were and are the inevitable consequence of the inherent cultural and genetic properties of ethnic minority groups, so beyond helping them to help themselves, nothing can be done about it. Nevertheless, public health responses were framed within such a cultural deficit model, one that locates both the problem and the solution in the behaviour of those ethnic groups at greater risk. So, for example, community leaders were mobilised to promote lockdown and social isolation policies, and to promote the value of vaccinations and reduce vaccine hesitancy.

The Framing of EVENS

In this context, the framing of EVENS was distinct. As discussed in the Introduction to this volume, EVENS was focused on the question of racial justice and how ethnic inequalities, underpinned by structural, institutional and interpersonal racism (Jones, 2000; Nazroo et al, 2020), shaped experiences of the COVID-19 pandemic and in turn were themselves shaped by the pandemic and the policies put in place to manage it. To do this, and to do it within a reasonable timeframe, while maintaining a robust scientific approach to the generation of evidence, EVENS was necessarily innovative in a number of ways. Three dimensions of this innovation were particularly important: the approach to data collection, population coverage and topic coverage. These innovative features were anchored by several principles that shaped the design, which were as follows:

- The survey design would allow statistical inference to be made.
- Questionnaire coverage would be developed in collaboration with academic and non-academic users of the data.
- The survey could be conducted within a short timeframe.
- The mode of survey delivery could accommodate social distancing, shielding and other lockdown measures.
- The achieved sample would cover a wider range of ethnic groups than that typically achieved in ethnically boosted surveys.

Our approach to data collection was, of course, shaped by social distancing policies and the movements into and out of lockdown as the COVID-19 pandemic evolved. This precluded face-to-face recruitment of participants and in-person interviews, which led to the decision to use online, social networking and campaigning approaches to recruitment, and to do this in partnership with voluntary, community and social enterprise (VCSE) organisations serving ethnic minority populations, and to primarily collect data using online and telephone methods (some interviews with Roma and Gypsy/Traveller participants were conducted face to face).

This also allowed us to think innovatively about population coverage. Traditional approaches to sampling ethnic minority people for surveys involve focusing fieldwork in areas with a high proportion of ethnic minority residents and the (often indirect) screening of a large number of households to identify eligible sample members. As well as requiring considerable resources, such an approach does not cover, or sample, people living in areas with smaller proportions of ethnic minority residents, an issue that is particularly important in relation to the inclusion of those living in areas that are wealthier and that are more rural. In addition, it also typically results in a focus on larger, geographically more concentrated and more visible ethnic minority groups – Black African, Black Caribbean, Indian, Pakistani and Bangladeshi groups. By taking an online and campaigning approach to sampling, we were able to recruit anyone who defined themselves as a member of an ethnic minority group, regardless of which group or where they lived, and to (slightly) broaden the ethnic minority groups covered beyond UK 2021 Census categories to include both a White Eastern European group and a Jewish group. This led to EVENS having unrivalled coverage of ethnic minority people living in Britain, even if the statistical theory and approach lying behind this were complex (and innovative), as was outlined in Chapter 2.

These two innovations in sampling and population coverage led to EVENS generating a non-probability survey, one where participants have an unknown (or even zero) probability of inclusion. Even if such samples are framed within quotas to ensure that they cover key demographic characteristics (say, age, gender and region of residence), they are typically not seen as appropriate to use when making generalisations about the population as a whole, so to draw statistical inference. This is because of unknown biases resulting from characteristics that are associated with a likelihood to take part in the survey. However, methods have been developed to compensate for selection bias in non-probability samples (Elliot and Valliant, 2017; Chen et al, 2019; Saunders and Shlomo, 2021), and we further developed and applied these methods to generate survey weights that can be used to enable statistical inference to be drawn. This approach, which was described in Chapter 2, involved using a quasi-randomisation approach to calculate survey weights that are based on propensity score matching to integrate the non-probability sample with a probability reference sample, alongside calibration to population benchmarks. This thereby compensates for selection and coverage biases.

Nevertheless, in practice these innovations also led to three important limitations with the survey. First, the speed with which the survey was conducted, coupled with a reliance on online recruitment and interviewing methods, meant that the EVENS data have relatively few participants aged older than 65. This gap could not be corrected using statistical methods, so the analyses in this volume are restricted to those aged 18-65. This is important, because there are likely to be differences in the level and nature of ethnic inequalities across generations and age groups. In effect, this means that it is possible that the findings presented here understated the extent of ethnic inequalities in Britain. Second, the survey implementation was designed to allow ethnic minority and White British people to be interviewed over the same period, something that was crucially important as the COVID-19 pandemic and policies to manage it evolved during the period of fieldwork. However, because they were sampled in different ways (see Chapter 2), aligning the timing of the recruitment of the two samples proved very difficult, with the White British sample recruited relatively early in the EVENS data collection period (during the second lockdown), and the ethnic minority sample recruited at a fairly even rate across the whole period, with an additional sample recruited at the end of the period (in October and November 2021). Third, the statistical approach to weighting has been experimental, and occurred before the 2021 Census findings on the ethnic composition of the UK population were made available. This means that the weights used for the analysis reported here are provisional, although they will be finalised in time for the release of the data for general use.

The final important innovation implemented by EVENS was in relation to topic coverage. Here, the experiences of ethnic minority people were centred in the design process, rather than adopting a more generic approach to topic coverage. So, the questionnaire had sections on identity, citizenship and belonging, on experiences of racism and discrimination, and on participation in politics, civic activities and protest. In addition, other more traditional sections, such as those on housing, education, employment and health, were tailored to enable a focus on ethnic inequality. Importantly, to ensure that the questionnaire content was relevant to the lives of the very diverse ethnic groups covered in the survey, it was co-designed with our partner VCSE organisations, who made substantial and important contributions to questionnaire content. This, then, allowed us to generate an interdisciplinary data source that could be used to investigate a wide range of research and policy questions.

A final piece of context for EVENS is to place it within the history of national surveys of the lives of ethnic minority people living in the UK. Although there have been many surveys of ethnic minority people, the majority have not been national, and while there have been many national surveys that have oversampled groups of ethnic minority people, many have either had a particular topic focus (such as the 1999 and 2004 Health Surveys for England (Erens et al, 2000; Sproston and Mindell, 2006) or have had a more generalist focus rather than one specifically framed around the question of ethnic inequality. The exceptions are the four surveys carried out by the Policy Studies Institute and its predecessor, Political and Economic Planning. The first of these, entitled *Racial Discrimination in England*, was conducted in the mid-1960s (Daniel, 1968) at what now seems like a relatively early phase of migration from Commonwealth and former Commonwealth countries. This was also a time when overt discrimination against ethnic minority people was commonplace, having just only been subjected to legislation by the first Race Relations Act, which in December 1965 made discrimination on the grounds of 'colour, race, or ethnic or national origins' in public places an offence. The second survey was entitled *Racial Disadvantage in Britain*

(Smith, 1977) and was carried out in the mid-1970s. Its findings suggested that ethnic inequalities had not improved over the previous ten years, despite the introduction of legislation and the relative economic prosperity of the time. The third survey, which took place in the early 1980s, shifted titles and was called *Black and White Britain* (Brown, 1984). It was set in an era of industrial decline, high rates of unemployment and, as its title implies, when anti-racist movements were framed by the notion of political blackness.[1] The fourth survey was conducted in the mid-1990s (Modood et al, 1997), a time when the emerging success of some non-White ethnic minority groups was becoming visible, most notably that of those Indian people who had initially settled in East Africa, but had been forced to migrate from there in the late 1960s and early 1970s. Its title reintroduced the term 'disadvantage', but in a more qualified sense, it was called *Ethnic Minorities in Britain: Diversity and Disadvantage*. If we place EVENS as the fifth in this trajectory of surveys, we can see that, like its predecessors, it: reflected the historical context in which it was carried out; was innovative in its approach to data collection; expanded the range of ethnic groups under consideration; and expanded the topics it covered. Unlike the predecessor surveys, we move away from the word 'disadvantage' in the title of this report, and explicitly reference 'racism' and 'inequality'. By placing EVENS as the fifth in this series of important surveys, our purpose, in part, is to emphasise the importance of such surveys in documenting ethnic inequalities and how they are shaped by racism. We will return to this point later in the chapter. Before then, we provide a summary of some of the key messages that have emerged from this volume.

Key findings

Experiences of racist assault and racial discrimination are widespread

A newly developed measure capturing direct experiences of racism was implemented in the EVENS questionnaire. Conceptually this overlapped with other measures, and some of the items were drawn from existing studies, but it was distinct in covering all of the following: racial assault (verbal, physical and damage to property); racial discrimination in institutional settings; racial discrimination in social settings; and expectations of racial discrimination. Crucially, it captured experiences at different time periods across participants' lives. In comparison with studies that focus only on some dimensions of experience or only on particular time points in a participant's life (for example, the last year), the findings using this more comprehensive set of measures show that ethnic minority people experience strikingly high levels of exposure to racist assault and racial discrimination.

Over a third of ethnic minority participants reported having experienced one or more racist assaults (verbal, physical or damage to property) over their lifetimes, with one in six reporting having experienced a physical assault. Responses from ethnic minority participants also indicated widespread experience of discrimination within institutional settings – close to a third of ethnic minority people reported experiencing racial discrimination in education, a similar proportion reported racial discrimination in employment, and around a fifth reported experiences of racial discrimination when seeking housing. Considering social settings, close to a third of ethnic minority participants reported experiences of racial discrimination in public, and almost one in six ethnic minority people report experiencing racial discrimination from neighbours. Moreover, more than one in five reported experiencing discrimination from the police.

Of course, the extent of these experiences of racism and racial discrimination varied across the groups covered by EVENS. Gypsy/Traveller, Roma, Jewish and the five Black ethnic groups reported very high rates of experiencing racism. For example, over half the respondents from the Gypsy/Traveller, Jewish and Any other Black ethnic groups reported having experienced a physical racist assault, while racial discrimination from the police was reported by more than two fifths of the Black Caribbean and Any other Black ethnic groups, and by more than a third of the Roma and the Gypsy/Traveller ethnic groups. Racial discrimination in public places was experienced by close to half of the Gypsy/Traveller and the Black Caribbean ethnic groups, and more than two fifths of the any Other Black and White and Black Caribbean ethnic groups. In contrast, experiences of racist assault and racial discrimination were much lower for the White Irish, White Eastern European and Any other White ethnic groups, perhaps indicating the importance of being able to present as, and being socially assigned as, White. Nevertheless, people within the first two of these groups did report substantial experiences of racism, with, for example, more than one in ten of the White Irish group and more than one in 20 of the White Eastern European group having reported experiencing a racist assault, and two fifths of the White Irish group and a third of the White Eastern European group having reported experiencing discrimination within one of the institutional and social settings covered by the questionnaire.

Context, and the ways in which this shapes the racialisation of particular ethnic groups, is, of course, crucial. Experiences of racism continued throughout the pandemic, with around 14% of ethnic minority people reporting experiencing some form of racist assault, and over 10% reporting experiencing racial discrimination in public settings. Notably, the risk of experiencing racial discrimination for people in the Chinese, Other Asian and the White Eastern European groups increased during the pandemic relative to the other ethnic minority groups included in the survey. Indeed, for the period of the COVID-19 pandemic, people from the Chinese ethnic group, alongside those from the Roma and the Gypsy/Traveller ethnic groups, had the highest rates of reporting increased police activity within their community and the highest rates of reporting being stopped by the police.

Ethnic minority people report high levels of engagement in political and civic life

EVENS included coverage of levels of political trust, interest in politics, political affiliation, and support for BLM. BLM is, of course, a direct response to the widespread experiences of racist assault and racial discrimination just outlined and EVENS found high levels of support for BLM across most ethnic minority groups included in the survey. More than three quarters of participants in the Black Caribbean, Black African, Arab, White Irish, Pakistani and Indian groups expressed support for BLM, as did almost three quarters of the Bangladeshi group, around two thirds of the Jewish, Chinese, Any other Black and the various mixed ethnic groups, and just over half of the White British ethnic group. Lower levels of support for Black Lives Matter were found among people from Roma, Gypsy/Traveller and White Eastern European backgrounds, but nevertheless more than a quarter of the Roma group and close to two fifths of the Gypsy/Traveller and White Eastern European groups did express support. It is also important to note that only a small minority of people in each ethnic group reported that they opposed BLM.

We do not know from these analyses why there was variation in support for BLM across ethnic groups. This, in part, might reflect the salience of experiences relevant to the movement, with those groups experiencing the highest levels of racism and of racial discrimination from the police possibly more like to support BLM. It might also reflect the extent to which experiences of racism for a group are recognised and validated by the public at large, as well as within the movement. So, for the Gypsy/Traveller and the Roma ethnic groups, it may be that, despite high levels of exposure to racist assault and racial discrimination, there is a sense of their experiences not being picked up by and represented within the campaigning activities of BLM.

Interestingly, despite experiences of racism, and social and economic disadvantage, most ethnic minority people reported higher levels of trust in national, regional and local governments compared with White British people. Similarly, other indicators of political engagement, such as interest in politics and having a political party affiliation, did not indicate a political alienation of ethnic minority people. So, as for the measures of trust, people in most ethnic minority groups had higher levels of political engagement than their White British counterparts. The exceptions were the Roma, Gypsy/Traveller and White Eastern European ethnic groups, mirroring the findings for support for BLM and suggesting that such support might be an element of wider political engagement in British politics.

Perhaps not surprisingly, given the wider coverage of ethnic minority groups in EVENS compared with other surveys, the findings demonstrate considerable variation across groups in terms of affiliation to political parties. The Pakistani, Bangladeshi, Black African and Black Caribbean ethnic groups reported the highest support for the Labour Party. Relatively high rates of support for Labour were also found among the Indian, Arab, and the various mixed, Other Asian and Roma ethnic groups. The Conservative Party had the highest share of support from the Jewish group, but also had relatively high levels of support from the Chinese, Any Other Black and Any Other ethnic groups, while the highest levels of support for the Liberal Democrats were found for the White Eastern European, Chinese and White Irish groups.

Ethnic minority groups face ongoing economic inequalities

When considering economic inequalities, it is important to pay attention to both a full range of outcomes, covering different dimensions of economic wellbeing, and how these vary differentially across ethnic minority groups – a nuanced account is needed. EVENS has the necessary comprehensive coverage of both ethnic groups (as already detailed) and outcomes. For example, it allowed us to assess labour force participation rates and employment rates (both covering the whole population aged 18–65), unemployment rates (focused on only those who were in the labour force), precarious employment, financial situation (including financial hardship and worries about finances), level of education and changes in these outcomes during the COVID-19 pandemic. It is also important to document the different patterns found for women and for men.

One of the most striking findings from EVENS is that during the COVID-19 pandemic, ethnic inequalities in labour market outcomes did not increase substantially. So, labour market changes occurring during the pandemic, such as change in occupation, movement into unemployment, furlough, increased working hours and pay reduction, did not vary greatly across ethnic groups. However, we also did not see a decrease in ethnic inequalities; they persisted into the period of the COVID-19 pandemic. For instance, Pakistani women and men continued to report high unemployment rates relative to White British women and men, and Bangladeshi, Gypsy/Traveller and Roma men had a higher risk than White British men of being in precarious employment (that is, with temporary and zero-hours contracts, or solo self-employed). Precarious employment is a particularly important outcome in contemporary labour markets, indicating insecurity of employment (Clark and Ochmann, 2022). It may be that the government's job retention scheme (furlough) coupled with the employment sectors within which ethnic minority workers are concentrated (such as health and social care, and transport and delivery services) mitigated the risk of an increase on average in ethnic inequalities in the labour market, without reducing these inequalities.

The picture is not positive in relation to ethnic inequalities in finances. On average, ethnic minority groups fare well in comparison to the White British group in relation to educational attainment (although this is markedly not the case for the Mixed White and Black Caribbean, Gypsy/Traveller and Roma ethnic groups). Some ethnic minority groups (the Jewish, Any other White and Indian ethnic groups) fare well in relation to having professional and higher administrative managerial jobs compared to White British people (though Roma, Gypsy/Traveller, Mixed White and Black Caribbean and White Eastern European people are much more likely to be in semi-routine and routine occupations). However, substantial ethnic inequalities are apparent in relation to financial situations. This is marked by higher proportions with financial difficulties (further exacerbated by the COVID-19 pandemic – many ethnic minority groups reported close to double the rates of financial difficulties in the pandemic compared to the pre-pandemic period), high rates of benefits receipt (indicating high levels of financial hardship) and high rates of being worried about finances. Of course, the financial situation should relate directly to educational level, labour market participation and type of job held. The fact that we do not see as straightforward a translation of academic and labour market resources into financial wellbeing for ethnic minority groups as we see for White British people points to both the need to consider the complexity of underlying processes and, as previously discussed, the ways in which processes related to racism impact on outcomes. Therefore, it is worth noting that despite the relative stability of occupational outcomes for ethnic minority people compared with White British people after the start of the COVID-19 pandemic, all ethnic minority groups experienced more income instability than the White British group during this period. Ethnic minority groups were more vulnerable to the negative financial consequences of the COVID-19 pandemic compared to the White British group, in addition to experiencing longstanding inequalities prior to the pandemic.

Ethnic inequalities persist in housing circumstances, but ethnic minority people have and retain strong attachments to their place of residence

Findings from EVENS evidenced inequalities in five inter-related dimensions of housing: household tenure, household types, overcrowding and space, residential mobility, and levels of belonging. The findings demonstrate distinct levels of material deprivation across almost all ethnic minority groups compared with the White British group, the exceptions being the White Irish, Jewish and, to a lesser extent, Indian ethnic groups.

In terms of tenure, findings from EVENS show that no ethnic minority group had a higher rate of home ownership (without or with a mortgage) than the White British group. The lowest rates of owning a home were found for the White Eastern European, Mixed White and Black Caribbean, Black African and Arab groups, who also had high rates of renting. Renting indicates a level of housing instability and could be especially damaging during the COVID-19 pandemic when paired with the financial hardships and uncertainties described earlier.

Levels of overcrowding, and consequent pressure on space in households, were higher within ethnic minority groups than White British groups, and this is a particular issue for three-generation households that are more common in the Pakistani and Roma ethnic groups. In contrast, the rate of living in detached housing was highest for the White British, Arab, White Irish and Indian ethnic groups, who were three times more likely to live in such housing than the Black African, Black Caribbean and Bangladeshi ethnic groups. Ethnic minority people were disadvantaged in terms of access to outdoor space at home. White British people had the highest rates of access to outdoor space at their property, while Arab, Chinese and Other Black people were four times more likely than White British people to be without outdoor space at home. Given its coverage of the experiences of Gypsy Traveller and Roma people, EVENS has also been able to uniquely document that the majority of Gypsy/Traveller people (almost three in five) and just over a quarter of Roma people lived in caravans and mobile homes.

Moving house during the pandemic – an indication of housing precarity – was considerably more likely for Roma, Jewish, Other White, Indian, Mixed White and Asian, and Other Asian people, compared with White British people.

In terms of the local area, lack of access to open space was reported by more than one in ten people in the Pakistani, Mixed White and Asian, Chinese, Other Asian, Mixed White and Black African, and Other Black ethnic groups, compared to only one in 20 of the White British group. However, despite the on average poorer housing experiences of ethnic minority people, there was a widespread sense of belonging to the local area. Pakistani, Bangladeshi and Indian people were significantly more likely to report feelings of belonging to their local area than White British people. Interestingly, for all ethnic groups, apart from Roma, the majority of those who reported a change in belonging during the pandemic experienced increased attachment to the local area.

The COVID-19 pandemic has negatively impacted on some dimensions of ethnic inequalities in health

It has been well documented that the COVID-19 pandemic led to much higher risks of mortality among ethnic minority groups than among the

White British group. This is mirrored and further detailed in findings from EVENS. The odds of COVID-19 infection were higher compared with the White British group for the Gypsy/Traveller, Bangladeshi, Mixed White and Black African, Pakistani, Black African, White Eastern European (uniquely reported in the EVENS), White Irish, and Indian groups. Data from EVENS also demonstrated higher levels of COVID-related bereavement among many ethnic minority groups compared with the White British group, reflecting high mortality rates and indicating not only ethnic inequalities in mortality, but also ethnic inequalities in relation to the impact of the silent 'pandemic of grief' that occurred throughout the period.

Nevertheless, these ethnic inequalities in outcomes directly related to COVID-19 did not straightforwardly translate into ethnic inequalities in mental health and wellbeing. Levels of anxiety and depression were lower among people in the Black African, Chinese, White Eastern European and Any other Asian groups compared with the White British group. Similarly, people from the Gypsy/Traveller, Roma, Chinese and Black African ethnic groups were less likely to experience loneliness during the pandemic than the White British group, while the Roma, Bangladeshi, Black African, Pakistani and Indian groups had a lower chance of experiencing an increase in loneliness during the pandemic than the White British group. In contrast, a notable finding from EVENS was that a higher risk of depression and anxiety was found for the Arab group. There is very little additional evidence on the mental health of Arab people in Britain, which is a diverse population with complex and often traumatic migration histories.

We do not yet know, of course, what the longer-term impact of the COVID-19 pandemic will be on ethnic inequalities in health. In addition to the immediate direct effects of COVID-19 infection on health, measures introduced to manage the pandemic will have both short-term and long-term impacts on social and economic inequalities experienced by ethnic minority people. As discussed earlier, these impacts are patterned in complex ways across ethnic groups and across outcomes, but their general impact is to amplify ethnic inequalities. Such an amplification of socioeconomic inequalities, shaped by structural, institutional and interpersonal racism, is likely to increase ethnic inequalities in health.

Ethnic minority people have strong affiliations to both ethnic and national identities

This chapter has, to a certain extent, illustrated why the question of ethnic identity is so important. The ways in which ethnic identities are shaped by processes related to racism and, consequently, how this results in inequalities is a central component of the experiences of ethnic minority people in Britain. However, ethnic identity is also an important component of self-identification and affiliation to a group. EVENS demonstrated that across ethnic groups, ethnic identity was reported to be an important part of personal identity. This was particularly, but not only, the case for Black African, Black Caribbean, Pakistani, White Irish and Jewish groups, and least likely to be the case for the White British, White Eastern European and White Other groups.

In addition to felt identity, EVENS participants were asked how often they participated in practices relating to their ethnicity – the clothes they wore, the food they ate, and activities in general. Most people from ethnic minority groups reported regularly participating in such practices, while those in the White British group were the least likely to report participation, followed by White Irish and White Eastern European people. This perhaps signals the importance of such practices to one's sense of identity, particularly for those who were not members of White groups.

It is striking, though, that in addition to a strong affiliation to ethnic identity, EVENS data, along with data from other studies, show that ethnic minority people in Britain – people who have been racialised and minoritised within everyday contexts – remain strongly affiliated to a British identity. The sense of belonging to British society is very high across all groups, but particularly high among the Bangladeshi, Indian, Pakistani, Black African, Black Other, Arab and Jewish ethnic groups, as well as the White British group. The findings reported here for White Eastern European, Arab and Jewish people are particularly noteworthy – these populations have not been covered in other studies of national and ethnic identities.

In contrast to Britishness, a strong sense of belonging to English, Scottish and Welsh societies is less common among people from ethnic minority backgrounds compared with White British people. This might be a consequence of lower levels of inclusiveness for English/Scottish/Welsh national identities compared with the British national identity. For example, it has been suggested that the construction of Englishness is based more on an 'ethnic' rather than a 'civic' conceptualisation of identity (Leddy-Owen, 2014), so is more likely to be considered in terms of ancestry and Whiteness rather than citizenship. In this regard, it is interesting to note that EVENS data indicate that White Eastern Europeans are almost equally likely to report a strong sense of belonging to British and English national identities.

EVENS was also unique in including an open – free text – question on ethnic identity, asked before other questions on ethnic group membership and strength of ethnic and national identity. A meaningful proportion of participants chose not to answer this question – about a third across all groups – and a further substantial proportion used variants of official or administrative terms to describe their identities – about half across all groups. The common use of administrative language to describe their ethnicity by EVENS participants is likely to reflect how embedded these terms are in everyday life in Britain, but also demonstrates how official categories do represent at least part of how we conceive of our identities – there was extensive development work to produce and consequently refine these categories. Responses from the remainder of the sample (about one in five) illustrate how people tend to think about their ethnicity when they are not bound by, or go beyond, predefined categories. In some cases, this was a reflection of the inadequacy of administrative categories to reflect the complexity of people's identities, including complex migration histories and families with multiple ethnic origins. It also reflected the importance of subnational places to people's identities and the complex ways in which ethnicity is related to experiences of persecution and oppression.

The implications of these findings for the policy agenda within Britain and beyond

The evidence presented in this volume points to four key conclusions:

1. Ethnic inequalities remain for a wide range of economic, social and health outcomes. They were present before the beginning of the COVID-19 pandemic and either persisted or increased during the pandemic.
2. These social, economic and health inequalities operate jointly across people's life courses. While some might show evidence of some improvement – for example, outcomes related to education – these improvements are not translated into improvements in other domains of people's lives.
3. Despite this, ethnic minority people are able to maintain both a strong sense of affiliation to their ethnic identity and to a national British identity. They also maintain a strong engagement in political and civic life, reflected, perhaps, in a strong attachment to their places of residence.
4. Underlying both these inequalities and the nature of ethnic identities are pervading and very common experiences of racism and racial discrimination.

These summary conclusions do not, of course, reflect the depth, breadth and nuance of the evidence produced by EVENS, and the variations it shows across and within ethnic groups, including those documented for the first time by the study. Nevertheless, they do tell the story of ethnic inequality and how it is shaped by processes related to structural, institutional and interpersonal racism. This evidence is at odds with the conclusions and recommendations made by the report from the Commission on Race and Ethnic Disparities (2021) and the UK government's response to that report found in *Inclusive Britain* (Race Disparity Unit, 2022). Both of these downplay – indeed, deny – the significance of racism to our society, and instead emphasise individual, cultural and group deficits within an imagined framework to promote social mobility. The ambition seems to be to even out inequalities across population groups and places (but not to reduce inequality) without paying attention to the fundamental causes of these inequalities. This is, perhaps, not surprising in relation to the recent and current political context in the UK, where we are faced with a series of ongoing and evolving policies related to culture, citizenship, community, segregation and migration that are populist and disregard the evidence base. Such policies further and fundamentally undermine the social status of ethnic minority people and communities, reinforce processes of racialisation, and have a strong potential to negatively impact on and reinforce the social, economic and health inequalities documented here and elsewhere.

Nevertheless, the stark ethnic inequalities seen in the impact of the COVID-19 pandemic, along with the killing of George Floyd and the subsequent resurgence of BLM, has raised awareness of the significance of ethnic inequalities across the full range of social, public and private institutions in the UK. Questions have been asked about everything from deaths in custody, unequal health outcomes and failures of education systems, to the ways in which histories of colonisation, slavery and empire are embedded in our cultures and celebrated by our monuments and in the commemorations of our history. Indeed, during the BLM protests in 2020, we had a series of public statements in support of race equality from a large proportion of private, public and governmental organisations. These are, of course, the institutions that shape lives, both in terms of their provision of key services and because they provide employment opportunities for the majority of the workforce. They also bring together and amplify structural and interpersonal racism, and make them more salient (Nazroo et al, 2020). However, they are semi-autonomous and at arm's length from government, so are spaces where meaningful change can happen.

The positive note – one that has framed the design and conduct of EVENS – is that a careful and critical documentation of ethnic inequalities can lead to a contextually relevant and theoretically informed analysis of the causes of these inequalities. This book is the beginning of such a descriptive mapping of ethnic inequalities. The evidence generated by such work can then be translated into action by the leadership teams of those institutions who want to change the ways in which their organisations generate and amplify, rather than mitigate and redress, ethnic inequalities. This is an ambitious task; it requires thinking critically about the functions of institutions, acknowledging how such functions are rooted in the colonial histories of institutions, resulting in interconnected systems of structured racial inequity, and setting about to transform those functions and the way in which they are implemented using a model that is informed by a decolonisation agenda – in other words, an agenda that acknowledges the existence, purpose and workings of racism in shaping the lives of its citizens and sets out to actively promote racial justice.

Here, of course, we run the risk of falling into the trap of *The Cruel Optimism of Racial Justice* (Meer, 2022). Meer argues that 'there is no likely end to the struggle for racial justice, only the promise this heralds and the desire to persevere, even despite knowledge of likely failure' (Meer, 2022: 1). This 'knowledge of likely failure' results from the evidence demonstrating that there has been little, or no, improvement in ethnic inequalities in Britain or elsewhere in the Global North. However, 'the desire to persevere', to combat racism, remains a powerful motivation for action. Consequently, our aspiration is that evidence on ethnic inequalities, generated by the innovative EVENS survey, coupled with informed critical analysis, such as that provided in this volume, can provide the framework to support the transformation of institutions, broader policy and society.

Returning to the questions laid out in the Introduction to this volume, the evidence generated by EVENS cannot tell us what a racially just society would look like. However, it does document the substantial ethnic inequalities in outcomes across a range of domains of life – Britain is not close to being a racially just society. EVENS has also demonstrated that during the COVID-19 pandemic, ethnic inequalities were maintained in many areas and extended in other areas. Perhaps a lesson to be learned is that during such crises – the current 'cost of living' crisis is another – the emphasis should be on policy interventions that take the opportunity to mitigate inequality.

Note

[1]   'blackness' is not capitalised here because, although it refers to the quality or state of identifying with Black ethnicities, it depicts identification with a socio-political movement that spans ethnicities, groups and categories, and is not considered a proper noun.

References

Abraham, T. (2021) 'Who do BAME Britons trust when it comes to COVID-19?' YouGov report. Available at: https://yougov.co.uk/topics/politics/articles-reports/2021/03/17/who-do-bame-britons-trust-when-it-comes-covid-19

Adam, E.K., Heissel, J., Zeiders, K., Richeson, J., Ross, E., Ehrlich, K. et al (2015) 'Developmental histories of perceived racial discrimination and diurnal cortisol profiles in adulthood: a 20-year prospective study', *Psychoneuroendocrinology*, 62: 279–91. doi: 10.1016/j.psyneuen.2015.08.018.

Ahmed, S. (1999) 'Home and away: narratives of migration and estrangement', *International Journal of Cultural Studies*, 2(3): 329–47. doi: 10.1177/136787799900200303.

Ahmed, S. (2007) 'A phonemonology of whiteness', *Feminist Theory*, 8(2): 149–68.

Aldrich, D.P. and Meyer, M.A. (2015) 'Social capital and community resilience', *American Behavioral Scientist*, 59(2): 254–69. doi: 10.1177/0002764214550299.

Alexander, C. (2018) 'Breaking black: the death of ethnic and racial studies in Britain', *Ethnic and Racial Studies*, 41(6): 1034–54. doi: 10.1080/01419870.2018.1409902.

Alexander, C. and Byrne, B. (2020) 'Introduction', in Byrne, B., Alexander, C., Khan, O., Nazroo, J. and Shankley, W. (eds) *Ethnicity, Race and Inequality in the UK: State of the Nation*. Bristol: Policy Press, pp 1–14.

Alexander, C., Chatterji, J. and Jalais, A. (2015) *The Bengal Diaspora: Rethinking Muslim Migration*. Abingdon: Routledge.

Allen, R., Wiśniowski, A., Aparicio Castro, A., Olsen, W.K. and Islam, M. (2021) 'The economic impact of the COVID-19 pandemic on ethnic minorities in Manchester'. Available at: https://www.research.manchester.ac.uk/portal/files/205812064/SSRN_id3949593.pdf.

Ali, S. and Heath, A. (2013) *Future Identities: Changing Identities in the UK – The Next 10 Years*. London: Government Office for Science.

Appleby, J. Kevin, and Donald Kerwin (eds) (2018) 2018 International Migration Policy Report: Perspectives on the Content and Implementation of the Global Compact for Safe, Orderly, and Regular Migration. New York: Scalabrini Migration Study Centers. https://doi.org/10.14240/ internationalmigrationrpt2018.

Ashe, S.D. (2021) *SHF Race Report. 40 Years of Tackling Racial Inequality in Britain*. Stuart Hall Foundation. Available at: https://www.stuarthallfoundation.org/wp-content/uploads/2021/01/SHF-Race-Report-2021.pdf

Aspinall, P. (1997) 'The conceptual basis of ethnic group terminology and classifications', *Social Science and Medicine*, 45(5): 689–98. doi: 10.1016/S0277-9536(96)00386-3.

Bailey, Z.D., Krieger, N., Agénor, M., Graves, J., Linos, N. and Bassett, M.T. (2017) 'Structural racism and health inequities in the USA: evidence and interventions', *The Lancet*, 389: 1453–63.

Barnett, K., Mercer, S.W., Norbury, M., Watt, G., Wyke, S. and Guthrie, B. (2012) 'Epidemiology of multimorbidity and implications for health care, research, and medical education: a cross-sectional study', *The Lancet*, 380(9836): 37–43. doi: 10.1016/S0140-6736(12)60240-2.

Barnett, P., Mackay, E., Matthews, H., Gate, R., Greenwood, H., Ariyo, K. et al (2019) 'Ethnic variations in compulsory detention under the Mental Health Act: a systematic review and meta-analysis of international data', *The Lancet Psychiatry*, 6(4): 305–17. doi: 10.1016/S2215-0366(19)30027-6.

Bastos, J.L., Celeste, R.K., Faerstein, E. and Barros, A. (2010) 'Racial discrimination and health: a systematic review of scales with a focus on their psychometric properties', *Social Science and Medicine*, 70(7): 1091–99. doi: 10.1016/j.socscimed.2009.12.020.

Bécares, L., Stafford, M., Laurence, J. and Nazroo, J. (2011) 'Composition, concentration and deprivation: exploring their association with social cohesion among different ethnic groups in the UK', *Urban Studies*, 48(13): 2771–87. doi: 10.1177/0042098010391295.

Bécares, L. (2015) 'Which ethnic groups have the poorest health?', in Jivraj, A. and Simpson, L. (eds) *Ethnic Identity and Inequalities in Britain: The Dynamics of Diversity*. Bristol: Policy Press, pp 123–40.

Bécares, L., Shaw, R., Katikireddi, S., Amele, S., Irizar, P., Kapadia, D. et al (2022) 'Racism as the fundamental cause of ethnic inequities in COVID-19 vaccine hesitancy: a theoretical framework and empirical exploration using the UK Household Longitudinal Study', *SSM – Population Health*, 19: 101150. doi: 10.1016/j.ssmph.2022.101150.

Battaglini, M., Burchardt, T., Obolenskaya, P. and Vizard, P. (2018) *Experience of Multiple Disadvantage among Roma, Gypsy and Traveller Children in England and Wales*. Centre for Analysis of Social Exclusion, LSE. Available at: https://econpapers.repec.org/RePEc:cep:sticas:/208

Benzeval, M., Burton, J., Crossley, T.F., Fisher, P., Jäckle, A., Low, H. et al (2020) 'The idiosyncratic impact of an aggregate shock: the distributional consequences of COVID-19'. Available at: https://papers.ssrn.com/sol3/papers.cfm?abstract_id=3615691

Bhopal, K. (2018) *White Privilege: The Myth of a Post-racial Society*. Bristol: Policy Press.

Bianchi, A., Shlomo, N., Schouten, B., Da Silva, D. and Skinner, C. (2019) 'Estimation of response propensities and indicators of representative response using population-level information', *Survey Methodology*, 45(2): 217–47.

Billari, F.C. and Liefbroer, A.C. (2010) 'Towards a new pattern of transition to adulthood', *Advances in Life Course Research*, 15: 59–75. doi: 10.1016/j.alcr.2010.10.003.

Bloch, A., Neal, S. and Solomos, J. (2013) *Race, Multiculture and Social Policy*. Basingstoke: Palgrave Macmillan.

Boccagni, P. and Kusenbach, M. (2020) 'For a comparative sociology of home: relationships, cultures, structures', *Current Sociology*, 68(5): 595–606. doi: 10.1177/0011392120927776.

Boliver, V. (2016) 'Exploring ethnic inequalities in admission to Russell Group universities', *Sociology*, 50(2): 247–66. doi: 10.1177/0038038515575859.

Bonnett, A. (2022) *Multiracism: Rethinking Racism in Global Context*. Cambridge: Polity Press.

Brondolo, E., Brady, N., Pencille, M., Beatty, D. and Contrada, R. (2009) 'Coping with racism: a selective review of the literature and a theoretical and methodological critique', *Journal of Behavioural Medicine*, 32(1): 64-88. doi: 10.1007/s10865-008-9193-0.

Brown, C. (1984) *Black and White Britain*. London: Heinemann.

Brown, P., Scullion, L. and Martin, P. (2013) *Migrant Roma in the United Kingdom: Population Size and Experiences of Local Authorities and Partners*. University of Salford. Available at: https://huddersfield.box.com/s/b3tv28x0e75yrkul7x9gdlank1jgk87a

Brun, C. and Fábos, A. (2015) 'Making homes in limbo? A conceptual framework', *Refuge*, 31: 5–17. doi: 10.25071/1920-7336.40138.

Brynin, M. and Longhi, S. (2015) *The Effect of Occupation on Poverty among Ethnic Minority Groups*. York: Joseph Rowntree Foundation.

Burgess, G. and Muir, K. (2020) 'The Increase in multigenerational households in the UK: the motivations for and experiences of multigenerational living', *Housing, Theory and Society*, 37(3): 322–38. doi: 10.1080/14036096.2019.1653360.

Busemeyer, M.R. (2022) 'The welfare state in really hard times: political trust and satisfaction with the German healthcare system during the COVID-19 pandemic', *Journal of European Social Policy*, 32(4). doi: 10.1177/09589287221085922.

Byrne, B. (2017) 'Testing times: the place of the citizenship test in the UK immigration regime and new citizens' responses to it', *Sociology*, 51(2): 323–8. doi: 10.1177/0038038515622908.

Byrne, B., Alexander, C., Khan, O., Nazroo, J. and Shankley, W. (2020) *Ethnicity, Race and Inequality in the UK: State of the Nation*. Bristol: Policy Press.

Carmichael, S. and Hamilton, C.V. (1967) *Black Power: Politics of Liberation in America*. New York: Random House.

Casey, L. (2016) *The Casey Review: A Review into Opportunity and Integration*. London: Department for Communities and Local Government.

Catney, G., Wright, R. and Ellis, M. (2021) 'The evolution and stability of multi-ethnic residential neighbourhoods in England', *Transactions of the Institute of British Geographers*, 46(2), 330–46. doi: 10.1111/tran.12416.

Chen, Y., Li, P. and Wu, C. (2019) 'Doubly robust inference with non-probability survey samples', *Journal of the American Statistical Association*, 115(532): 2011–21. doi: 10.1111/rssa.12696.

Chouhan, K. and Nazroo, L. (2020) 'Health inequalities', in Byrne, B., Alexander, C., Khan, O., Nazroo, J. and Shankley, W. (eds) *Ethnicity, Race and Inequality in the UK: State of the Nation*. Bristol: Policy Press, pp 73–92.

Clark, C. (2014) 'Glasgow's Ellis Island? The integration and stigmatisation of Govanhill's Roma population', *People, Place and Policy*, 8(1): 34–50. doi: 10.3351/ppp.0008.0001.0004.

Clark, K. and Ochmann, N. (2022) 'Good job, bad job, no job? Ethnicity and employment quality for men in the UK', IZA Discussion Paper No. 15099. Available at: https://ssrn.com/abstract=4114645

Clark, K. and Shankley, W. (2020) 'Ethnic minorities in the labour market in Britain', in Byrne, B., Alexander, C., Khan, O., Nazroo, J. and Shankley, W. (eds) *Ethnicity and Race in the UK: State of the Nation*. Bristol: Bristol University Press, pp 127–48.

Commission on Race and Ethnic Disparities (2021) *Commission on Race and Ethnic Disparities: The Report*. Available at: https://assets.publishing.serv ice.gov.uk/government/uploads/system/uploads/attachment_data/file/ 974507/20210331_-_CRED_Report_-_FINAL_-_Web_Accessible.pdf

Cook, E.J., Randhawa, G., Large, S., Guppy, A., Chater, A.M. and Pang, D. (2014) 'Who uses NHS Direct? Investigating the impact of ethnicity on the uptake of telephone based healthcare', *International Journal for Equity in Health*, 13(1): 1–9. doi: 10.1186/s12939-014-0099-x.

Corley, J., Okely, J.A., Taylor, A.M., Page, D., Welstead, M., Skarabela, B. et al (2021) 'Home garden use during COVID-19: associations with physical and mental wellbeing in older adults', *Journal of Environmental Psychology*, 73(2020): 101545. doi: 10.1016/j.jenvp.2020.101545.

Cribb, J., Waters, T., Wernham, T., Xu, X. and Payne, J. (2021) *Living Standards, Poverty and Inequality in the UK 2021*. Report No. R194. London: Institute for Fiscal Studies.

D'Orazio, M., di Zio, M. and Scanu, M. (2006) *Statistical Matching: Theory and Practice*. Hoboken, NJ: Wiley.

Daniel, W.W. (1968) *Racial Discrimination in England*. London: Penguin.

Dannefer, D. (2003) 'Cumulative advantage/disadvantage and the life course: cross-fertilizing age and social science theory', *Journals of Gerontology, Series B*, 58(6): S327-37. doi: 10.1093/geronb/58.6.S327.

Darlington, F., Norman, P., Ballas, D. and Exeter, D.J. (2015) 'Exploring ethnic inequalities in health: evidence from the Health Survey for England, 1998–2011', *Diversity and Equality in Health and Care*, 12(2): 54–65. doi: 10.21767/2049-5471.100032.

Datta, N. (2019) *Willing to Pay for Security: A Discrete Choice Experiment to Analyse Labour Supply Preferences*. London: Centre for Economic Performance, LSE.

Davies, B., Lalot, F., Peitz, L., Heering, M.S., Ozkececi, H., Babaian, J. et al (2021) 'Changes in political trust in Britain during the COVID-19 pandemic in 2020: integrated public opinion evidence and implications', *Humanities and Social Sciences Communications*, 8(1): 1–9. doi: 10.1057/s41599-021-00850-6.

De Bell, S., White, M., Gri, A., Darlow, A., Taylor, T., Wheeler, B. et al (2020) 'Spending time in the garden is positively associated with health and wellbeing: results from a national survey in England', *Landscape and Urban Planning*, 200: 103836. doi: 10.1016/j.landurbplan.2020.103836.

Department for Levelling Up, Housing and Communities (DLUHC) (2022) *Inclusive Britain: Government Response to the Commission on Race and Ethnic Disparities.* Available at: https://www.gov.uk/government/publications/inclusive-britain-action-plan-government-response-to-the-commission-on-race-and-ethnic-disparities/inclusive-britain-government-response-to-the-commission-on-race-and-ethnic-disparities

Devine, D., Gaskell, J., Jennings, W., and Stoker, G. (2021) 'Trust and the coronavirus pandemic: what are the consequences of and for trust? An early review of the literature', *Political Studies Review*, 19(2): 274–85. doi: 10.1177/1478929920948684.

Dawson, M.C. (1994) *Behind the Mule: Race and Class in African-American Politics.* Princeton: Princeton University Press.

Delaney, L., Fernihough, A. and Smith, J.P. (2013) 'Exporting poor health: the Irish in England', *Demography*, 50(6): 2013-35. doi: 10.1007/s13524-013-0235-z.

Demireva, N. and Heath, A. (2014) 'Diversity and the civic spirit in British neighbourhoods: an investigation with MCDS and EMBES 2010 data'. *Sociology*, 48(4): 643–62. doi: 10.1177/0038038513516695.

Department for Education (2014) *Promoting Fundamental British Values through SMSC.* Available at: https://www.gov.uk/government/publications/promoting-fundamental-british-values-through-smsc

Dominguez, T.P., Dunkel-Schetter, C., Glynn, L., Hobel, C. and Sandman, C. (2008) 'Racial differences in birth outcomes: the role of general, pregnancy, and racism stress', *Health Psychology*, 27(2): 194–203. doi: 10.1037/0278-6133.27.2.194.

Dorling, D. (2019) *Inequality and the 1%.* London: Verso.

Downes, D.J., Cross, A.R., Hua, P., Roberts, N., Schwessinger, R., Cutler, A.J. et al (2021) 'Identification of *LZTFL1* as a candidate effector gene at a COVID-19 risk locus', *Nature Genetics*, 53: 1606–15.

Elliot, M.R. and Valliant, R. (2017) 'Inference for nonprobability samples', *Statistical Sciences*, 32(2): 249–64.

Emirbayer, M. and Desmond, M. (2015) *The Racial Order.* Chicago: University of Chicago Press.

Erens, B., Primatesta, P. and Prior, G. (2000) *Health Survey for England: The Health of Minority Ethnic Groups 1999, Volumes I and II*. London: The Stationery Office.

Essed, P. (1991) *Understanding Everyday Racism: An Interdisciplinary Theory*. London: Sage.

Eurobarometer (2019) 'Discrimination in the European Union: special Eurobarometer 493 – Wave EB91.4'. Available at: https://europa.eu/eurobarometer/surveys/detail/2251

European Social Survey (2016) 'ESS8 - 2016 documentation report'. Available at: https://www.europeansocialsurvey.org/data/round-index.html

European Social Survey (2018) 'ESS9 - 2018 documentation report'. Available at: https://www.europeansocialsurvey.org/data/round-index.html

Eurostat (2014) *First and Second-Generation Immigrants: A Statistical Overview*. Luxembourg: European Union.

Fancourt, D., Bu, F., Mak, H.W. and Steptoe, A. (2020) *Covid-19 Social Study: Results Release 15*. Available at: https://www.nuffieldfoundation.org/wp-content/uploads/2020/04/COVID-19-social-study-results-1-July-2020.pdf

Fernandez-Reino, M. and Sumption, M. (2022) 'Citizenship and naturalisation for migrants in the UK'. The Migration Observatory. Available at: https://migrationobservatory.ox.ac.uk/resources/briefings/citizenship-and-naturalisation-for-migrants-in-the-uk

Financial Conduct Authority (2021) *Financial Lives 2020 Survey: The Impact of Coronavirus*. Available at: https://www.fca.org.uk/publication/research/financial-lives-survey-2020.pdf

Finney, N. (2011) 'Understanding ethnic differences in the migration of young adults within Britain from a lifecourse perspective', *Transactions of the Institute of British Geographers*, 36(3): 455–70. doi: 10.1111/j.1475-5661.2011.00426.x.

Finney, N. and Simpson, L. (2009) *Sleepwalking to Segregation: Challenging Myths of Race and Migration*. Bristol: Policy Press.

Finney, N. and Jivraj, S. (2013) 'Ethnic group population change and neighbourhood belonging in Britain', *Urban Studies*, 50(16): 3323–41. doi 10.1177/0042098013482497.

Finney, N. and Harries, B. (2015) 'Which ethnic groups are hardest hit by the "housing crisis"?', in Jivraj, S. and Simpson, L. (eds) *Ethnic Identity and Inequalities in Britain: The Dynamics of Diversity*. Bristol: Policy Press, pp 141–60. doi: 10.2307/j.ctt1t89504.15.

Ford, R. (2011) 'Acceptable and unacceptable immigrants: how opposition to immigration in Britain is affected by migrants' region of origin', *Journal of Ethnic and Migration Studies*, 37(7): 1017–37. doi: 10.1080/1369183X.2011.572423.

Fortier, A.-M. (2021) *Uncertain Citizenship: Life in the Waiting Room*. Manchester: Manchester University Press.

Fortin, N., Lemieux, T. and Torres, J. (2016) 'Foreign human capital and the earnings gap between immigrants and Canadian-born workers', *Labour Economics*, 41: 104–19. doi: 10.1016/j.labeco.2016.05.021.

Francis-Devine, B. (2022) *Unemployment by Ethnic Background*. London: House of Commons Library.

Frost, D., Catney, G. and Vaughn, L. (2022) '"We are not separatist because so many of us are mixed": resisting negative stereotypes of neighbourhood ethnic residential concentration', *Journal of Ethnic and Migration Studies*, 48(7): 1573–90. doi: 10.1080/1369183X.2021.1912590.

Funnell, C. (2015) 'Racist hate crime and the mortified self: an ethnographic study of the impact of victimization', *International Review of Victimology*, 21(1): 71–83.

Gardiner, L. and Slaughter, H. (2020) 'The effects of the coronavirus crisis on workers'. Resolution Foundation. Available at: https://www.resolution foundation.org/app/uploads/2020/05/The-effect-of-the-coronavirus-crisis-on-workers.pdf

Georgiadis, A. and Manning, A. (2011) 'Change and continuity among minority communities in Britain', *Journal of Population Economics*, 24: 541–68. doi: 10.1007/s00148-009-0288-x

Gilroy, P. (2013) *There Ain't No Black in the Union Jack*. Abingdon: Routledge.

Giuliani, M.V. (2003) 'Theory of attachment and place attachment', in Bonnes, M., Lee, T. and Bonaiuto, M. (eds) *Psychological Theories for Environmental Issues*. London: Routledge, pp 137–70.

Golash-Boza, T. (2016) 'A critical and comprehensive sociological theory of race and racism', *Sociology of Race and Ethnicity*, 2: 129–41.

Goldstein, D.A. and Wiedemann, J. (2022) 'Who do you trust? The consequences of partisanship and trust for public responsiveness to COVID-19 orders', *Perspectives on Politics*, 20(2): 412–38. doi: 10.1017/S1537592721000049.

Gower, J.C. (1971) 'A general coefficient of similarity and some of its properties', *Biometrics*, 27(4): 857–71. doi: 10.2307/2528823.

Groves, R.M. and Heeringa, S.G. (2006) 'Responsive design for household surveys: tools for actively controlling survey errors and costs', *Journal of the Royal Statistical Society: Series A*, 169(3): 439–57. doi: 10.1111/j.1467-985X.2006.00423.x.

Hamnett, C. and Reades, J. (2019) 'Mind the gap: implications of overseas investment for regional house price divergence in Britain', *Housing Studies*, 34(3): 388–406. doi: 10.1080/02673037.2018.1444151.

Han, Q., Zheng, B., Cristea, M., Agostini, M., Bélanger, J.J. and Gützkow, B. (2021) 'Trust in government regarding COVID-19 and its associations with preventive health behaviour and prosocial behaviour during the pandemic: a cross-sectional and longitudinal study', *Psychological Medicine*, 53(1): 149–59. doi: 10.1017/S0033291721001306.

Haque, Z., Bécares, L. and Treloar, N. (2020) *Over-exposed and Under-protected: The Devastating Impact of COVID-19 on Black and Minority Ethnic Communities in Great Britain*. Runnymede Trust. Available at: https://www. nhsbmenetwork.org.uk/wp-content/uploads/2020/08/Runnymede-Covi d19-Survey-report-v2-August-2020.pdf

Hardy, S.A., Pratt, M.W., Pancer, S.M., Olsen, J.A. and Lawford, H.L. (2011) 'Community and religious involvement as contexts of identity change across late adolescence and emerging adulthood', *International Journal of Behavioral Development*, 35(2): 125–35. doi: 10.1177/0165025410375920.

Harwood, H., Rhead, R., Chui, Z., Bakolis, I., Connor, L., Gazard, B. et al (2021) 'Variations by ethnicity in referral and treatment pathways for IAPT service users in South London', *Psychological Medicine*, 2: 1–12. doi: 10.1017/S0033291721002518.

Harvey, D. (2017) *The Ways of the World*. London: Profile Books.

Hayanga, B., Stafford, M. and Bécares, L. (2021) 'Ethnic inequalities in healthcare use and care quality among people with multiple long-term health conditions living in the United Kingdom: a systematic review and narrative synthesis', *International Journal of Environmental Research and Public Health*, 18(23): 12599. doi: 10.3390/ijerph182312599.

Haycox, H. (2022) 'Policy paradoxes and the Vulnerable Persons Resettlement Scheme: how welfare policies impact resettlement support', *Critical Social Policy*. doi: 10.1177/02610183221088532.

Heath, A.F., Fisher, S.D., Sanders, D. and Sobolewska, M. (2011) 'Ethnic heterogeneity in the social bases of voting at the 2010 British general election', *Journal of Elections, Public Opinion and Parties*, 21(2): 255–77. doi: 10.1080/17457289.2011.562611.

Heath, A.F., Fisher, S.D., Rosenblatt, G., Sanders, D. and Sobolewska, M. (2013) *The Political Integration of Ethnic Minorities in Britain*. Oxford: Oxford University Press.

Heckman, J. and Landersø, R. (2021) *Lessons from Denmark about Inequality and Social Mobility*. Cambridge, MA: National Bureau of Economic Research. doi: 10.3386/w28543.

Holly, S., Hashem Pesaran, M. and Yamagata, T. (2011) 'The spatial and temporal diffusion of house prices in the UK', *Journal of Urban Economics*, 69(1): 2–23. doi: 10.1016/j.jue.2010.08.002.

Hooghe, M. and Quintelier, E. (2014) 'Political participation in European countries: the effect of authoritarian rule, corruption, lack of good governance and economic downturn', *Comparative European Politics*, 12(2): 209–32. doi: 10.1057/cep.2013.3.

hooks, b. (1984) *Feminist Theory: From Margin to Center*. Boston, MA: South End Press.

Hu, Y. (2020) 'Intersecting ethnic and native–migrant inequalities in the economic impact of the COVID-19 pandemic in the UK', *Research in Social Stratification and Mobility*, 68: 100528. doi: 10.1016/j.rssm.2020.100528.

Huddy, L. and Khatib, N. (2007) 'American patriotism, national identity, and political involvement', *American Journal of Political Science*, 51(1): 63–77. doi: 10.1111/j.1540-5907.2007.00237.x.

Hughes, M.E., Waite, L.J., Hawkley, L.C. and Cacioppo, J.T. (2004) 'A short scale for measuring loneliness in large surveys', *Research on Aging*, 26(6): 656–72. doi: 10.1177/0164027504268574.

Hussain, A. and Miller, W. (2006) *Multicultural Nationalism: Islamophobia, Anglophobia, and Devolution*. New York: Oxford University Press.

ICNARC (2020) *ICNARC Report on COVID-19 in Critical Care*, 24 April. Available at: https://www.icnarc.org/Our-Audit/Audits/Cmp/Reports

Im, J., Ho Cho, I. and Kim, J.K. (2018) 'FHDI: an R package for fractional hot deck imputation', *The R Journal*, 10(1): 140–54.

Ipsos MORI (2020) 'Attitudes to racism in Britain'. Research for *The Economist*. Available at: https://www.ipsos.com/en-uk/half-britons-support-aims-black-lives-matter-movement

Jackson, S.B., Stevenson, K.T., Larson, L.R., Peterson, M.N. and Seekamp, E. (2021) 'Outdoor activity participation improves adolescents' mental health and well-being during the COVID-19 pandemic', *International Journal of Environmental Research and Public Health*, 18(5): 2506. doi: 10.3390/ijerph18052506.

Jennings, W., Stoker, G. Valgarðsson, V., Devine, D. and Gaskell, J. (2021) 'How trust, mistrust and distrust shape the governance of the COVID-19 crisis', *Journal of European Public Policy*, 28(8): 1174–96. doi: 10.1080/13501763.2021.1942151.

Jivraj, S. and Simpson, L. (2015) *Ethnic Identity and Inequalities in Britain: The Dynamics of Diversity*. Bristol: Policy Press.

Johnston, N. (2021) 'Who can vote in UK elections?' House of Commons Library Briefing Paper CBP08985. Available at: https://commonslibrary.parliament.uk/research-briefings/cbp-8985

Jones, C.P. (2000) 'Levels of racism: a theoretic framework and a gardener's tale', *American Journal of Public Health*, 90(8): 1212–15. doi: 10.2105/ajph.90.8.1212.

Kalton, G. and Kasprzyk, D. (1986) 'The treatment of missing survey data', *Survey Methodology*, 12(1): 1–16.

Kalton, G. and Kish, L. (1984) 'Some efficient random imputation methods', *Communications in Statistics-Theory and Methods*, 13: 1919–39. doi: 10.1080/03610928408828805.

Kapadia, D. and Bradby, H. (2021) 'Ethnicity and health', in Chamberlain, K. and Lyons, A.C. (eds) *Routledge International Handbook of Critical Issues in Health and Illness*. Abingdon: Routledge, pp 183–96.

Kapadia, D., Nazroo, J. and Clark, K. (2015) 'Have ethnic inequalities in the labour market persisted?', in Jivraj, S. and Simpson, L. (eds) *Ethnic Identity and Inequalities in Britain: The Dynamics of Diversity*. Bristol: Policy Press, pp 161–80.

Kapadia, D., Zhang, J., Salway, S., Nazroo, J., Booth, A., Villarroel-Williams, N. et al (2022) *Ethnic Inequalities in Healthcare: A Rapid Evidence Review.* London: NHS Race and Health Observatory. Available at: https://www.nhsrho.org/wp-content/uploads/2022/02/RHO-Rapid-Review-Final-Report_v.7.pdf

Karlsen, S. and Nazroo, J.Y. (2002a) 'Agency and structure: the impact of ethnic identity and racism on the health of ethnic minority people', *Sociology of Health and Illness*, 24(1): 1–20, doi: 10.1111/1467-9566.00001.

Karlsen, S and Nazroo, J.Y. (2002b) 'Relation between racial discrimination, social class, and health among ethnic minority groups', *American Journal of Public Health*, 92(4): 624–31. doi: 10.2105/AJPH.92.4.624.

Karlsen, S. and Nazroo, J.Y. (2004) 'Fear of racism and health', *Journal of Epidemiology and Community Health*, 58: 1017–18.

Karlsen, S. and Nazroo, J.Y. (2006) 'Measuring and analyzing "race", racism and racial discrimination', in Oakes, J. and Kaufman, J. (eds) *Methods in Social Epidemiology*. San Francisco: Jossey-Bass, pp 86–111.

Karlsen, S and Nazroo, J.Y. (2015) 'Ethnic and religious differences in the attitudes of people towards being "British"', *The Sociological Review, 63*, 759–81. doi: 10.1111/1467-954X.12313.

Kasarda, J.D. and Janowitz, M. (1974) 'Community attachment in mass society', *American Sociological Review*, 39(3): 328–39. doi: 10.2307/2094293.

Katikireddi, S.V., Lal, S., Carrol, E.D., Niedzwiedz, C.L., Khunti, K., Dundas, R. et al (2021) 'Unequal impact of the COVID-19 crisis on minority ethnic groups: a framework for understanding and addressing inequalities', *Journal of Epidemiology and Community Health*, 75(10): 970–74. doi: 10.1136/jech-2020-216061.

Kim, J.K. (2011) 'Parametric fractional imputation for missing data analysis', *Biometrika*, 98(1): 119–32. doi: 10.1093/biomet/asq073.

Kim, J.K. and Fuller, W.A. (2004) 'Fractional hot deck imputation', *Biometrika*, 91(3): 559–78. doi: 10.1093/biomet/91.3.559.

Kressin, N.R., Raymond, K.L. and Manze, M. (2008) 'Perceptions of race/ethnicity-based discrimination: a review of measures and evaluation of their usefulness for the health care setting', *Journal of Health Care for the Poor and Underserved*, 19(3): 697–730. doi: 10.1353/hpu.0.0041.

Krieger, N., Smith, K., Naishadham, D., Hartman, C. and Barbeau, E. (2005) 'Experiences of discrimination: validity and reliability of a self-report measure for population health research on racism and health', *Social Science and Medicine*, 61(7): 1576–96. doi: 10.1016/j.socscimed.2005.03.006.

Lane, P. and Smith, D. (2021) 'Mid-term review – UK Roma national integration strategy: Roma at the intersection of ethnic-inclusive, post-racial and hyper-ethnic policies', *Journal of Contemporary European Studies*, 29(1): 73–83. doi: 10.1080/14782804.2019.1626226.

Landrine, H., Klonoff, E., Corral, I., Fernandez, S. and Roesch, S. (2006) 'Conceptualizing and measuring ethnic discrimination in health research', *Journal of Behavioral Medicine*, 29(1): 79–94. doi: 10.1007/s10865-005-9029-0.

Leddy-Owen, C. (2014) '"It's true, I'm English … I'm not lying": essentialized and precarious English identities', *Ethnic and Racial Studies*, 37(8): 1448–66. doi: 10.1080/01419870.2012.705010.

Liberal Democrats (2019) '2019 general election manifesto'. Available at: https://www.libdems.org.uk/plan

Lukes, S., de Noronha, N. and Finney, N. (2019) 'Slippery discrimination: a review of the drivers of migrant and minority housing disadvantage', *Journal of Ethnic and Migration Studies*, 45(17): 3188–206. doi: 10.1080/1369183X.2018.1480996.

Lymperopoulou, K. and Parameshwaran, M. (2015) 'Is there an ethnic group educational gap?', in Jivraj, A. and Simpson, L. (eds) *Ethnic Identity and Inequalities in Britain: The Dynamics of Diversity*. Bristol: Policy Press, pp 118–98. doi: 10.2307/j.ctt1t89504.17.

Maehler, D.B. (2022) 'Determinants of ethnic identity development in adulthood: a longitudinal study', *British Journal of Developmental Psychology*, 40(1): 46–72. doi: 10.1111/bjdp.12384.

Malik, S. and Shankley, W. (2020) 'Arts, media and ethnic inequalities', in Byrne, B., Alexander, C., Khan, O., Nazroo, J. and Shankley, W. (eds) *Ethnicity, Race and Inequality in the UK: State of the Nation*. Bristol: Policy Press, pp 167–88.

Manning, A. and Rose, R. (2021) 'Ethnic minorities and the UK labour market', *CentrePiece*: 1–5. Available at: https://cep.lse.ac.uk/pubs/download/cp603.pdf

Manning, A. and Roy, S. (2010) 'Culture clash or culture club? National identity in Britain', *Economic Journal*, 120(542): F72–100. doi: 10.1111/j.1468-0-0297.2009.02335.x.

Mansfield, K.E., Mathur, R., Tazare, J., Henderson, A.D., Mulick, A.R., Carreira, H. et al (2021) 'Indirect acute effects of the COVID-19 pandemic on physical and mental health in the UK: a population-based study', *The Lancet Digital Health*, 3(4): e217–30. doi: 10.1016/S2589-7500(21)00017-0-0.

Mao, G., Fernandes-Jesus, M., Ntontis, E. and Drury, J. (2021) 'What have we learned about COVID-19 volunteering in the UK? A rapid review of the literature', *BMC Public Health*, 21(1): 1–15. doi: 10.1186/s12889-021-11390-8.

Marques, P., Santos Silva, A., Quaresma, Y., Resende Manna, L., de Magalhaes Neto, N. and Mazzoni, R. (2021) 'Home gardens can be more important than other urban green infrastructure for mental well-being during COVID-19 pandemics', *Urban Forestry & Urban Greening*, 64: 127268. doi: 10.1016/j.ufug.2021.127268.

Martin, N. and Khan, O. (2019) 'Ethnic minorities at the 2017 British general election'. Available at: https://assets.website-files.com/61488f992 b58e687f1108c7c/61c3125671c8d5a0ce3c59c5_2017%20Election%20B riefing%20(1).pdf

Massey, D. (1992) 'A place called home?', *New Formations*, 7: 3–15.

Mathur, R., Rentsch, C.T., Morton, C.E., Hulme, W.J., Schultze, A., MacKenna, B. et al (2021) 'Ethnic differences in SARS-CoV-2 infection and COVID-19-related hospitalisation, intensive care unit admission, and death in 17 million adults in England: an observational cohort study using the OpenSAFELY platform', *The Lancet*, 397(10286): 1711–24. doi: 10.1016/S0140-6736(21)00634-6.

Maxwell, R. (2009) 'Caribbean and South Asian identification with British society: the importance of perceived discrimination', *Ethnic and Racial Studies*, 32(8): 1449–69. doi: 10.1080/01419870802604024.

Maxwell, R. (2010a) 'Trust in government among British Muslims: the importance of migration status', *Political Behavior*, 32(1): 89–109. doi: 10.1007/ s11109-009-9093-1.

Maxwell, R. (2010b) 'Evaluating migrant integration: political attitudes across generations in Europe', *International Migration Review*, 44(1): 25–52. doi: 10.1111/j.1747-7379.2009.00797.x.

Maxwell, R. (2012) *Ethnic Minority Migrants in Britain and France: Integration Trade-offs*. Cambridge: Cambridge University Press.

May, T., Aughterson, H., Fancourt, D. and Burton, A. (2021) '"Stressed, uncomfortable, vulnerable, neglected": a qualitative study of the psychological and social impact of the COVID-19 pandemic on UK frontline keyworkers', *BMJ Open*, 11(11): E050945. doi: 10.1136/ bmjopen-2021-050945.

McKee, K., Moore, T. and Crawford, J. (2015) *Understanding the Housing Aspirations of People in Scotland*. Edinburgh: Scottish Government.

Meer, N. (2022) *The Cruel Optimism of Racial Justice*. Bristol: Policy Press.

Mikolai, J., Keenan, K. and Kulu, H. (2020) 'Intersecting household-level health and socio-economic vulnerabilities and the COVID-19 crisis: an analysis from the UK', *SSM – Population Health*, 12: 100628. doi: 10.1016/j.ssmph.2020.100628.

Modood, T., Berthoud, R., Lakey, J., Nazroo, J., Smith, P., Virdee, S. et al (1997) *Ethnic Minorities in Britian: Diversity and Disadvantage*. London: Policy Studies Institute.

Nandi, A. and Platt, L. (2014) *Britishness and Identity Assimilation among the UK's Minority and Majority Ethnic Groups* (No. 2014-01). ISER Working Paper Series.

Nandi, A. and Platt, L. (2020) 'The relationship between political and ethnic identity among UK ethnic minority and majority populations', *Journal of Ethnic and Migration Studies*, 46(5): 957–79. doi: 10.1080/ 1369183X.2018.1539286.

Nazroo, J.Y. (1997) *The Health of Britain's Ethnic Minorities*. London: Policy Studies Institute.

Nazroo, J.Y. (2021) 'The central role of racism in shaping the life experiences of ethnic minority people in the UK', in Revolving Doors Agency (ed) *The Knot: An Essay Collection on the Interconnectedness of Poverty, Trauma, and Multiple Disadvantage*. London, Lankelly Chase, pp 40–9. Available at: https://lankellychase.org.uk/wp-content/uploads/2021/02/RDA_The-Knot_Essay-collection_FINAL.pdf

Nazroo, J.Y. and Bécares, L. (2020) 'Evidence for ethnic inequalities in mortality related to COVID-19 infections: findings from an ecological analysis of England and Wales', *BMJ Open*, 10(12): e041750. doi: http://dx.doi.org/10.1136/bmjopen-2020-041750.

Nazroo, J.Y. and Bécares, L. (2021) *Ethnic Inequalities in COVID-19 Mortality: A Consequence of Persistent Racism*. Runnymede/CoDE Covid Briefings. Available at: https://www.runnymedetrust.org/publications/ethnic-inequalities-in-covid-19-mortality-a-consequence-of-persistent-racism

Nazroo, J. and Karlsen, S. (2003) 'Patterns of identity among ethnic minority people: Diversity and commonality', *Ethnic & Racial Studies*, 26(5): 902–30. doi: 10.1080/0141987032000109087.

Nazroo, J.Y., Bhui, K. and Rhodes, J. (2020) 'Where next for understanding race/ethnic inequalities in severe mental illness? Structural, interpersonal and institutional racism', *Sociology of Health and Illness*, 42(2): 262–76. doi: 10.1111/1467-9566.130012.

Nazroo, J.Y., Falaschetti, E., Pierce, M. and Primatesta, P. (2009) 'Ethnic inequalities in access to and outcomes of healthcare: analysis of the Health Survey for England', *Journal of Epidemiology & Community Health*, 63(12): 1022–7. doi: 10.1136/jech.2009.089409.

Nesdale, D. and Mak, A.S. (2003) 'Ethnic identification, self-esteem and immigrant psychological health', *International Journal of Intercultural Relations*, 27(1): 23–40. doi: 10.1016/S0147-1767(02)00062-7.

OECD (2021) 'Trust in government (indicator)'. Available at: https://data.oecd.org/gga/trust-in-government.htm

Office for Health Improvements and Disparities (2022) *COVID-19 Mental Health and Wellbeing Surveillance Report: 3. Measures of Anxiety, Depression, Loneliness and Life Satisfaction*. Available at: https://www.gov.uk/government/publications/covid-19-mental-health-and-wellbeing-surveillance-report/3-triangulation-comparison-across-surveys

Office for National Statistics (ONS) (2020) 'Coronavirus (COVID-19) related deaths by ethnic group, England and Wales: 2 March 2020 to 10 April 2020'. Available at: https://www.ons.gov.uk/peoplepopulationandcommunity/birthsdeathsandmarriages/deaths/articles/coronavirusrelateddeathsbyethnicgroupenglandandwales/2march2020to10april2020

ONS (2021a) SOC 2020. The current Standard Occupational Classification for the UK, published in three volumes. Available at: https://www.ons.gov.uk/methodology/classificationsandstandards/standardoccupationalclassificationsoc/soc2020

ONS (2021b) 'Coronavirus (COVID-19) case rates by socio-demographic characteristics, England: 1 September 2020 to 25 July 2021'. Available at: https://www.ons.gov.uk/peoplepopulationandcommunity/healthandsocialcare/conditionsanddiseases/bulletins/coronaviruscovid19caseratesbysociodemographiccharacteristicsengland/1september2020to25july2021

ONS (2021c) 'Deaths involving COVID-19 by religious group, England: 24 January 2020 to 28 February 2021'. Available at: https://www.ons.gov.uk/peoplepopulationandcommunity/birthsdeathsandmarriages/deaths/articles/deathsinvolvingcovid19byreligiousgroupengland/24january2020to28february2021

ONS (2021d) 'Updating ethnic contrasts in deaths involving the coronavirus (COVID-19), England: 24 January 2020 to 31 March 2021'. Available at: https://www.ons.gov.uk/peoplepopulationandcommunity/birthsdeathsandmarriages/deaths/articles/updatingethniccontrastsindeathsinvolvingthecoronaviruscovid19englandandwales/24january2020to31march2021

ONS (2022) 'List of ethnic groups'. Available at: https://www.ethnicity-facts-figures.service.gov.uk/style-guide/ethnic-groups

ONS, Social Survey Division (2020) 'Annual Population Survey, January–December, 2019', [data collection], UK Data Service, 4th edn. Accessed 13 April 2022. doi: 10.5255/UKDA-SN-8632-4.

ONS, Social Survey Division (2021) 'Annual Population Survey, January–December, 2020', [data collection], UK Data Service, 4th edn. Accessed 13 April 2022. SN: 8789, doi: 10.5255/UKDA-SN-8789-4.

Pan, D., Sze, S., Minhas, J.S., Bangash, M.N., Pareek, N., Divall, P. et al (2020) 'The impact of ethnicity on clinical outcomes in COVID-19: a systematic review', *EClinicalMedicine*, 23: 100404. doi: 10.1016/j.eclinm.2020.100404.

Parker, K., Horowitz, J.M. and Anderson, M. (2020) 'Amid protests, majorities across racial and ethnic groups express support for the Black Lives Matter movement'. Pew Research Center. Available at: https://www.pewresearch.org/social-trends/2020/06/12/amid-protests-majorities-across-racial-and-ethnic-groups-express-support-for-the-black-lives-matter-movement

Parsons, S. and Wiggins, R.D. (2020) *Trust in Government and Others during the COVID-19 Pandemic – Initial Findings from the COVID-19 Survey in Five National Longitudinal Studies.* London: UCL Centre for Longitudinal Studies. Available at: https://cls.ucl.ac.uk/wp-content/uploads/2020/10/Trust-in-government-and-others-during-the-COVID-19-pandemic-%E2%80%93-initial-findings-from-COVID-19-survey.pdf

Peach, C. (1998) 'South Asian and Caribbean ethnic minority housing choice in Britain', *Urban Studies*, 35(10): 1657–80. doi: 10.1080/0042098984097.

Peach, C. (ed) (1994) *Ethnicity in the 1991 Census. Volume 2 – The Ethnic Minority Populations of Great Britain.* London: HMSO.

Phan, V., Singleton, C., Bryson, A., Forth, J., Ritchie, F., Stokes, L. et al (2022) 'Accounting for firms in ethnicity wage gaps throughout the earnings distribution'. IZA Discussion Paper No. 15284. https://doi.org/10.2139/ssrn.4114869

Phillips, C. (2010) 'Institutional racism and ethnic inequalities: an expanded multilevel framework', *Journal of Social Policy*, 40: 173–92.

Phillips, D. and Harrison, M. (2010) 'Constructing an integrated society: historical lessons for tackling Black and minority ethnic housing segregation in Britain', *Housing Studies*, 25(2): 221–35. doi: 10.1080/02673030903561842.

Phinney, J. (1992) 'The multigroup ethnic identity measure: a new scale for use with adolescents and youth adults from diverse groups', *Journal of Adolescent Research*, 7(2): 156–76. doi: 10.1177/074355489272003.

Phinney, J. and Chavira, V. (1995) 'Parental ethnic socialization and adolescent coping with problems related to ethnicity', *Journal of Research on Adolescence*, 5(1): 31–53. doi: 10.1207/s15327795jra0501_2.

Pierce, M., Hope, H., Ford, T., Hatch, S., Hotopf, M., John, A. et al (2020) 'Mental health before and during the COVID-19 pandemic: a longitudinal probability sample survey of the UK population', *The Lancet Psychiatry*, 7(10). doi: 10.1016/S2215-0366(20)30308-4.

Platt, L. and Warwick, R. (2020) 'COVID-19 and ethnic inequalities in England and Wales', *Fiscal Studies*, 41(2): 259–89. doi: 10.1111/1475-5890.12228.

Public Health England (2020) *Disparities in the Risk and Outcomes of COVID-19.* Gateway number: GW-1447. Available at: https://assets.publishing.service. gov.uk/government/uploads/system/uploads/attachment_data/file/908434/ Disparities_in_the_risk_and_outcomes_of_COVID_August_2020_update.pdf

Purcell, N.J. and Kish, L. (1980), 'Postcensal estimates for local areas (or domains)', *International Statistical Review*, 48: 3–18. doi: 10.2307/1402400.

Putnam, R.D. (2007) 'E pluribus unum: diversity and community in the twenty-first century: the 2006 Johan Skytte Prize Lecture', *Scandinavian Political Studies*, 30(2): 137–74. doi: 10.1111/j.1467-9477.2007.00176.x.

R Core Team (2022) 'R: a language and environment for statistical computing'. R Foundation for Statistical Computing, Vienna, Austria. Available at: https://www.R-project.org

Race Disparity Unit (2022) *Policy Paper, Inclusive Britain: Government Response to the Commission on Race and Ethnic Disparities.* Available at: https://www. gov.uk/government/publications/inclusive-britain-action-plan-government-response-to-the-commission-on-race-and-ethnic-disparities/inclusive-britain-government-response-to-the-commission-on-race-and-ethnic-disparities

Radloff, L.S. (1977) 'The CES-D scale: a self-report depression scale for research in the general population', *Applied Psychological Measurement*, 1(3): 385–401. doi: 10.1177/014662167700100306.

Rex, J. and Moore, R. (1967) *Race, Community and Conflict: A Study of Sparkbrook*. New York: Oxford University Press.

Rhodes, J. and Brown, L. (2019) 'The rise and fall of the "inner city": race, space and urban policy in postwar England', *Journal of Ethnic and Migration Studies*, 45(17): 3243–59. doi: 10.1080/1369183X.2018.1480999.

Rienzo, C. and Fernandez-Reino, M. (2021) *Migrants in the UK Labour Market: An Overview*. University of Oxford, Migration Observatory. Available at: https://migrationobservatory.ox.ac.uk/wp-content/uploads/2019/07/MigObs-Briefing-Migrants-in-the-UK-labour-market-an-overview.pdf

Roberts, R.E., Phinney, J. S., Masse, L.C., Chen, Y.R., Roberts, C.R. and Romero, A. (1999) 'The structure of ethnic identity of young adolescents from diverse ethnocultural groups', *Journal of Early Adolescence*, 19(3): 301–22. doi: 10.1177/0272431699019003001.

Rumbaut, R.G. (2005) 'Sites of belonging: acculturation, discrimination, and ethnic identity among children of immigrants', in Wiesner, T.S. (ed) *Discovering Successful Pathways in Children's Development: Mixed Methods in the Study of Childhood and Family Life*. Chicago: University of Chicago Press, pp 111–64.

Runnymede Trust and the Radical Statistics Race Group (1980) *Britain's Black Population*. London: Heinemann.

Saunders, C. and Shlomo, N. (2021) 'A new approach to assess the normalization of differential rates of protest participation', *Quality and Quantity*, 55(1): 79–102.

Schouten, B. and Shlomo, N. (2017) 'Selecting adaptive survey design strata with partial R-indicators', *International Statistical Review*, 85(1): 143–63. doi: 10.1111/insr.12159.

Scottish Government (2022) 'Coronavirus (COVID-19): public attitudes and behaviours'. Available at: https://www.gov.scot/publications/public-attitudes-behaviours-around-coronavirus-april-update

Shankley, W. and Finney, N. (2020) 'Ethnic minorities and housing in Britain', in Byrne, B., Alexander, C., Khan, O., Nazroo, J. and Shankley, W. (eds) *Ethnicity, Race and Inequality in the UK: State of the Nation*. Bristol: Policy Press, pp 149–66.

Shankley, W. and Williams, P. (2020) 'Minority ethnic groups, policing and the criminal justice system in Britain', in Byrne, B., Alexander, C., Khan, O., Nazroo, J. and Shankley, W. (eds) *Ethnicity, Race and Inequality in the UK: State of the Nation*. Bristol: Policy Press, pp 51–72.

Simon P. (2008) 'The choice of ignorance: the debate on ethnic and racial statistics in France', *French Politics, Culture & Society*, 26(1): 7–31.

Simon P. (2017) 'The failure of the importation of ethno-racial statistics in Europe: debates and controversies', *Ethnic and Racial Studies*, 40(13): 2326–32. doi: 10.1080/01419870.2017.1344278.

Simpson, L. and Finney, N. (2009) 'Spatial patterns of internal migration: evidence for ethnic groups in Britain', *Population, Space and Place*, 15(1): 37–56. doi: 10.1002/psp.497.

Simpson, L., Gavalas, V. and Finney, N. (2008) 'Population dynamics in ethnically diverse towns: the long-term implications of immigration', *Urban Studies*, 45(1): 163–83. doi: 10.1177/0042098007085106.

Singh, P.P., Srivastava, A., Sultana, G.N.N., Khanam, N., Pathak, A., Suravajhala, P. et al (2021) 'The major genetic risk factor for severe COVID-19 does not show any association among South Asian populations', *Scientific Reports*, 11: 12346.

Smith, D.J. (1977) *Racial Disadvantage in Britain*. London: Penguin.

Sobolewska, M. and Barclay, A. (2021) The Democratic Participation of Ethnic Minority and Immigrant Voters in the UK. Available at: https://www.jrrt.org.uk/wp-content/uploads/2021/11/The_Democratic_Participation_of_Ethnic_Minority_and_Immigrant_Voters_in_the_UK.pdf

Sobolewska, M. and Shankley, W. (2020) 'Politics and representation', in Byrne, B., Alexander, C., Khan, O., Nazroo, J. and Shankley, W. (eds) *Ethnicity, Race and Inequality in the UK: State of the Nation*. Bristol: Policy Press, pp 189–202.

Solomos, J. (2003) 'Rethinking Racial Inequality', *Ethnicities*, 3(2): 269–73. doi: 10.1177/1468796803003002006.

Spitzer, R.L., Kroenke, K., Williams, J.B. and Löwe, B. (2006) 'A brief measure for assessing generalized anxiety disorder: the GAD-7', *Archives of Internal Medicine*, 166(10): 1092–97. doi: 10.1001/archinte.166.10.1092.

Sproston, K. and Mindell, J. (2006) *Health Survey for England 2004: The Health of Minority Ethnic Groups*, vol 1. London: The Information Centre.

Sproston, K. and Nazroo, J.Y. (2002) *Ethnic Minority Psychiatric Illness Rates in the Community (EMPIRIC)*. London: The Stationery Office.

StataCorp (2019) *Stata Statistical Software: Release 16*. College Station, TX: StataCorp LLC.

Stevenson, C., Wakefield, J.R.H., Felsner, I., Drury, J. and Costa, S. (2021) 'Collectively coping with coronavirus: local community identification predicts giving support and lockdown adherence during the COVID-19 pandemic', *British Journal of Social Psychology*, 60(4): 1403–18. doi: 10.1111/bjso.12457.

Stopforth, S., Bécares, L., Nazroo, J. and Kapadia, D. (2021a) 'A life course approach to understanding ethnic health inequalities in later life: an example using the United Kingdom as national context', in *The Routledge Handbook of Contemporary Inequalities and the Life Course*. Abingdon: Routledge, pp 383–93.

Stopforth, S., Kapadia, D., Nazroo, J. and Bécares, L. (2021b) 'Ethnic inequalities in health in later life, 1993–2017: the persistence of health disadvantage over more than two decades', *Ageing and Society*: 1–29. doi: 10.1017/S0144686X2100146X.

Stopforth, S., Kapadia, D., Nazroo, J. and Bécares, L. (2022) 'The enduring effects of racism on health: understanding direct and indirect effects over time', *SSM – Population Health*, 19: 101217. doi: 10.1016/j.ssmph.2022.101217.

Sturgis, P., Brunton-smith, I., Kuha, J., Jackson, J., Sturgis, P., Brunton-smith, I. et al (2014) 'Ethnic diversity, segregation and the social cohesion of neighbourhoods in London', *Ethnic and Racial Studies*, 37(8): 1286–309. doi: 10.1080/01419870.2013.831932.

Tajfel, H. and Turner, J.C. (1979) 'An integrative theory of intergroup relations', in Austin, W.G. and Worchel, S. (eds) *The Social Psychology of Intergroup Relations*. Monterey, CA: Brooks/Cole Publishing Company, pp 56–65.

Teorell, J., Dahlberg, S., Holmberg, S., Rothstein, B., Alvarado Pachon, N. and Axelsson, S. (2020) *The Quality of Government Standard Dataset, Version Jan20*. University of Gothenburg: Quality of Government Institute. doi: 10.18157/qogstdjan20.

Thompson, C.W., Roe, J., Aspinall, P., Mitchell, R., Clow, A. and Miller, D. (2012) 'More green space is linked to less stress in deprived communities: evidence from salivary cortisol patterns', *Landscape and Urban Planning*, 105(3): 221–9. doi: 10.1016/j.landurbplan.2011.12.015.

Topriceanu, C.C., Wong, A., Moon, J.C., Hughes, A.D., Bann, D., Chaturvedi, N. et al (2021) 'Evaluating access to health and care services during lockdown by the COVID-19 survey in five UK national longitudinal studies', *BMJ Open*, 11(3). doi: 10.1136/bmjopen-2020-045813.

Tremblay, M.S., Gray, C., Babcock, S. and Barnes, J. (2015) 'Position statement on active outdoor play', *International Journal of Environmental Research and Public Health*, 12(6): 6475–505. doi: 10.3390/ijerph120606475.

Turner, J.C. (2010) 'Towards a cognitive redefinition of the social group', in Postmes, T. and Branscombe, N.R. (eds) *Rediscovering Social Identity*. London: Psychology Press, pp 210–34.

Umaña-Taylor, A.J. (2011) 'Ethnic identity', in Schwartz, S.J., Luyckx, K. and Vignoles, V.L. (eds) *Handbook of Identity Theory and Research*. New York: Springer Science and Business Media, pp 791–809.

Understanding Society (2022) Data Dashboard: Covid-19. Available at: https://www.understandingsociety.ac.uk/topic/covid-19/ data-dashboard

Utsey, S.O. (1998) 'Assessing the stressful effects of racism: a review of instrumentation', *Journal of Black Psychology*, 24(3): 269–88. doi: 10.1177/00957984980243001.

Van Hout, M.-C. and Staniewicz, T. (2011) 'Roma and Irish Traveller housing and health: a public health concern', *Critical Public Health*, 22(2): 193–207. doi: 10.1080/09581596.2011.594872.

Vanneman, R.D. and Pettigrew, T.F. (1972) 'Race and relative deprivation in the urban United States', *Race & Class*, 13(4): 461–86. doi: 10.1177/030639687201300404.

Victor, C.R., Martin, W. and Zubair, M. (2012) 'Families and caring among older people in South Asian communities in the UK: a pilot study', *European Journal of Social Work*, 15(1): 81–96. doi: 10.1080/13691457.2011.573913. Available at: http://www.jstor.org/stable/25791719

Voogt, R.J. and Saris, W.E. (2003) 'To participate or not to participate: the link between survey participation, electoral participation, and political interest', *Political Analysis*, 11(2): 164–79. doi: 10.1093/pan/mpg003.

Wallace, S., Nazroo, J. and Bécares, L. (2016) 'Cumulative effect of racial discrimination on the mental health of ethnic minorities in the United Kingdom', *American Journal of Public Health*, 106(7): 1294–300. doi: 10.2105/AJPH.2016.303121.

Walter, B. (2001) *Outsiders Inside: Whiteness, Place and Irish Women*. London: Routledge.

Warikoo, N. (2005) 'Gender and ethnic identity among second-generation Indo-Caribbeans', *Ethnic and Racial Studies*, 28(5): 803–31. doi: 10.1080/01419870500158752.

Warner, M., Burn, S. Stoye, G., Aylin, P.P., Bottle, A. and Propper, C. (2021) 'Socioeconomic deprivation and ethnicity inequalities in disruption to NHS hospital admissions during the COVID-19 pandemic: a national observational study', *BMJ Quality & Safety*, 31(8): 590–8. doi: 10.1136/bmjqs-2021-013942.

Weinberg, J. (2022) 'Trust, governance, and the Covid-19 pandemic: an explainer using longitudinal data from the United Kingdom', *Political Quarterly*, 93(2): 316–25. doi: 10.1111/1467-923X.13131.

Williams, M. and Husk, K. (2013) 'Can we, should we, measure ethnicity?', *International Journal of Social Research Methodology*, 16(4): 285–300. doi: 10.1080/13645579.2012.682794.

Williams, D.R. (1996) 'Race/ethnicity and socioeconomic status: measurement and methodological issues', *International Journal of Health Services*, 26(3): 483–505. doi: 10.2190/U9QT-7B7Y-HQ15-JT14.

Williams, D.R. and Mohammed, S.A. (2009) 'Discrimination and racial disparities in health: evidence and needed research', *Journal of Black Psychology*, 39(6): 532–59. doi: 10.1177/0095798412461808.

Williams, D.R., Neighbors, H.W. and Jackson, J.S. (2003) 'Racial/ethnic discrimination and health: findings from community studies', *American Journal of Public Health*, 93(2): 200–8. doi: 10.2105/AJPH.93.2.200.

Witteveen, D. (2020) 'Sociodemographic inequality in exposure to COVID-19-induced economic hardship in the United Kingdom', *Research in Social Stratification and Mobility*, 69: 100551. doi: 10.1016/j.rssm.2020.100551.

Wohland, P., Rees, P., Norman, P., Lomax, N. and Clark, S. (2018) 'NEWETHPOP – ethnic population projections for UK local areas 2011–2061'. UK Data Archive. Available at: https://reshare.ukdataservice.ac.uk/852508

Xu, J., Shim, S., Lotz, S. and Almeida, D. (2004) 'Ethnic identity, socialization factors, and culture-specific consumption behavior', *Psychology & Marketing*, 21(2): 93–112. doi: 10.1002/mar.10117.

YouGov COVID-19 tracker (2022) 'Imperial College London YouGov Covid 19 behaviour tracker data hub'. Available at: https://github.com/YouGov-Data/covid-19-tracker

Yuval-Davis, N., Varjú, V., Tervonen, M., Hakim, J. and Fathi, M. (2017) 'Press discourses on Roma in the UK, Finland and Hungary', *Ethnic and Racial Studies*, 40(7): 1151–69. doi: 10.1080/01419870.2017.1267379.

Zahariadis, N., Petridou, E., Exadaktylos, T. and Sparf, J. (2021) 'Policy styles and political trust in Europe's national responses to the COVID-19 crisis', *Policy Studies*, 44(1): 46–67. doi: 10.1080/01442872.2021.2019211.

Zwysen, W. and Demireva, N. (2018) 'An examination of ethnic hierarchies and returns to human capital in the UK', *Social Inclusion*, 6(3): 6–33. doi: 10.17645/si.v6i3.1457.

Zwysen, W., Di Stasio, V. and Heath, A. (2021) 'Ethnic penalties and hiring discrimination: comparing results from observational studies with field experiments in the UK', *Sociology*, 55(2): 263–82. doi: 10.1177/0038038520966947.

Index

References to figures appear in *italic* type; those in **bold** type refer to tables.